KT-440-319

Contributors

Pam Foley is a Senior Lecturer in Children and Families at The Open University's Faculty of Health and Social Care. Her practice background is in women's and children's health. Her teaching and research focuses on child and family social policy and on European models of children's services.

Nick Frost is Professor of Social Work (childhood, children and families) at the Faculty of Health and Social Sciences, Leeds Metropolitan University. Nick is a qualified and registered social worker, and practised in local authority social work settings for 15 years before commencing his academic career. Nick has published widely in the fields of child welfare and professional learning and he was recently appointed as Chair of North Yorkshire Safeguarding Children Board.

Stephen Leverett is a Lecturer in Children and Young People at The Open University's Faculty of Health and Social Care. His practice background is in social care and social work. He teaches policy and practice for work with children, young people and families and conducts pedagogical research in antenatal and health and social care education.

Andy Rixon is a Lecturer in Children and Young People at The Open University's Faculty of Health and Social Care. His practice background is as a social worker and in local authority training and development. His teaching and researches interests are in practice with children, young people and families, critical best practice in social work and social work education.

Bill Stone works on a freelance basis as a social work consultant with a mixed portfolio of practice, research, training and consultancy. He is the independent social work representative on the Law Society's Children's Law Subcommittee, chairs adoption and fostering panels, and is a consultant for the Churches' Child Protection Advisory Service

Other Contributors

This series of three books forms part of The Open University module *Working together for children* and has grown out of debates and discussions within the undergraduate teaching team working at the University. We would like to thank the following for their critical reading and invaluable feedback: Judith Argles, Brigitte Beck-Woerner, Sheila Campbell, Maurice Crozier, Hasel Daniels, Sue Dumbleton, Helen Evans, Trevor Evans, Louise Garrett, Gill Goodliff, Gloria Potter, Lin Miller, Robin McRoberts, Kate New, Lindsay O'Dell, Janet Seden and our developmental testers. We would also like to thank our focus group, our editors Carol Price, Alison Cadle, Kate Hunter, Mary Franklin, and Beccy Dresden, our team assistants Val O'Connor and Caroline Holdaway, and our External Assessor, Denise Hevey, who has provided insightful and timely comments at every turn.

We should especially like to acknowledge the contribution of our Module Manager, Tabatha Torrance, who has guided, assisted and supported the module team throughout.

North Kent College
The Learning Technology Centre
Tel: 01322 629615

2 7 OCT 2016

Lower Higham Road
Gravesend
DA12 2JJ

Changing children's services

NORTH KENT COLLEGE

Learning Technology Centre
Gravesend Campus

Direct Telephone Line: 01322 629615
Direct e-mail address: LTC_Gravesend@northkent.ac.uk

This book has been issued for **four weeks**
Fines will be charged for late returns

050902

Working together for children

This innovative series brings together an interdisciplinary team of authors to provide an accessible collection of ideas, debates, discussions and reflections on childhood, practice and services for children. The books have been designed and written as illustrative teaching texts, giving voice to children's and practitioners' own accounts as well as providing research, policy analysis and examples of good practice. These books are aimed at students, practitioners, academics and educators across the wide range of disciplines associated with working with children.

There are three books in the *Working together for children series*:

- *Connecting with children: developing working relationships*, edited by Pam Foley and Stephen Leverett

- *Promoting children's wellbeing: policy and practice*, edited by Janet Collins and Pam Foley

- *Changing children's services: working and learning together*, edited by Pam Foley and Andy Rixon

Changing children's services:
working and learning together

Edited by Pam Foley and Andy Rixon

21 OCT 2016

£22.99

362.7 FOL

050902

Published by
Policy Press
University of Bristol
Fourth Floor, Beacon House
Queen's Road, Clifton
Bristol BS8 IQU
United Kingdom
http://www.policypress.org.uk

in association with

The Open university
Walton Hall, Milton Keynes
MK7 6AA
United Kingdom

First published 2008. Second edition published 2014.

Copyright © 2014 The Open University

All rights reserved. No part of this publication may be reproduced, stored in a retrieval system, transmitted or utilised in any form or by any means, electronic, mechanical, photocopying, recording or otherwise, without written permission from the publisher or a licence from the Copyright Licensing Agency Ltd. Details of such licences (for reprographic reproduction) may be obtained from the Copyright Licensing Agency Ltd, Saffron House, 6–10 Kirby Street, London EC1N 8TS; website http://www.cla.co.uk/

Edited and designed by The Open University.

Printed in the United Kingdom by Bell & Bain Ltd, Glasgow.

This book forms part of the Open University module *KE312 Working together for children*. Details of this and other Open University modules can be obtained from the Student Registration and Enquiry Service, The Open University, PO Box 197, Milton Keynes MK7 6BJ, United Kingdom (tel. +44 (0)845 300 60 90; email general-enquiries@open.ac.uk).

http://www.open.ac.uk

British Library Cataloguing in Publication Data

A catalogue record for this book is available from the British Library.

Library of Congress Cataloging-in-Publication Data

A catalog record for this book has been requested.

ISBN 978 1 4473 1379 3

2.1

Contents

Introduction

Since writing the first edition of this book an environment of constant change has become no less a fact of life for all those working with children and families. The contemporary context has evolved as we have moved out of an era of expanding investment in many areas of services for children into an era where shrinking resources is the more common experience – for both economic and political reasons. The aims and methods of the Labour governments were rapidly overtaken by new political realities, not just in Westminster but in the increasingly diverse governments and assemblies across the UK. Attempting to analyse these changes within children's services at any one time requires grappling with trends and directions, both overt and underlying, in a shifting area of social and political thinking. The wellbeing of children remains a central concern for each successive government, as part of an abiding set of questions about how we should live. While things never stand still, the themes of this book have continued to be relevant – how does change affect practitioners, their workplaces, the families they work with and the relationship between children, young people, their parents and the state? Equally, as the necessity of practitioners working in more integrated ways has continued, it remains important to question what this really means, whether it actually works and how might it work better. In this new edition we have taken the opportunity to update and expand some of these debates.

Both rhetoric and realities continue to coexist within the modernisation programmes that periodically sweep through public services. For contemporary children's services, delivering on choice, standards and targets has meant a series of significant reorganisations across rather than just within traditional practice boundaries. The argument that improvements to services require the sweeping away of established patterns of working has remained explicit. For some this means a reintegration of services for children and families which should never have become so divided; such a reintegration is the only means by which to achieve real improvements. For others this is a strategy that could undermine existing roles, expertise and values. Agencies merging and co-locating, teams integrating, practitioners expanding their range of responsibilities or taking lead roles in new teams, and the invention of new kinds of practitioners are all consequences of these changes. Inevitably such fundamental challenges continue to raise a host of issues and uncertainties about roles and responsibilities, workplace cultures, the ethics of care and people's own identities as practitioners.

The critical political and ethical questions embedded in children's welfare and protection ask fundamental questions of adult organisations and institutions. No one would argue that even radical restructuring is the answer to many of the really important issues in relation to children's wellbeing. It is crucial to remain aware of the 'bigger picture' as deeper structural factors remain highly influential. Evidence pointing to the potential role of significant inequality on the wellbeing of children in the UK (Wilkinson and Pickett, 2009) has been acknowledged by politicians of different political persuasions but this has not led to the set of coordinated policies needed to address it. Instead deep-rooted social issues have been more likely to be addressed through targeting 'troubled families' and early intervention in the lives of children. The measurement of early interventions and short-term outcomes is emphasised at the expense of other long-term concerns for children, such as low social mobility in the UK (Blanden et al., 2005) and the unflattering comparisons of children's wellbeing in the UK with children's wellbeing in other European countries that have been made (UNICEF, 2013).

The challenge for children's services, whose primary focus must be to show improvements in the wellbeing of children, is first, to work with broad trans-disciplinary concepts (such as 'wellbeing') using trans-disciplinary knowledge and understandings and second, to demonstrate respect for and attention to the interests and goals of a good childhood for all children in the UK. All this must take place within what Beck (2000) has called a 'risk society' characterised by manufactured, often un-boundaried, uncertainties about the future (Beck, 2000), which all too easily become linked with children and young people.

Many changes that define the modern world, such as the digital revolution, are having a major impact upon children's lives and children's services, with both good and bad consequences. Policy and practice directions and developments can be knocked off course by particular events involving children and are frequently taken up by the media, where anxieties about childhood remain a major preoccupation. Our society continues to experience a series of 'moral panics', those orchestrated scares engineered by various agents to regulate the behaviour of people or groups who appear to threaten social values (Ungar, 2008). The projection of fears onto childhood and youth will continue to influence the working practices within children's services.

Practitioners can be aware of these adult anxieties as they go through a series of stages: a condition or episode seen as a threat to society's values is presented by the media, responded to by establishment figures, pronounced upon by experts, and a way of coping evolves or the condition either disappears or escalates (Krinsky, 2008). Adult anxieties, sentimental or instrumental, are reflected, for example, in the extent to which children's services can become over-focused on futures and outcomes at the expense of measures that can improve children's present quality of life.

What remains at the heart of all work with children and families is the ability to create and sustain good working relationships. The need for a range of communication and interpersonal skills is not always given sufficient priority in the education, training and qualifications of the many groups of practitioners now working with children. A clear emphasis on connecting with children and developing good relationships highlights essential 'qualities' such as being respectful, being concerned, being trustworthy, being self-aware, being resilient, 'being there' and being, at times, able to form extraordinary relationships with children and families. Practitioners working across boundaries need these skills as much as others – interagency working equally requires interpersonal skills.

Practice relationships are complex, each located in particular kinds of context or setting and reflecting the wider sphere of child–adult relations. As mentioned earlier, relationships need to be developed and maintained in often feverish atmospheres when public concern becomes heightened in response to cruelty or sexual abuse. Practitioners need to acquire greater insight and better understandings of children's and young people's lives. They also need to develop greater insight into each other's roles and ways of understanding the world. Both of these should be underpinned by a knowledge of critical theories to establish a basis for challenging dominant theories or assumptions about children in contemporary society.

Good working relationships should be rooted in an understanding that children are a distinct social group and childhood is an important period of life in its own right. It can also be helpful to recognise children's agency and appreciate that children themselves play a part in the shaping of children's services and in the development of the skills of practitioners. Such views of children and young people are no longer either new or radical, and many of the changes under way in children's services are increasingly informed by these kinds of ideas. Attributing an evolving capacity for reason to children can only strengthen democratic relationships and values. However, children's rights and children's and young people's participation are still far from universally embedded in processes and structures. A rights perspective is not always sufficient, participation is not always meaningful and there is room for doubt that altering the status of childhood in these kinds of ways is the key.

Other potentially revealing questions are now being debated, relating to the expansion and contraction of the welfare state in the UK or the contrast between children's services in the UK and those that are the result of the different social and pedagogical practices in other parts of Europe (Cameron and Moss, 2011). Once there is some disruption of current understandings of what certain groups of practitioners do, there is room for creative and productive transformations of practice by both generalist and specialist practitioners, for the benefit of the children with whom they work.

This book explores and explains the emphasis on integrated working in children's services, and it also examines both the combining of skilled individuals and the development of skills within an individual. It also intends to raise some key critical questions. To what extent are the barriers at all levels to agencies and practitioners working together really being addressed? How sure can we be that there is more to be gained than to be lost? What in the education of teachers, social workers, family support workers, early years workers and the many others who work with children prepares them for this kind of work and helps them to meet the expectations it gives rise to? Are there other skills that are more important and frequently absent? Do we really know that integrated working delivers better outcomes for children and their families? There are many critical questions for us to explore.

This book also addresses the issue of the knowledge and skills needed by those working with children, and asks questions about where the best place is to find them and how best to teach and learn them. Multi-professional teams will bring multiple understandings of the issues to their work with children. Questions have arisen about addressing the divisions between different disciplines of key importance to work with children, including sociology, psychology, childhood and family studies, health, social care and education. Is the answer to these questions a necessity for common skills and knowledge for everyone working in children's services in order for integration to work? Is integrated learning the key to integrated working? The nature of learning itself seems crucial here, as theories of informal learning such as that of 'communities of practice' (Wenger, 1998) illustrate some of the limitations of formal learning and the alternative ways in which new knowledge and skills are generated.

This series of books focuses on the nought-to-twelve age group, and throughout we have placed an emphasis on the value of children's voices. We have, however, omitted children's ages, unless they are particularly relevant, to avoid reproducing the 'age and stage' thinking that has often obscured children's individual capacities and capabilities. In fact, we hope to encourage people with an interest in childhood to look outwards and consider how this important period in people's lives connects with the rest of the life course. We also value the views of practitioners and have drawn upon their insights into the changing world of practice in which they find themselves. Writers and practitioners from a variety of disciplines have contributed to this book, and this is reflected in the diversity of language and terminology.

In the first, updated chapter we look at change as a backdrop to the rest of the book. This chapter considers in particular the impact of change since a modernising tone was set by recent governments. This impact is explored from the point of view of voluntary as well as statutory services, and from the standpoint of children and families as well as of practitioners. The chapter also analyses broader sources of change beyond the political and policy arena. Highlighting a key theme of the book, there is a particular focus on the relationship between change and interagency working.

In Chapter 2 we again pick up on one of the key themes of this book, the accelerating move towards integrated ways of working in children's services. Interagency working has several notable features, including addressing health promotion and social care issues through community agencies, extended schools and community schools, and more sustained and focused work with and support for parents. This is now to be achieved through a range of practitioners working in interagency teams of various designs, often in common settings, although policy also sometimes simultaneously suggests this is best achieved through the multi-skilling of the individual worker. Starting from the perspective of children and families, this chapter outlines some of the range of drivers behind interagency working and how these changes manifest themselves, particularly in terms of partnership working, between agencies but also with children and families. It goes on to explore the challenges and issues that have been experienced by practitioners engaged in the process of establishing closer working together.

In the third chapter we look at how working together has involved supporting and working in partnership with parents and carers. This chapter focuses on the political context in which parenting is experienced and the impact of the context of parenting, including gender, social networks and inequality. The concept of capital is debated, examining different forms – economic, human, emotional and social. These forms of capital are then explored in relation to how parenting support is defined and the ways practitioners can work with parents.

Chapter 4 investigates the question of whether more integrated forms of working 'work'. It looks at the different perspectives from which this question could be asked; is it a matter of improved outcomes for children? Better processes for families and practitioners? Or a question of a more efficient use of resources? Considering the widespread acceptance that interagency working must be the best way to organise and deliver services, the evidence is not extensive; but the available research and the lessons that can be drawn from it is considered in detail here.

It is the 'learning together' of the book title that is the focus of Chapter 5. While raising the level of education, training and qualifications across the children's workforce has been a major aim of policy, this chapter examines how it is that practitioners can and do learn. Learning is viewed from a range of perspectives, exploring both formal learning and theories of social learning such as the concept of 'communities of practice'. The importance of learning from the expertise that children and families possess about their own lives is also emphasised here. The chapter continues the interagency theme, touching on the role of both pre- and post-qualifying education and training.

The central idea underpinning the final chapter, 'Children's services: the changing workplace', is to explore the idea that changes to practitioners and practice are closely related to changes that take place in the institutions and workplaces that children and families experience every day. So this chapter explores how workplaces respond to pressure to change from 'below' (service users and practitioners) and from 'above' (policy makers), and how the expansion of children's services and the continuing series of reports into abuse rooted in particular workplaces led to the rapid development of audit, regulation and managerialism.

Challenging and changing interagency organisational cultures is, it is argued, crucial if there is to be any chance of responding to both the contemporary and future challenges likely for children's services.

References

Beck, U. (2000) 'Risk society revisited: theory, politics and research programmes' in Adam, B., Beck, U. and Van Loon, J. (eds), *The Risk Society and Beyond: Critical Issues for Social Theory*, London, Sage.

Blanden, J., Gregg, P. and Machin, S. (2005) *Intergenerational Mobility in Europe and North America: A Report Supported by the Sutton Trust* [Online]. Available at http://cep.lse.ac.uk/about/news/IntergenerationalMobility.pdf (accessed 6 December 2013).

Cameron, C. and Moss, P. (2011) *Social Pedagogy and Working with Children and Young People, Where Care and Education Meet*, London, Jessica Kingsley Publishers.

Krinsky, C. (ed) (2008) *Moral Panics over Contemporary Children and Youth*, London, Ashgate.

Ungar, S. (2008) 'Don't know much about history: a critical examination of moral panics over student ignorance' in Krinsky (ed) (2008) *Moral Panics over Contemporary Children and Youth*, London, Ashgate.

Unicef Report Card 11 (2013) [Online]. Available at http://www.unicef-irc.org/Report-Card-11/ (accessed 6 December 2013).

Wenger, E. (1998) *Communities of Practice: Learning, Meaning, and Identity*, Cambridge, Cambridge University Press.

Wilkinson, R. and Pickett, K. (2009) *The Spirit Level: Why More Equal Societies Almost Always Do Better*, London, Allen Lane.

Chapter 1 Working with change

Andy Rixon

Introduction

One of the defining features of working in children's services is change. Changing organisations, policies, procedures and expectations seem to be a constant feature of life for many practitioners. Government, national and local, constantly creates new policies, or recreates old ones, to try and deal with problems new as well as familiar. Political philosophies fluctuate in their beliefs about where solutions are to be found. As a result, resources grow, shrink and change direction; and relationships between statutory, private and third sectors are realigned. Practitioners with 'established' roles are expected to adapt; new practitioners' roles evolve or are created. At the same time, society and social relations do not stand still – relationships between service 'providers' and 'receivers' are less clear-cut. Even our understanding of children and childhood itself is subject to change over time.

Change is the theme of this chapter – its sources and its impact on practitioners and the children and families with whom they work. Amongst a variety of changes, we will explore in particular the interrelationship between change and interprofessional ways of working – a key theme of this book. While interagency and interprofessional working are not new phenomena, they are continuing to be a major theme in the organisation of early twenty-first century services for children in the UK. The creation of new agency structures, the emergence of lead professionals and 'common' frameworks suggest that change in the direction of closer 'working together' for children is unlikely to slow down.

Core questions

- How is the landscape of children's services changing?
- What are the implications of change for practitioners, children and their families?
- What are the factors that are influencing change?
- What is the relationship between change, and interagency and interprofessional working?

1 Continuous improvement – continuous change?

While the evolution of services for children is inevitable and in many cases highly desirable, the specific agenda of change is one that appears to have been actively encouraged – the government desire for 'continuous improvement' increasingly became equated to the need for continuous change. The tone for the start of the twenty-first century was set by such policy documents as *Modernising Government*:

> We must make clear that additional investment comes with strings attached and is conditional on achieving improved results through modernisation. We must encourage a commitment to quality and continuous improvement, and ensure that public bodies know how to turn this commitment into results. And we must work in partnership with the independent audit bodies and inspectorates, so that we all focus on the goal of improving the value delivered to the public.
>
> (Cabinet Office, 1999, p. 35)

Public services were criticised for impeding the improvement in quality by sticking to working practices that were seen as too traditional in a fast-changing world. As well as reinforcing the need for change, this extract also suggests the mechanisms by which improvements were to be measured, such as regulation, targets, audit and inspection. The modernising theme was experienced across the UK as it was taken forward into new devolved governments and assemblies that in turn created their own currents of change. Change was experienced in all sectors, for example the Modernisation Agency which also placed 'continuous improvement' at the heart of the NHS (Pinnock and Dimmock, 2003). The NHS in England has since seen the rise – and in most cases demise – of GP fundholding, strategic health authorities, primary care trusts, clinical commissioning groups and foundation hospitals, to name but a few examples. The modernisation programme led to a review of public administration in Northern Ireland which involved restructuring the commissioning agents and consolidating the providing agents, reducing the number of Health and Social Care Trusts from 17 to 5. Schools in England similarly experienced the effects of the 2010 coalition government's belief in 'whole-system reform' with both 'profound structural change and rigorous attention to standards' (Department for Education (DfE), 2010, p. 7).

Thinking point 1.1: What major changes are you aware of in children's services, either personally or professionally? What do you think has been the effect of these changes, both positive and negative?

Modernisation has also frequently been underpinned by developments in information and communication technology (ICT) and government-inspired large-scale ICT projects and databases. Few practitioners have escaped the increasing proportion of time spent on the computer.

Partly as a consequence of such changes and the initiatives and reviews that flow from them, organisations which provide services for children often seem to be in a state of permanent internal reorganisation:

> 'We have no sooner settled down from the last reorganisation than they wanted to change the boundaries again and everything gets another shaking up.'
>
> (Social worker, personal communication)

New councils or new directors of services may also want to 'make their mark' through changing the organisation and structure of service delivery.

While practitioners will support the principle of improving services, reorganisations can generate much cynicism amongst staff and have a substantial impact upon morale. The extent to which improvement is achieved through structural change, for example, is often unclear. A study of a major local government reorganisation of local authorities in Scotland, Wales and England in the 1990s identified a profound impact on the work undertaken by one of the agencies – social services. Little evidence of savings was found, compared to the upheaval in terms of loss of expertise and morale (Craig and Manthorpe, 1999a). A study of local government reorganisations in England has argued that structural change has disruptive effects on organisational outcomes and has negative consequences at least in the short term (Andrews and

Boyne, 2012). The impact can be far-reaching although not always negative:

> Such reorganisations can also mean a redrawing of geographical boundaries between different agencies disrupting established systems and power relationships. While changes of this nature are frequently experienced negatively, it has been noted that they can sometimes create new opportunities for innovative working.
>
> (Craig et al., 2000)

A changing environment inevitably calls for organisations to adapt. Banks argues that some voluntary sector organisations illustrate a 'professional entrepreneurial' response where some 'private sector' approaches, for example in fund-raising, are blended with 'public service ideals' (2004, p. 189). The growth of social enterprise represented a further change in the landscape of the care sector and a new twist on this blend. While the forms that social enterprise have taken are diverse – ranging from registered charities and cooperatives to limited companies – the entrepreneurial response is explicit even if they have been defined as businesses with primarily social objectives – 'social enterprises are distinctive because their social or environmental goals are central to what they do' (Social Enterprise Coalition, 2007, p. 4).

Practice box 1.1

PLUS

PLUS (formerly Playplus) is a voluntary organisation based in Stirling that supports disabled children and young people aged 5–26 in play and social activities, and more recently in inclusion in schools. One of its founders, who has written on the topic (Dumbleton, 2005), says that the project was 'born out of a chance remark' about the invisibility of disabled children in public play spaces – spaces which in fact were not all that appealing to non-disabled children: 'If public play areas were unattractive, unappealing and dangerous for non-disabled children, what of those who had additional support needs?'

Several examples of their experiences are used in this chapter to highlight the evolution of such projects, the influence of funding, and changing relationships between agencies.

The initial impetus for Playplus came from an informal group operating in a political climate in which local government had given legitimacy to the public funding of childcare. ...

Partnerships with other agencies are the means by which as normal a life as possible can be achieved for children and young people whose needs fall outwith the norm. For Playplus, the positive political climate and, particularly, the existence of the play development officer were crucial. The presence of a council officer gave the project legitimacy with professionals and funders and facilitated the early interagency working – such as the use of school premises – on which the continued development of the organisation has depended.

(Source: Dumbleton, 2005, pp. 36–39)

Inclusive play activities are accessible through groups such as PLUS

In a study of family centres in England, Tunstill et al. found change to be a consistent feature of their work, pressures for change coming from three main sources (Tunstill et al., 2007, p. 122):

- 'pressures exerted by central government through new policy directions'
- 'pressures from local government through changing funding policies, including cuts in finance'

- the 'changing priorities of partner agencies in both the voluntary and statutory sectors'.

Of the 344 family centres reviewed, three-fifths reported experiences of organisational restructuring or a 'services review', or having completely changed the nature of their work (Tunstill et al., 2007). The direction of their work moved towards more targeted and interventionist work with less open access provision. New services reflected shifts in government policy focusing on areas such as parenting education, homework clubs, support for teenage mothers and preparation to enable parents to return to work. This could again change the ethos of family centres as in some cases neighbourhood work decreased while that in assessment and child protection increased (Tunstill et al., 2007).

The funding arrangements to support these changes were often experienced as complicated and time-consuming, and seem to have become an area of expertise in their own right:

> 'Funding arrangements are becoming more complex and the expertise required to write funding bids and fill in complicated returns for different funding sources has also become more complex.'

> 'Funding can take up an eternity each year.'

> (Family centre workers quoted in Tunstill et al., 2007, p. 130)

Funding cycles can also get continually shorter – see Practice box 1.3.

As well as the funding complexity, all agencies have been required to demonstrate the success of their work in terms of outcomes, usually linked to explicit targets. Most areas of local government and the health service have had the experience of appearing in contentious league tables, exposing the extent to which their targets have been hit or missed. Banks (2004) linked these developments to the emergence of what was then a new form of accountability. Practitioners have always been accountable both to the children and the families with whom they work, and to the wider public. Banks argues, however, that the emphasis on public accountability has grown, 'requiring the production of quantifiable outputs and outcomes' in order not just to improve practice but 'to show a good job has been done' and value for money has been achieved (Banks, 2004, p. 151). This has been paralleled by an expansion in administration and proceduralisation. One key finding of the public inquiry into failings in patient care in a hospital in Mid-Staffordshire was that the focus had been on finance and meeting targets as the main measure of performance rather than on professional compassion and the real quality of care (Francis, 2013).

A frequent criticism of outcome targets concerns the potential distortions that can arise as the focus of work shifts to meet them – creating some dilemmas for practice. MacBeath et al. (2007) noted a particularly serious version of this effect in their study of schools facing 'exceptionally challenging circumstances':

> As headteachers frequently testified, they had very short-term targets and some senior leaders saw this as a moral conflict that they wrestled with on a daily basis. Should they deploy the best teachers and invest the greatest efforts on those young people most likely to pay dividends in terms of critical benchmark?
>
> (MacBeath et al., 2007, p. 101)

The impact of top-down managerialism, audit and inspections is explored further in Chapter 6.

Some target setting by the government has focused attention on areas where practice has been in need of improvement. The educational progress of Looked After children, for example, has long been identified as an area of concern (Jackson, 1987, 2010) and a government target for improvement (DH, 1998; DfE, 2012).

Practice box 1.2

PLUS and changing policy agendas

It was the emphasis on prevention that precipitated [a] significant shift in Playplus's relationship with its local authority partners. In 2002/03 Stirling Council increased its funding allocation to Playplus by more than 50% ... and ensured that Playplus moved from being possibly available to children, but with no commitment or obligation to provide a particular level of service, to an entitlement model – which was designed to 'prevent' some children from needing a formal social work assessment. ...

This funding development has meant a move to greater accountability for the organisation. The outcomes of the service are

---

> no longer measured in 'child hours' but in provision and uptake of each child's entitlement to support. Playplus's target is to work with 90% of the disabled children aged 5–19 in the Stirling Council area
>
> ...
>
> This greater accountability has also 'bought' for funders a place on the Management Board ... Developments in the wider world of social care have also impacted on Playplus which is registered with the Care Commission as a support service and is inspected against the relevant care standards.
>
> (Dumbleton, 2005, pp. 42–43)

In contrast to the experience of change as a result of a loss of funding, some family centres experienced change due to an increase in resources (Tunstill et al., 2007). Contracting resources in some sectors, new funding emerging in others, has been a pattern reflected throughout all sectors of children's services; however there are also longer term trends that have a more radical impact on their overall shape. The early twenty-first century saw an overall significant investment in sectors such as early years through the Sure Start programme. This decade-long trend came to an end in 2008. A combination of economic difficulties and changing political priorities saw deep cuts in government spending and local authority budgets. The language of 'austerity' rather than investment has shaped subsequent planning in children's services.

Policy makers do sometimes acknowledge, in theory, that constant change is not always required:

> In creating a healthcare system fit for the 21st century we are not interested in change for change's sake and we are inclined to distrust structural change as a distraction from the key issues and challenges.
>
> (Scottish Executive, 2003, p. 9)

This statement seems to have been part of an attempt to establish a distinction between the Scottish and English approaches to the structure of healthcare. In the document cited above this is located in Scottish 'collectivism' being a central feature rather than the key driver being 'choice' as in England. This distinction highlights the influence of broader national and political philosophies in shaping the way services are structured and practitioners work together.

1.1 Reacting and resisting

Thinking point 1.2: Can you think of the last significant change that happened where you worked (in any workplace)? How did you respond?

Although change has positive as well as negative features, the discussion above acknowledges that some changes have a stressful impact on practitioners; issues of morale, for example, clearly emerged from the local authority reorganisations. A number of studies have tried to categorise in different ways how practitioners respond. Charles and Butler (2004), for example, argue that in the face of change practitioners are forced to adopt strategies that try to balance their work ideals with the realities of the working environment. They illustrate this through identifying the impact on social workers of factors such as deprofessionalisation, increasing bureaucracy and risk management, arguing that a cycle of 'accommodation' can become established which, by requiring the suppression of feelings, can have negative consequences for both workers and those they work with. The authors encourage the use of a more reflective form of practice that enables practitioners to be aware of this effect and seek other more positive strategies (Charles and Butler, 2004).

Troman and Woods argue that there is a 'considerable body of work which links teacher stress with the wholesale restructuring of national education systems' (2000, p. 255). Through a series of interviews with teachers, they identify significant points in teachers' lives where they responded to stress through choosing one of a range of strategies. Key strategies, they suggest, are submitting to imposed changes (retreatism), attempting to find ways of reducing workloads or stress (downshifting), or making the most of new opportunities (self actualisation). Research into the resilience of teachers in maintaining their commitment to teaching has highlighted the importance of factors such as the working environment and quality of leadership (Gu and Day, 2013).

Rogers and Reynolds focus on internal psychological processes and argue that it can be helpful to distinguish between change and transition:

Change is external and transition is internal, although there are many external indicators of the internal states. People in transition may move through recognisable stages from denial and resistance, to exploration and commitment, although not always in that order.

(Rogers and Reynolds, 2003a, p. 104)

Practitioners protesting alongside service users against changes they see as detrimental to services

Lack of change and challenge can lead to institutionalised provision and poor practice and values. Any group of practitioners, in certain circumstances, can become complacent about current practice or not understand the need for change. In the extreme, damaging practices can be maintained, illustrated by enquiries into the abuse of children in care, for example, children's homes in North Wales investigated in the 1990s (Waterhouse, 2000) and again in 2013.

In interviews with a range of social care professionals, Banks (2004, p. 189) also identifies a range of possible responses to change, including 'reluctant conformity' and 'principled quitting', but she also stresses the strategies of resisting or challenging change both individually and collectively. Practitioners can resist change if they see it as having negative consequences for families, for example the closure of a particular resource, or if decisions have been made contrary to the conclusions of consultation with children and families. Advocates of the need to develop a 'new' form of professional practice suggest that this needs to incorporate collective action in the broader social context, including users of the services the professionals are involved in providing (Banks, 2004). This issue has long been debated in social work and argued for in other professional areas. Change does not have to be a one-way street; practitioners can also actively lead change in children's services where they see how services can be improved.

Practitioners may sometimes feel at the mercy of constant policy changes; however, top-down change is of course mediated through the realities of organisational and individual practice. Practitioners can be relatively powerful in interpreting policy when working directly with children and their families; this is embodied in the idea of face-to-face practitioners being 'street-level bureaucrats' (Lipsky, 1980). Change may not always have the consequences originally intended as various levels of reinterpretation are passed through on the policy trajectory (Bowe et al., 1992).

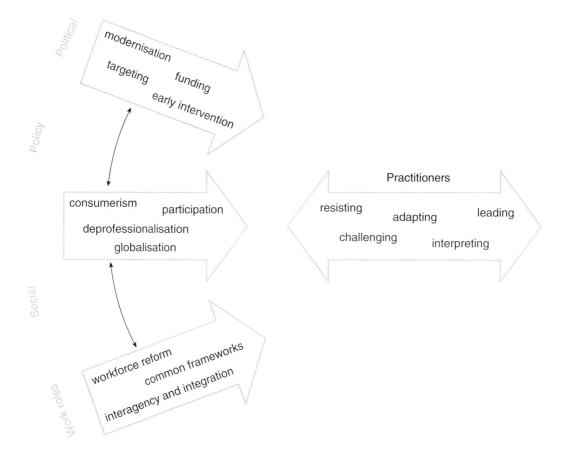

Examples of drivers for change and the response of practitioners

Key points

1   The early twenty-first century has seen a concerted drive towards modernisation of the delivery of children's services, stressing the need for change and continuous improvement.

2   Organisational change can be a positive force to improve practice but is often experienced as destabilising.

3   Practitioners experiencing change can adopt a range of strategies both reactive and proactive.

2 Practitioners, families and the changing workforce

The experience of change is common across the children's workforce in virtually all settings, regardless of levels of training or history of professionalism. Any separation between the professional and the 'non-','semi-' or 'para-' professional will be largely artificial, but there can be particular issues for some groups of staff that have, or are aspiring to, the 'professional' label. The ideas of identity, ethics and culture are arguably more relevant to this second group. Changes and challenges to long- established practices and traditional ways of working will be felt more acutely by some groups of practitioners than others.

Thinking point 1.3: What do you think have been the main changes, over the last ten years, in any professional role with which you are familiar in work with children (for example, for teachers, doctors, health visitors or social workers)?

Workforce structures in children's services have been changing significantly. Teachers, for example, have in the past had the classroom to themselves, but now share their working environment with other practitioners – teaching assistants and support staff (with a whole range of different titles), and volunteers. Between 2000 and 2012 the number of teaching assistants providing additional learning resources in the classroom in England increased from 79,000 to 232,300 (National Statistics, 2013) while the number of teachers has remained relatively stable. This trend has been mirrored across the UK to varying degrees.

Teaching and classroom assistants have made a valuable contribution to children's education, including enabling the greater inclusion of disabled children within mainstream schooling. With schools managing budgets, there are also implications in the relative cost of different staff groups. The cost of resources is often an important factor driving change that may not be made explicit.

These changes are mirrored in other areas of practice with children. Social work assistants, once common, were significantly reduced in number as the emphasis on the importance of qualified staff increased. Yet they have re-emerged in many teams in order to do tasks that are seen as not essential for social workers to undertake. Similarly, calls to the 'duty' social work team have increasingly been answered by a trained administrator rather than a social worker. In nursing and midwifery too, healthcare assistants undertake many roles that were previously the preserve of their more highly trained colleagues.

Children work with an increasing variety of practitioners in schools

Thinking point 1.4: How well qualified do you think practitioners need to be who are working with children in children's centres and schools, teaching sports or listening to children read?

Closely tied into these changes are challenges to what it means to be a professional. What is it, for example, that distinguishes the teaching of a teacher from the 'helping' of others working in the classroom? Where are the clear boundaries? Does it matter whether or not they are maintained? Certainly this lack of clarity has been shown in a number of studies (for example, Russell et al., 2005) creating issues on both sides, with support staff, for example, feeling that their role is not fully recognised or rewarded in terms of status or pay:

'I would like to see an end to the two-tier system of support staff. Qualified and unqualified both doing the same job but with a huge difference in salary! I am responsible for the teaching of the groups I work with.'

(Teaching assistant quoted in Russell et al., 2005, p. 185)

The emergence of such new roles can be both liberating and threatening. Teachers have broadly welcomed support staff, yet they have not in the past been trained for collaborative working (Open University, 2005). This pattern is repeated in other settings, leaving the complexities of working relationships to be sorted out in the front line of practice.

Fortunately children meanwhile seem to adapt without necessarily needing to distinguish the boundaries:

'Well the helpers seem to help out and do what the teacher does and the teacher seems to mostly teach children. But sometimes the helpers teach children.'

(School pupil quoted in Eyres et al., 2004, p. 157)

This trend has been fuelled by the policies of successive governments, which have challenged working practices in health, education and social care. The agenda of 'modernising' the public sector which we explored earlier emphasised flexibility and choice to replace what were portrayed as old-style public service 'monoliths' (DH, 2002). New types of 'social care professional' were advocated that would also cross established divisions between professionals and knowledge bases:

Family care workers combining the skills of the health visitor and the social worker to provide family support in times of trouble.

(DH, 2002, webpage)

The central role of this multi-skilled key worker has continued to be promoted; a family support worker who can deliver practical help, emotional support, and parenting education alongside their co-ordination role (Lloyd et al., 2011). The idea of a lead professional (or key worker, designated professional, etc.), who can be drawn from any discipline, has become increasingly central to new configurations of services.

These trends can seem to be contradictory. In becoming a graduate occupation and having a regulatory body, social work has arguably increased its 'professional' status. At the same time, some commentators argue that it has been subject to these same forces of modernisation. As the emphasis on procedures, bureaucracy, managerialism and outcome targets has grown, so the ability of social workers to use independent professional judgement, or find creative solutions, can be reduced (Lymbery and Butler, 2004; Munro, 2011).

Practitioners without a 'professionalised' history or identity have become increasingly involved in acquiring training and qualifications as part of the drive to improve the skills level of the children's workforce. A central part of the modernisation agenda was the recognition that qualifications across the workforce varied but were at a low level in some sectors (Children's Workforce Development Council (CWDC), 2006). The variety of qualifications and awarding bodies was also seen as confusing and led to the development of an integrated qualification framework. Again, the aim was to shift the emphasis from 'traditional professional boundaries to ensuring that the child's needs are met by someone with the right skills, whatever their job title or position in the organisation' (DH, 2005, p. 43).

Virtually all practitioners have experienced the rising expectations of qualifications and skills, a further illustration of which is the raising of the professional status of early years workers through the introduction of foundation degrees, the establishment of the early years professional, and subsequently the early years teacher. In Scotland a degree-level qualification was introduced for managers in early years settings (QAA Scotland, 2007).

The introduction and establishment of new professional groups to work in an arena where another group of professionals already operates can again be seen as a threat as well as an opportunity. This is illustrated by one of the unions representing teachers in their initial response to the development of a professional qualification to be seen as equivalent to their own:

'The Government has made it clear the early years qualification is not a substitute for a teaching qualification. Therefore, early years professionals should not be substitutes for teachers. Their role needs to be clearly defined.'

(Steve Sinnott, General Secretary, National Union of Teachers, quoted in Bloom, 2006, webpage)

2.1 Professionals in (late) modern society

The change and anxiety for all those working with children and families is also occurring within a broader social context where the 'status' of professionals is changing and being challenged. Scrutiny and criticism by the public and media can be intense: there are cases for damages in the court for negligence or 'failed' operations, or for compensation to children who were not protected from abuse. Professional claims to deploy 'expert' knowledge 'fairly' have been, and continue to be, undermined by high-profile enquiries. The trust in the ethics of professionals, that they will always act in the best interests of their patients or clients, is called into question.

We are all increasingly encouraged to see ourselves as 'consumers' of services, with greater choice. Consumers have a different relationship with professionals from 'clients' or 'patients'.

'Patients' have in some cases been encouraged by government to become 'experts' on their own conditions, and information available on the internet allows us all to believe that we can usefully acquire and apply expertise previously in the sole domain of the professional. This potentially enables a renegotiation of the power relationship between doctor and patient, teacher and parent, social worker and child.

Parents have been encouraged to have an increasing say in the running of schools, and parental 'power' has moved towards being equated with that of professional teacher. For example in 2010 the Conservative/ LibDem coalition government in England promoted the idea of Free Schools, which were to be state funded but not under local democratic control (in the Academies Act 2010). They could be set up and run by parents, teachers, charities or businesses 'in response to what local people say they want' (DfE, 2013). The relevant government website contained instructions for applying to set up your own school.

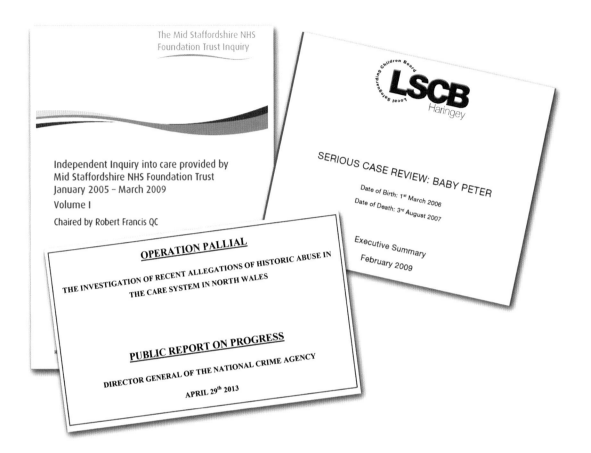

High-profile inquiries can lead to further loss of trust in professionals

Cultural capital is a concept from sociology which refers to those forms of knowledge a person may have which gives them an advantage in society; for example, parents can give children the attitude and knowledge or 'cultural capital' that enables them to be comfortable and successful in the education system.

Of course in practice it is likely that this power will be easier to access for some parents, who have the appropriate **cultural capital**, than others. Without this, changes such as Free Schools are in danger of reinforcing rather than breaking down social barriers, leading to educational, inequalities. Factors such as gender, ethnicity, class and social exclusion all influence the reality of this change. The importance of recognising these factors in work with parents and the role of different forms of capital is discussed in Chapter 3.

Most new developments in children's services require all practitioners to involve parents and children, encouraging accountability and greater participation. Their rights to involvement have been built into new partnership structures. This degree of participation can have many positive benefits, but shifting power relations clearly have an impact on practitioners and can create uncertainty if it is unclear what the shape of new relationships will be. Increasing participation is an issue not only of positioning people as consumers of services or even of strengthening children's rights, although fundamental, but also of changing and challenging perspectives on children themselves. Practitioners are increasingly recognising children's **agency** and the fact that, if supported and enabled, children can, and want to, be involved in decisions that affect their lives (Leverett, 2008). The increasing adoption of schools councils, for example, supports children's rights and encourages active participation in schools. The 'Rights of Children and Young Persons (Wales) Measure' (2011) placed a duty on Welsh Ministers to have due regard to the rights and obligations in the United Nations Convention on the Rights of the Child when making decisions about all proposed new policies or legislation. The extent to which these developments pose a challenge will fall differently on different professions and individual practitioners within them, depending on their training, histories and value systems.

Agency is a term used in sociology to describe action by an individual or group that may transform the world around them.

Practitioners have also been directed to challenge each other's expertise. In analysing the inquiry into the death of Victoria Climbié (Laming, 2003), Parton (2004) argues that the inquiry report illustrates the breakdown of certainty over medical diagnosis:

> Not only does the report demonstrate numerous examples where 'erroneous' medical diagnosis and communications had a tragic impact on the way the case was handled by other professionals, but it also clearly argues that medical diagnosis and opinion must not be treated at face value and uncritically. Social workers, police officers and other doctors were all found culpable in this respect.
>
> (Parton, 2004, p. 87)

The whole place of experts and expertise has been questioned more widely in a society seemingly infused with risk and uncertainty (Beck, 2004). The confidence that professionals have 'the answers' has been undermined not just as a result of challenges in the media but because of the multiplicity of other views and choices that now seem to have equal validity. A late modern or postmodern perspective would suggest that society no longer has the required shared value base:

> we could argue that dominant scientific values and the practices which harness scientific methods – such as medicine – have lost their privileged position as explanatory systems. They have become

just one more set of claims about what is true and have to battle it out with other truth claims – for example, those of alternative therapies such as homeopathy or acupuncture.

(Jones and Tucker, 2000, p. 10)

Professional expertise is seen not to have provided all the solutions to the problems experienced by society. We have lost our belief in the inevitability of progress (Beck, 2004).

This shift can be overstated. As noted above in the example of schools, late-modern perspectives leave little room for the enduring influences of social and economic class (Atkinson, 2007). Science and medicine continue to be powerful discourses in society and some professionals maintain privilege and power. In fact many of the social professions have sought to demonstrate clearer 'scientific' evidence for their decisions and judgements. An emphasis on 'evidence-based practice' has become increasingly significant for a wide range of practitioners. However, it is clear that relations between professionals and children and their families, and between professionals and other professionals, are on shifting ground.

Other social and economic phenomena impact upon professional practice. The increasing complexity of family structures and relationships calls into question the skills of practitioners to engage effectively (Featherstone, 2004). Globalisation has radically altered society through economic change, labour force mobility, and more fluid and uncertain work patterns. UK society has become more ethnically and culturally diverse, as reflected in practitioners themselves as well as those they work with. The reality of this changing context for practice is demonstrated by Nigel Parton (2004) in his comparison of two inquiries into child abuse thirty years apart. While superficially the inquiries into the deaths of the two girls Maria Colwell (in 1973) and Victoria Climbié, and the role played by the child protection agencies involved, may seem similar, Parton points out the radically different environments in which they took place. The Climbié inquiry reveals a social complexity marked by globalisation and individualisation not evident previously. Social workers, for example, themselves from a variety of countries, were working with large numbers of asylum-seeking families in organisations with increasingly complex procedures and systems of information technology (Parton, 2004).

Technological change has continued to be profound, notably the broadening and speeding up of communication and access to knowledge. The growth of social media has enabled the generation of sophisticated user content that further blurs the boundaries of expert knowledge. It can also challenge the boundaries of child / adult knowledge and power. The growth of new technology may have provided more data, but also a potential source of further distancing of the professional from the service user. Recent reviews of social work have questioned the extent to which input of data substitutes for the relational nature of work with children and families (Munro, 2011).

2.2 The impact of change on children and families

Practice box 1.3

PLUS

Other changes experienced by Plus illustrate the ups and downs of funding arrangements, changing patterns of partnership working and the impact of change on disabled children and their families.

There have been changes external to the projects that have had an impact on what we deliver at PLUS. Some have been positive. For example, we've attracted some new funding, the funding that has been able to allow us to support pre-school children and work across the Forth Valley for example. However ... the local authority is going through quite an extensive review of the services that they deliver at present, consequently this has resulted in a fairer charging policy coming into place. Some young people have been deemed as not eligible for our service anymore and as a result have had to drop out.

One of the organisations we have worked very closely with over the past six years have actually recently just told us that their funding is coming to an end and they've been unable to secure future funding. This partnership that we've had with them has allowed approximately 13 to 15 young people on a weekly basis to access a youth group immediately after school. It's a drop-in organisation or a drop-in centre for teenagers. It's very hard to find something that's out of school care for young people to attend when they're in their teenage years and this

---

> organisation has been able to really fill that hole. Unfortunately, we will now lose that as a support for our young people.
>
> For the first time, we've been given funding for nine months as opposed to the usual 12 months. So you can understand with nine months' funding it's quite difficult for us to plan ahead, it's quite difficult for us to work out how can we sustain what we're delivering.
>
> (Susan Roger, Plus CEO, 2013)

Our focus so far has been on the challenges for practitioners of these currents of change but they inevitably affect the experience of children and their families as well. The evaluation of the impact of past local government reorganisations discussed above also noted this effect. While services were on the whole maintained during the period of change, it nevertheless seemed to increase feelings of powerlessness:

> Users and carers, furthest removed from the process of reform, felt most vulnerable and least able to affect the way in which it occurred.
>
> (Craig and Manthorpe, 1999b, webpage)

Even within the changing environment of user participation and 'parent power', large-scale change can be undertaken without participation, even clearly against the wishes of families using services. Major restructuring is rarely 'user-led'. Women, for example, may not feel they have any control over what they see as deteriorating health-visiting services, whatever the policy rationale for this and similar changes (Russell and Drennan, 2007).

Other trends affect the relationship between families and practitioners. While some parents are able to have a greater say in the running of schools, for example, some policies have made them more responsible for their children's education. James and James (2001) suggested that developments such as contracts between home and school led to a 'narrowing of the gap' between education at school and in the family. Similarly, we may become 'expert patients', but consequently we may also be increasingly taking on the responsibility for risk, and its associated anxiety (Beck, 2004).

While striving for 'continuous improvement' often results in constant change, research suggests that parents and children value the continuity of services and of individual workers:

> Several children and carers highlighted the negative impact of losing valued relationships with workers when time-limited interventions were withdrawn. Parents of children receiving mentoring support were concerned about the high turnover of staff and volunteers, which impacted on the relationships that the children were able to develop with their mentors.
>
> (Pinnock and Evans, 2007, p. 9)

Interviews in this study reinforce the consistent finding that the establishment of trusting relationships with practitioners is a key element of effective service delivery, and that such relationships often require time to become established. Short-term services and staff turnover clearly work against this potential. Practitioners in the study were rightly concerned about whether long-term preventative services perpetuate dependency, and stressed the empowerment of families. However, given the policy emphasis on prevention, the study reveals the 'potential mismatch' between the views of practitioners and of children and their parents about the role of preventative services (Pinnock and Evans, 2007, p. 9).

Children's worlds are affected by these changes. For example, as we have seen, they have had to adapt to a range of adults being involved in supporting their learning in the classroom in addition to teachers. These trends may also result in children having the most contact with the least qualified staff – for example, children most in need of special assistance working primarily with assistants rather than teachers.

Children and their families can equally be agents of change, as they have been in relation to services for disabled children, for example, and may often be frustrated by the slow pace of it (Charlesworth, 2003). Work by Action for Children illustrates ways in which children and young people can be involved in designing recruitment advertisements and interviewing staff, although support and development are needed to ensure this makes a lasting change to prevailing cultures (Action for Children, 2009).

Children and young people agreeing their feedback after interviewing candidates for the Group Director of Children's Services (Swindon)

Practice box 1.4

Children in Northern Ireland (CiNI) is the regional umbrella body for the children's sector across Northern Ireland, providing information, policy, training, participation and advocacy services to member organisations in their direct work with and for children and young people.

...

Change can happen rapidly within the children's sector and this was certainly the case for CiNI with the securing of additional funding from the Department of Health, Social Services and Public Safety to support the implementation of an innovative training initiative. In acknowledgment of the increasing numbers of children with complex health needs and the lack of childcare to meet the demands of children with disabilities, the funding was used to develop and deliver a training programme for childminders, day-care and after school staff, parents and family members (such as grandparents). One of the significant changes for CiNI was the additional stakeholders to be included in the training – parents and grandparents. A reassessment of previous training was carried out, and subsequent changes to where and when the training was to be delivered were taken into account in light of the new stakeholders' involvement.

(Adapted from Children in Northern Ireland, 2013)

Key points

1   The composition of the children's workforce has been changing, causing a renegotiation of the boundaries between established and emerging roles.

2   Change has partially been fuelled by the desire to enhance the levels of qualifications and skills of the practitioners working with children.

3   Practitioners in 'professional' roles have also experienced challenges to their status and expertise as a result of broader social change and enquiries that have exposed them to criticism.

4   Children and their families are creating change through their increased participation in the development of services although not all are able to participate equally.

5   Children and their families can experience changes within children's services as disruptive to relationships.

3 Change and interagency working

The developments in interprofessional and interagency working are an integral part of some of the changes discussed above. Breaking down existing boundaries between established roles is a central feature of many of the drivers for change.

A number of the succeeding chapters will explore interagency working in more detail – its rationale, problems, effectiveness, and not least, its confusing terminology – but our intention here is to focus on just some of the issues raised for practitioners by this aspect of change.

3.1 'Being confident enough to let go'

Just as there can be a multiplicity of roles operating in areas that were once the jurisdiction of just one practitioner, it seems inevitable that changes arising from explicit requirements for interagency and interprofessional working will add an extra level of complexity. Practitioners bring with them a professional self-identity but also anxieties about their position and status. This seems particularly important if, as some commentators argue, one element of successful working together is the need for workers to each have confidence in their own professional identity.

> Another respondent argued that professionals need to be confident enough in their professional identity to let go of previous affiliations: 'People [in our team] don't seem to feel as though their identity is just totally wrapped up with where they've come from, with their professional background. I think that [attitude] harnesses the strengths rather than identifies the weaknesses'.
>
> (Anning et al., 2010, p. 72)

Teaching assistants can work with children using particular techniques drawn from those used by speech therapists

However, change can produce many more sources of threat and anxiety, and many things that practitioners may need to 'let go' of. One issue can be the erosion of what might have been seen as central elements of 'their role'. Anning et al. (2010), in their study of five multi-professional teams in children's services, cite the example of speech therapists training education staff to help children with language problems. This was due to the increasing integration of children's services within schools, but has also influenced by a shortage of speech therapists.

Such blurring of roles can be even more problematic if this is seen as a move from specialism to genericism:

> 'I still want to offer a professional service from a health perspective.'
>
> (Nurse quoted in Banks, 2004, p. 135)

> 'Yes I am a nurse, I don't write reports for court. Only stuff to do with health.'
>
> (Nurse quoted in Anning et al., 2010, p. 66)

> 'You get a blurring of professional roles which I think is dangerous. Because at the end of the day social workers think they know what nurses and doctors do, but they don't. Similarly nurses ... think they know what social workers do, but they don't.'
>
> (Social worker quoted in Davies, 2003, p. 203)

The emphasis placed on flexibility does not contradict the place of specialist knowledge; integrated teams often still value the contribution of different expertise.

The issue of labels can be particularly symbolic for some workers, both in terms of feelings about their own status:

'First of all we called ourselves project workers, which I absolutely hated, because that says we could be someone who had been employed as a volunteer you know, off the streets, without qualifications.'

(Practitioner quoted in Anning et al., 2010, p. 72)

and perhaps too for relationships with families they are working with:

'I feel happy with the label but I'm not sure that the community fully understands the label. I think it can be a little confusing.'

(Practitioner quoted in Anning et al., 2010, p. 73)

This perhaps mirrors the experience of practitioners labelling 'service users'– for both groups, how you are labelled may have important consequences, not least for accessing resources.

Within the confusion of terminology, Banks (2004) argues that this 'letting go' could be characterised as the crucial distinction between multi- professional and interprofessional working:

Carrier and Kendall (1995, p. 10) distinguish multiprofessional working, where the traditional forms and divisions of professional knowledge and authority are retained, from interprofessional, where there is a willingness to share and give up exclusive claims to specialist knowledge if the needs of service users can be better met by members of other professional groups. Many community-based teams are currently somewhere between multiprofessional and interprofessional, with tensions apparent as they shift along the continuum.

(Banks, 2004, p. 127)

Some of the research studies mentioned above do cite examples of professionals who were able to emerge from these challenges with a positive sense of a new identity and ultimately accept new labels. Anning et al. (2010) noted practitioners in a child development team who adapted to the change:

'I think myself and the physio do a lot of role blurring in terms of treating the child as a whole in certain aspects but I don't feel threatened by that. I know some people might.'

(Anning et al., 2010, p. 74)

and practitioners in a Child and Adolescent Mental Health Service (CAMHS) team who were open to letting go of old identities and adopting such new labels:

'I don't see myself as an ex-teacher or a counsellor. I see myself as a CAMH worker.'

(Anning et al., 2010, p. 73)

Professionals who struggled through the pain of transformation to the gains of a new professional identity reported an enhanced sense of 'who I am'.

(Anning et al., 2010, p. 75)

Thinking point 1.5: Can you apply any of these issues to your own role or the role of someone you know working with children?

3.2 Lead professionals and common cores

Given the significance of labels, the emergence of the 'lead professional' label seems a particularly important development. This is another strand of change within the children's workforce in the twenty-first century.

Some of the impetus for this has come from children and parents, who have argued that the professional system has been too complicated, requiring them to relate to too many people. This argument has long been advanced in relation to services for disabled children (Watson et al., 2002), but the principle of a single worker liaising between family and a network of practitioners has been adopted not just for disabled children (see, for example, HM Treasury/DfES, 2007) but more widely as a response to the coordination of services from a range of agencies (Scottish Executive, 2006; CWDC, 2009).

The importance of the family's perspective was always acknowledged in principle:

> You and your child will have a say in who should be the lead professional.
>
> (DfES, 2005a, p. 2)

However, the extent of this 'say' remains to be tested in the response of agencies, individuals and the rapid staff turnover experienced in areas of children's services.

This lead role may not be a radical departure from other incarnations of key workers or key professionals and link workers, but the scale of its use has become much more widespread in children's services. This change is not necessarily a 'blurring' of roles as it is not anticipated that this 'lead' will provide all services, but that they will be the initial point of contact, liaising with other professionals where necessary. However, in theory, and in practice, it was always envisaged that a wide range of practitioners could perform this role. In Scotland consultation on the proposal for lead professionals reflected the view that 'the lead professional should be appointed based on the needs of an individual child' and noted that 'the role should not automatically fall to social work' (Scottish Executive, 2006). And in another lead role in relation to 'troubled families':

> [E]ffective family intervention workers come from a wide range of backgrounds including housing, police, voluntary sector, youth offending, nursing, psychology and social work. Suitability for this type of work has a lot to do with attitudes and interpersonal skills as well as any particular professional background.
>
> (Department for Communities and Local Government, 2012, p. 30)

The specific skills needed for this role to work as it should, include forming relationships both with children and their families and with other professionals. Practitioners in this role have emphasised the importance of listening, empathy, counselling skills, and gaining confidence and trust, that is, core interpersonal skills rather than specialist knowledge (Halliday and Asthana, 2004).

Here is one perspective on the core skills identified for success as a lead professional:

- Strong communication skills including diplomacy and sensitivity to the needs of others
- An ability to establish successful and trusting relationships with children, young people and families, and to communicate without jargon
- An ability to empower children, young people and families to work in partnership with other practitioners and to be able to make informed choices about the support they require and receive
- The capacity to support children, young people or parents/ carers in implementing a range of strategies to enable them to achieve their potential
- An ability to establish effective and professional relationships with colleagues from different backgrounds
- An ability to convene meetings and discussions with different practitioners
- An ability to translate their own knowledge and understanding into effective practice
- An ability to work in partnership with other practitioners to deliver effective interventions and support for children, young people and families.

(DfES, 2005b, webpage)

3.3 Managing to change

Organisational change is discussed in more detail in Chapter 6. Clearly, however, one key factor in children's services is the way change is managed. Various models of working with change are available, but they all usually stress the need for an understanding of the way people react to change and strategies for gaining the commitment of staff.

'I can see the importance of change and you learn from it ... It is important to acknowledge feelings and to help people by valuing what they have achieved: from that and their strengths change can come. People need time to look at what they are afraid of and to go through change with their feelings acknowledged.'

('Under-eights' project manager quoted in Seden, 2003, p. 112)

	Loss	Gain
Personal	Feeling deskilled	New co-training opportunities
	Clarity of role	Interesting challenges
	Current colleagues	Better communication with the practitioners with whom I mainly work
Organisational	Confusion	Better service for children
	Reorganisation costs	Access to new resources

A balance sheet for change: a simple way of working with practitioners to unpick the gains and losses they experience through the change process. (Adapted from Rogers and Reynolds, 2003b)

Recognition of the importance of the role of managers seems equally true of working across boundaries:

Our work in this field suggests that perhaps the key variable in implementing effective practice is the leadership offered by managers. Effective leadership is an essential and challenging element in developing effective joined-up working. It involves individuals who can work in the new, ever-changing world of joined-up working that involves networking and boundary crossing.

(Frost and Lloyd, 2006, p. 13)

North Kent College
The Learning Technology Centre
Tel: 01322 629615

2 7 OCT 2016

Lower Higham Road
Gravesend
DA12 2JJ

Anning et al. (2010) suggest that a manager needs to be 'a chameleon', constantly able to adapt to change. Tronto (2001) has argued that this ability is true for all practitioners and that working within a constantly changing environment is a key element of professional competence:

> It also requires the capacity to act in a constantly changing world and be both cautious and confident about changing conditions.
>
> (Tronto, 2001, quoted in Banks, 2004, p. 182)

Key points

1 Bringing practitioners together from different backgrounds can be challenging to established roles. Interprofessional working can also lead to the creation of new identities.

2 Government policy has increasingly stressed the common elements of skills and knowledge for all those working with children, including the development of lead roles.

3 Research with integrated teams suggests that there is a balance to be struck between retaining professional identity and being able to work flexibly beyond traditional professional boundaries.

4 The successful management of change is a key skill needed by practitioners and managers alike.

Conclusion

Change is an experience common to all practitioners to varying degrees, and impacts on their work individually and their ability to work together. It may be that an understanding of change and its gains and losses can help practitioners reflect on and react to the forces impacting upon them. This can include the role that children and families play themselves in initiating and contributing to change. It is also important to recognise that all work undertaken with children, their families and carers takes place within the broad social arena, which will continue to throw up new and complex challenges in the future as in the past.

References

Action for Children (2009) *The Right Choice: Involving Children and Young People in Recruitment and Selection*, London, Action for Children. Also available online at http://www.actionforchildren.org.uk/media/43263/the-right-choice.pdf (accessed 11 July 2013).

Andrews, R. and Boyne, G. (2012) 'Structural change and public services; the impact of the reorganisation process in English local government', *Public Administration*, vol. 90, no. 2, pp. 297–312.

Anning, A., Cottrell, D., Frost, N., Green, J. and Robinson, M. (2010) *Developing Multiprofessional Teamwork for Integrated Children's Services* (2nd edn), Maidenhead, Open University Press.

Atkinson, W (2007) 'Anthony Giddens as Adversary of Class Analysis', *Sociology*, vol. 41, pp. 533–549.

Banks, S. (2004) Ethics, *Accountability and the Social Professions*, Basingstoke, Palgrave Macmillan.

Beck, U. (2004) *Risk Society: Towards a New Modernity*, London, Sage.

Bloom, A. (2006) 'Fears new nursery staff will squeeze out teachers', *Times Educational Supplement*, 1 December, available online at http://www.tes.co.uk/search/story/?story_id=2316493 (accessed 7 September 2007).

Bowe, R., Ball, S., and Gold, A. (1992) *Reforming Education and Changing Schools: Case Studies in Policy Sociology*, London, Routledge.

Cabinet Office (1999) *Modernising Government*, London, The Stationery Office.

Carrier, J. and Kendall, I. (1995) 'Professionalism and interprofessionalism in health and community care: some theoretical issues' in Owens, P., Carrier, J. and Horder, J. (eds) *Interprofessional Issues in Community and Primary Health Care*, Basingstoke, Macmillan.

Charles, M. and Butler, S. (2004) 'Social workers' management of organisational change' in Lymbery, M. and Butler, S. (eds) *Social Work Ideals and Practice Realities*, Basingstoke, Palgrave Macmillan.

Charlesworth, J. (2003) 'Managing across professional and agency boundaries' in Seden, J. and Reynolds, J. (eds) *Managing Care in Practice*, London, The Open University/Routledge, pp. 139–164.

Children in Northern Ireland (2013) *Response to: Towards a Childcare Strategy A Consultation Document*, Belfast, CiNI.

Children's Workforce Development Council (CWDC) (2006) *Early Years Professional National Standards* [online]. Available at http://www.cwdcouncil.org.uk/pdf/Early%20Years/EYP_National_Standards_July_2006.pdf (accessed 3 September 2007).

Children's Workforce Development Council (CWDC) (2009) *Coordinating and Delivering Integrated Services for Children and Young People, the Team Around the Child (TAC) and the Lead Professional: A Guide for Managers*, Leeds, CWDC.

Craig, G., Hill, M., Manthorpe, J., Tisdall, K., Monaghan, B. and Wheelaghan, S. (2000) 'Picking up the pieces: local government reorganisation and voluntary sector children's services', *Children & Society*, vol. 14, no. 2, pp. 85–97.

Craig, G. and Manthorpe, J. (1999a) *Unfinished Business? Local Government Reorganisation and Social Services,* Bristol, The Policy Press.

Craig, G. and Manthorpe, J. (1999b) *The Impact of Local Government Reorganisation on Social Services Work,* [online], Joseph Rowntree Foundation. Available at http://www.jrf.org.uk/knowledge/findings/government/999.asp (accessed 2 January 2008).

Davies, C. (2003) 'Workers, professions and identity' in Henderson, J. and Atkinson, D. (eds) *Managing Care in Context*, London, The Open University/Routledge.

Department for Communities and Local Government (DCLG) (2012) *Working with Troubled Families: A Guide to the Evidence and Good Practice*, London, DCLG.

Department for Education (DfE) (2010) *The Importance of Teaching: The Schools White Paper* 2010, Foreword by the Secretary of State for Education, London, Crown Copyright.

Department for Education (DfE) (2012) *Outcomes for Children Looked After by Local Authorities in England, as at 31 March 2012* [online], DfE National Statistics. Available at https://www.gov.uk/government/uploads/system/uploads/attachment_data/file/191969/SFR32_2012Text.pdf (accessed 26 June 2013).

Department for Education (DfE) (2013) *Free Schools* [online]. Available at http://www.education.gov.uk/schools/leadership/typesofschools/ freeschools (accessed 8 August 2013).

Department for Education and Skills (DfES) (2005a) *Every Child Matters: What is the Common Assessment Framework?* [online]. Available at http:// www.everychildmatters.gov.uk/_files/ 9C0FA5C9D5787362C313926CDD6D7E4F.pdf (accessed 2 January 2008).

Department for Education and Skills (DfES) (2005b) *Every Child Matters: Lead Professional* [online]. Available at http://www. everychildmatters.gov.uk/deliveringservices/leadprofessional (accessed 2 January 2008).

Department of Health (DH) (1998) *Quality Protects: Framework for Action*, London, DH/The Stationery Office.

Department of Health (DH) (2002) *Speech by the Rt Hon Alan Milburn MP, 16th October 2002: Reforming Social Services* [online]. Available at http://www.dh.gov.uk/en/News/Speeches/Speecheslist/DH_4031620 (accessed 3 September 2007).

Department of Health (DH) (2005) *Report from the National Clinical Director for Children on the Development of the National Service Framework for Children, Young People and Maternity Services*, London, DH.

Dumbleton, S. (2005) 'Widening opportunities for disabled children in Stirling: a voluntary body initiative' in Glaister, A. and Glaister, B. (eds) *Inter-Agency Collaboration – Providing for Children*, Edinburgh, Dunedin Academic Press, pp. 36–46.

Eyres, I., Cable, C., Hancock, R. and Turner, J. (2004) '"Whoops, I forgot David": children's perceptions of the adults who work in their classrooms', *Early Years*, vol. 24, no. 2, pp. 149–162.

Featherstone, B. (2004) *Family Life and Family Support: A Feminist Analysis*, Basingstoke, Palgrave Macmillan.

Francis, R. (2013) *Report of the Mid Staffordshire NHS Foundation Trust Public Inquiry* [online], London, The Stationery Office. Available at http://www.midstaffspublicinquiry.com/report (accessed 8 August 2013).

Frost, N. and Lloyd, A. (2006) 'Implementing multi-disciplinary teamwork in the new child welfare policy environment', *Journal of Integrated Care*, vol. 14, no. 2, pp. 11–17.

Gu, Q. and Day, C. (2013) 'Challenges to teacher resilience: conditions count', *British Educational Research Journal*, vol. 39, no. 1, pp. 22–44.

Halliday, J. and Asthana, S. (2004) 'The emergent role of the link worker: a study in collaboration', *Journal of Interprofessional Care*, vol. 18, no. 1, pp. 17–28.

HM Treasury/Department for Education and Skills (DfES) (2007) *Aiming High for Disabled Children: Better Support for Families*, London, HM Treasury/DfES.

Jackson, S. (1987) 'Residential care and education', *Children & Society*, vol. 2, pp. 335–350.

Jackson S. (2010) *Education for Social Inclusion: Can we Change the Future for Children in Care?* London, University of London, Institute of Education.

James, A.L. and James, A. (2001) 'Tightening the net: children, community, and control', *British Journal of Sociology*, vol. 52, no. 2, pp. 211–228.

Jones, L. and Tucker, S. (2000) 'Exploring continuity and change' in Brechin, A., Brown, H. and Eby, M.A. (eds) *Critical Practice in Health and Social Care*, London, The Open University/Sage, pp. 3–24.

Laming, Lord (2003) *The Victoria Climbié Inquiry*, London, The Stationery Office.

Leverett, S. (2008) 'Children's participation' in Foley, P and Leverett, S. (eds) (2008) *Connecting with Children: Developing Working Relationships*, Bristol, The Policy Press.

Lipsky M (1980) *Street Level Bureaucracy: Dilemmas of the Individual in Public Services*, New York, Russell Sage.

Lloyd, C., Wollny, I., White, C., Gowland, S. and Purdon, S. (2011) *Monitoring and Evaluation of Family Intervention Services and Projects between February 2007 and March 2011* [online], Research Report DFE-RR174, Department for Education. Available at https://www.gov.uk/government/uploads/system/uploads/attachment_data/file/184031/DFE-RR174.pdf (accessed 21 August 2013).

Lymbery, M. and Butler, S. (eds) (2004) *Social Work Ideals and Practice Realities*, Basingstoke, Palgrave Macmillan.

MacBeath, J., Gray, J., Cullen, J., Frost, D., Steward, S. and Swaffield, S. (2007) *Schools on the Edge: Responding to Challenging Circumstances*, London, Paul Chapman.

Munro, E. (2011) *The Munro Review of Child Protection: Final Report: A Child Centred System*, London, Department for Education.

National Statistics (2013) *School Workforce in England: November 2012* [online], London, Department for Education. Available at https://www.gov.uk/government/uploads/system/uploads/attachment_data/file/193090/SFR_15_2013.pdf (accessed 25 June 2013).

Open University (2005) E111 *Supporting learning in primary schools*, Study Topic 1, 'Teaching assistants today', Milton Keynes, The Open University.

Parton, N. (2004) 'From Maria Colwell to Victoria Climbié: reflections on public inquiries into child abuse a generation apart', *Child Abuse Review*, vol. 13, no. 2, pp. 80–94.

Pinnock, K. and Evans, R. (2007) 'Developing responsive preventative practices: key messages from children's and families' experiences of the Children's Fund', *Children & Society* [online]. Available at http://www.blackwell-synergy.com/doi/full/10.1111/j.1099–0860.2007.00081.x (accessed 22 October 2007).

Pinnock, M. and Dimmock, B. (2003) 'Managing for outcomes' in Henderson, J. and Atkinson, D. (eds) *Managing Care in Context*, London, The Open University/Routledge, pp. 257–282.

QAA Scotland (2007) *The standard for childhood practice*, available online at <http://www.sssc.uk.com/doc_details/1050-the-standard-for-childhood-practice>, accessed 12 July 2013.

Roger, S. (2013) Personal communication to The Open University.

Rogers, A. and Reynolds, J. (2003a) 'Leadership and vision' in Seden, J. and Reynolds, J. (eds) *Managing Care in Practice*, London, The Open University/Routledge, pp. 57–82.

Rogers, A. and Reynolds, J. (2003b) 'Managing change' in Seden, J. and Reynolds, J. (eds) *Managing Care in Practice*, London, The Open University/Routledge.

Russell, A., Blatchford, P., Bassett, P., Brown, P. and Martin, C. (2005) 'The views of teaching assistants in English key stage 2 classes on their role, training and job satisfaction', *Educational Research*, vol. 47, no. 2, pp. 175–189.

Russell, S. and Drennan, V. (2007) 'Mothers' views of the health visiting service in the UK: a web-based survey', *Community Practitioner*, vol. 80, no. 8, pp. 22–26.

Scottish Executive (2003) *Partnership for Care: Scotland's Health White Paper*, Edinburgh, Scottish Executive.

Scottish Executive (2006) *Getting It Right for Every Child: Proposals for Action – Analysis of Consultation Responses*, Edinburgh, Scottish Executive.

Seden, J. (2003) 'Managers and their organisations' in Henderson, J. and Atkinson, D. (eds) *Managing Care in Context*, London, The Open University/Routledge, pp. 105–132.

Social Enterprise Coalition (2007) *Health Business: A Guide to Social Enterprise in Health and Social Care* [online]. Available at http://www.socialenterprise.org.uk/documents/Healthy_Business.pdf (accessed 2 January 2008).

Troman, G. and Woods, P. (2000) 'Careers under stress: teacher adaptations at a time of intensive reform', *Journal of Educational Change*, vol. 1, no. 3, pp. 253–275.

Tronto, J. (2001) 'Does managing professionals affect professional ethics? Competence, autonomy and care' in DesAutels, P. and Waugh, J. (eds) *Feminists Doing Ethics*, Lanham, MD, Rowman & Littlefield, pp. 187–202.

Tunstill, J., Aldgate, J. and Hughes, M. (2007) *Improving Children's Services Networks: Lessons from Family Centres*, London, Jessica Kingsley.

Waterhouse, S. (2000) *Lost in Care: Report of the Tribunal of Inquiry into the Abuse of Children in Care in the Former County Council Areas of Gwynedd and Clwyd since 1974*, London, The Stationery Office.

Watson, D., Townsley, R., Abbott, D. and Latham, P. (2002) *Working Together? Multi-agency Working in Services to Disabled Children with Complex Health Care Needs and Their Families: A Literature Review*, Birmingham, Handsel Trust.

Chapter 2 Towards integrated working

Bill Stone and Pam Foley

Introduction

An expectation that agencies and their practitioners will work increasingly closer together has crossed all areas of children's services. This has ranged from closer strategic partnerships to bringing a range of practitioners together in highly integrated teams. This chapter explores the concepts of interagency and integrated working, and analyses the reasons why this trend has become such a major feature of policy and practice in work with children, and, in an era which sees a refocusing of children's services on what are understood as their core responsibilities, the problems and issues that have arisen in the process.

Core questions

- Why, from the perspective of children and their families, are interagency working and more integrated ways of working important?
- What are meant by 'interagency', 'interprofessional' and the many other terms in this area?
- What is the policy context and what are the key drivers for integrating work?
- What are some of the key issues and difficulties arising from increasingly integrated working?
- What skills are needed to ensure children and families remain at the centre of integrated working?

1 Starting with a child and their family

1.1 The experience of children and families

A theme throughout several chapters in this book will be the exploration of whether, and how, different agencies and practitioners can work more effectively together to enhance the wellbeing of children and families. 'Working together' for children might sound a straightforward enterprise, and sometimes this may be the case.

However, from the point of view of the child and their family who can expect to be at the centre of any reforms, things may look very different. We want to stress here therefore that any exploration of the subject should start with the experiences of children and families themselves.

> 'There are times that having all different people in my life is too much. I spend a lot of my time up the hospitals. I wish there were less appointments and less doctors to see.'
>
> (Child quoted in Turner, 2003, p. 21)

> 'At the beginning no-one explained that so many people would be visiting and phoning and that there would be so many appointments at the house. No-one told me what to expect, I'd like to have known more.'
>
> (Parent of child with disability quoted in Abbott et al., 2005, p. 231)

An example of the growing demand for better coordinated services has been that from children with disabilities and their families, whose experience frequently lies at one end of the continuum of interacting with multiple agencies and practitioners. In the past, families with children with disabilities have on average had contact with at least ten different professionals over the course of a year, and attended at least twenty appointments at hospitals or clinics (Care Co-ordination Network UK, 2001, cited in Townsley et al., 2004, p. 3). For children with complex healthcare needs, these numbers can be much higher, leading to a bewildering situation:

> The sheer number of professionals who may be involved in supporting a disabled child in the community can often lead to a lack of continuity and coordination and may leave families uncertain about who to contact regarding specific problems.
>
> (Townsley et al., 2004, p. 3)

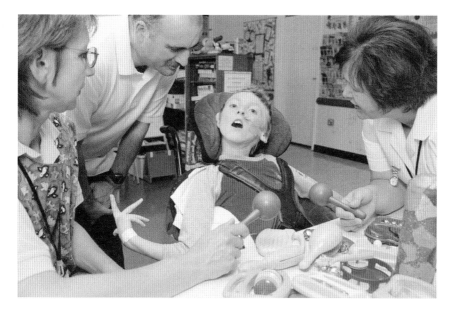

Some children and families have to deal with numerous appointments and assessments with many different practitioners

It is clear that many children with a disability understand the need to see a range of people and value the contribution they make to their welfare (Turner, 2003). However, their experience of fragmented services, the numbers of people involved and the lack of 'child-centredness' provide a clear example of how the work of different practitioners needs to be well coordinated (Turner, 2003). This can include the value of having just one practitioner to liaise with, who in turn helps to coordinate services on their behalf (Abbott et al., 2005).

Different policy makers across the UK have attempted to address the fragmentation and uncoordinated nature of services. For example the Scottish Government introduced Getting it right for every child (known as GIRFEC) (Scottish Government, 2013), which was explicit about agencies working together. Their website explains the implications of this approach for practitioners as follows:

- Putting the child or young person at the centre and developing a shared understanding within and across agencies

- Using common tools, language and processes, considering the child or young person as a whole, and promoting closer working where necessary with other practitioners

(Scottish Government, 2013)

Analysis of what primarily drives different agencies and practitioners to work more closely together tends to be dominated by discussion of government policy and finance, so it is important to recognise that one force for change can and should originate from children and families. Starting with children's views is also a reminder that, when asked, they can have plenty to say about their lives. Rather than play a part as an 'object of concern', albeit with expertise on their own lives, they need to be active participants in contributing to the shape of services and the construction of solutions. Supported by an emphasis on children's rights, this standpoint conceptualises children as agents who have their own views and opinions about the adults and the institutions with which they interact. Research with children with a disability and young people by Turner (2003) for the Welsh Assembly clearly demonstrated that they have a wealth of views on the type of practice they would like to experience and the sort of services they would like to see.

Consultation with children and young people in care in England similarly illustrated how they can comment on issues directly relating to interagency service delivery (DfES, 2007). For example, while the increased sharing of information about children is widely seen in policy terms as important to enabling better working together, children clearly express their concerns about who has access to this information. They were equally able to comment on the idea of lead professionals and the proposal that they should hold their own budgets (generally positively on both proposals) (DfES, 2007).

Discussion about the difficulties for practitioners from different agencies or professionals working together to meet agreed standards and to respond to what children and families say is required usually focuses primarily on structures or issues of knowledge base, workplace and professional cultures, values and attitudes. But the way in which different practitioners view children – and construct their ideas of childhood – adds an additional layer. How children's services are constructed depends in part on how childhood is constructed (Moss and Petrie, 2002). Positioning children as 'in need' of such things as care, control and education rather than focusing on children's evolving capacities can call into question the current configuration of services. The context of reorganising services is not just about different relationships between services but also about 'a new relationship with children themselves' (Cohen, 2005, p. 10).

It is also crucial to ascertain the perspective of parents and carers, who will usually be there for the child when all the professionals have gone home. Their ongoing participation in the development of services is also crucial. The partnership structures discussed below that require the inclusion of parents in most new development have gone some way towards recognising this, although the extent to which this has impacted on services is variable.

1.2 The contexts of children's wellbeing

There are many different perspectives on what children and families need, what their capabilities are and how their wellbeing can be promoted. Despite this diversity of views, most practitioners would agree that all aspects of children's lives are inextricably linked. A child is a whole person whose life cannot be divided up into different segments, with each segment considered separately. A child's social and emotional development cannot, for example, be easily split off from her or his physical health. There has been a growing body of evidence in child development theory demonstrating that children's overall development is influenced by a whole range of other factors in the wider environment in which they live (Aldgate, 2006; Fawcett, 2000). These influences range from immediate family relationships through school to broader elements of the community and wider society. This 'ecological' model, developed in particular by Bronfenbrenner (1979), has become highly influential and provides a useful theoretical framework for understanding the interrelatedness of all these factors.

One of the most striking things about looking at children's development in this way – both holistically and in an ecological context – is the implication that each practitioner's perspective on children's lives is valid and all their contributions are potentially important. Equally, this model suggests that no one profession has all the answers and no one perspective is definitive. In turn, these different sources of knowledge and practice need to be coordinated if the whole child is to be supported effectively. Herein lies one of the key challenges in working together for children.

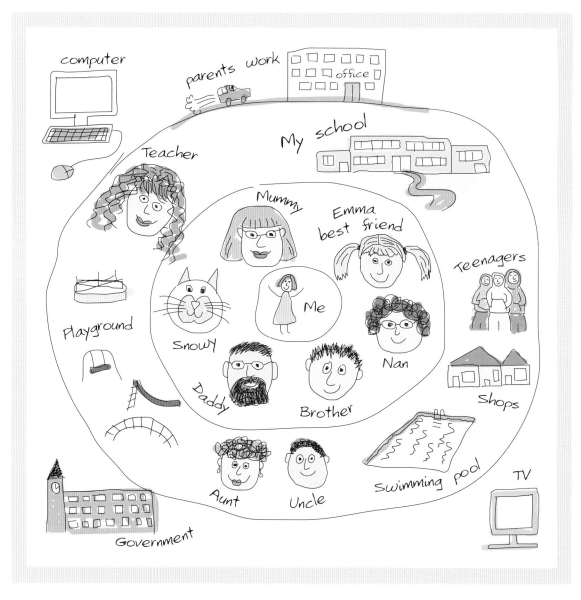

A child's view of her ecological context

The education and training of a range of practitioners involves becoming acquainted with a different body of theory and underpinning knowledge derived from one or more of the academic disciplines. Health visitors and early years workers, for example, will draw on child development theory to a greater extent than other practitioners. Social workers are likely to have knowledge of theories about family relationships such as systems theory, and may be informed by sociological theory more than other colleagues in the children's workforce. This knowledge and theory is inevitably selective and partial; no one discipline claims a complete or definitive understanding of the complexity of children's lives. It is a strength that the interdisciplinary nature of work with children and families is one of its defining features. These theoretical approaches, however, are not easily compatible or blended. Yet this is essential both for skilled and insightful practice and for any meaningful level of integrated working.

In addition, at the level of practice, those adults who are working with children are based in or work across a multitude of different settings: schools, health centres, play settings, children's centres, social work offices and community projects of all shapes and sizes. They are also employed by a variety of different agencies or working in a voluntary capacity. This obviously highlights the issues of communication and coordination.

To achieve anything substantial in terms of children's wellbeing, this diverse, scattered and somewhat fragmented children's workforce needs to be (as GIRFEC illustrated above) joined up around each individual child and his or her family. It is this difficult process of joining up, with all the potential for conflict, rivalry, miscommunication and misunderstanding that the process inevitably entails, that is explored in the rest of this chapter.

Key points

1 Explorations of the way practitioners work together should be informed by the voices of children and families and start with the realities of their lives.

2 A holistic view of children's lives provides a clear basis for the need for practitioners from different disciplines all having a contribution to make to children's wellbeing.

3 The interdisciplinary nature of children's services is a strength rather than a weakness.

2 The context for working together: discovering the key drivers

2.1 Defining our terms

We have already used the words 'interagency' and 'interprofessional'; before proceeding any further, some reference to the terminology problem is required.

Any discussion of the difficulties and complexities of practitioners 'working together' is not helped by the proliferation of terminology used to describe it. The entire field is characterised by what one commentator has called 'conceptual hybridity', that is, one concept being grafted onto another concept in a confusing way (Taylor et al., 2006, p. xi). Just some of the key words to be found in the writing on this subject are given below.

- Multi-agency/Cross-agency/Interagency/Trans-agency
- Multi-professional/Interprofessional/Interdisciplinary/Trans-disciplinary
- Coordination
- Cooperation
- Collaboration
- Partnerships
- 'Joined-up thinking' and 'Joined-up working'
- Cross-cutting
- Cross-boundary working
- Networks
- Integrated working

Thinking point 2.1: Can you define some of these terms in simple language? For example, what might be the difference between interprofessional, multi-agency and integrated working?

Even the language struggles to express with any clarity the complicated way in which concepts are being joined together, hence the proliferation of hyphens. Maybe that is also one explanation for the bewildering array of acronyms that one encounters in writing about this subject. We will not attempt to define the list of terms above, even if that were possible given the inconsistent way in which they are used; however, some could be usefully explored further. We should also clarify the terms adopted for this book to avoid adding to the confusion.

'Working together' and 'working across boundaries' are useful catch-all phrases; however, clearly many of these words are implying differing degrees of 'working together', and Frost (2005) suggested that some clarity can be brought to the subject by using the idea of a continuum of partnership. He argued that from all the possible terms that may be used, we can perhaps perceive a continuum from cooperation to integration, with partnership acting as an underlying theme:

no partnership   uncoordinated, free-standing services

level one   *co-operation* – services work together toward consistent goals and complementary services, while maintaining their independence

level two   *collaboration* — services plan together and address issues of overlap, duplication and gaps in service provision towards common outcomes

level three   *co-ordination* – services work together in a planned and systematic manner towards shared and agreed goals

level four   *merger/integration* – different services become one organisation in order to enhance service delivery

(Frost, 2005, p. 13)

This model has the merit of showing that there are different degrees of working together that operate within structures and organisations. For any practitioner working with children and families it should be possible to place her or his agency somewhere on this continuum. A 'network', for example, is often used to describe one configuration of practitioners which could be placed within this framework, as illustrated here in relation to a preferred configuration of interagency relationships being developed in Scotland:

> A linked group of professions and organisations from health care, social care and other agencies working together in a coordinated manner with clear governance and accountability arrangements.
>
> (Hudson, 2007, p. 6)

However, such a continuum may tend to imply that there is a natural progression in working together from one end to the other, and that integration is the final, hoped for, outcome. Many government policies across the UK have fuelled this idea of the desirability of integration at all levels – organisational to individual teams (see DfES, 2004, for example). However, full integration may in fact be neither possible nor desirable in some cases. An outcomes focus may help to bring some clarity here and prevent us from viewing interagency working as being an end in itself. If it is the outcomes for the child and their family that really matter, then the question should be: what is the best configuration for the development or delivery of a particular service?

Services for children and families across the UK are frequently reorganised. In England education and children's social services departments were brought together in the 2000s into a single 'children's services' designed in itself to lead to a greater degree of integration. Separate, self-contained 'silos' devoted to delivering a particular, focused service to children and their families were seen to be unhelpful in terms of providing a 'seamless service' to the end users and were replaced by more integrated structures. Such reorganisations may enable the structural difficulties of two services working together to be overcome (although this is by no means certain), but not necessarily the professional or disciplinary ones. As we have noted, practitioners within organisations, however they are constituted, interact drawing on different knowledge bases and values, etc. The idea of 'interprofessional' working therefore remains a distinct issue, even where teams are seemingly fully integrated. Such issues are evident in, for example, 'teams around the child'.

A team around the child is a multidisciplinary group of practitioners providing different services to a particular child or young person. Listed round the edge of this image are: Children's Team, Advocacy, Parenting, Play, Sure Start, Flying Start, Family Information Service, Communities 1st, Voluntary Organisations, Youth Service, Health, Schools, Police and Inclusion Services. (Blaenau Gwent County Borough Council)

The children's workforce is highly diverse. In addition to well-known professional groups such as teachers, social workers, children's nurses and so on, it also includes people in roles such as teaching assistants, early years workers, childminders, family support workers, play workers and foster carers. Other practitioners might work in a voluntary capacity in children's clubs, as Cubs and Brownies leaders, or in provision run by faith groups; most of these have not traditionally been seen as professionals but they can nevertheless play a highly significant role in children's lives. They are also seen to be working in an increasingly 'professional' way as training and regulation have grown. One example of this is the background criminal records checks that were introduced following the Bichard inquiry in 2004 (Bichard Inquiry Report, 2004). The scope of criminal records checks has subsequently been narrowed (with Criminal Records Checks carried out within the Disclosure and Barring Service) with regard particularly to the voluntary and community sector, although it is clear that voluntary agencies are still expected to adopt safe recruitment practice and do background checks on those with significant contact with children and vulnerable adults.

Issues around professionalism – who counts as a professional and why – are returned to later, but as the opening chapter made clear, our focus in this book is on the broader audience. Exploring 'working together for children' in this book is as much about 'inter-practitioner' working as that implied by any other terminology used in work with children.

2.2 Policy directions

The drive for agencies and their practitioners to work more closely together is not a new phenomenon. It has been around as long as there have been different groups of people providing services to children and families. But what is new is the extent of the emphasis on interagency, and increasingly integrated, working in recent approaches to the delivery of children's services.

It should first, however, be said that this approach has long been common in some areas, such as child protection (DH, 1989; DHSSPS 2003; HM Government, 2010; Scottish Government, 2010; Welsh Assembly Government, 2006). The complexities of a multiplicity of practitioners working to enhance the welfare of a child (in addition to the tendency for 'child-centredness' to be lost) are clearly illustrated in the arena of protecting and safeguarding children. Ineffective interagency working may not just result in unsatisfactory services but can have serious consequences for children.

The challenge for practitioners and their agencies working to protect children has long been to be able to work together in an effective way, sharing information and concerns, and planning and acting in a coordinated way. In the case of vulnerable children, where the stakes may be very high indeed, working together is even more critically important. In a complex, modern society where there is a whole range of services available to help and support children, this is inevitably difficult.

The death of Victoria Climbié and the landmark public inquiry that followed (Laming, 2003) provided a salutary example of how the network of agencies charged with safeguarding vulnerable children were not able to successfully protect a child. It is estimated that Victoria and her carers had contact with over seventy different professionals in the short period of time between her arrival in London from Paris and her death less than twelve months later. Numerous factors contributed to the inability of the child protection 'system' to intervene successfully in Victoria's life, including poor individual practice and lack of training and resources. However, the ineffective communication between agencies was identified, as in many inquiry reports before, as a significant contributor to the problem (Laming, 2003). Crucially, the inquiry report highlights the fact that the starting point for practitioners was rarely the child or her perspectives on her experience – Victoria was rarely seen as the central client in this case and rarely spoken to directly.

> Good communication, checking with partner agencies at the point of referral, and talking to the child as appropriate, must be the main way to decide how best to safeguard and promote a child's welfare.
>
> (Laming, 2003, p. 365)

Recognition of the need for agencies to work together has a long history in the UK. The Kilbrandon Report (Kilbrandon. 1964), for example, as well as establishing the system of children's panels in Scotland, also highlighted the role played by a whole variety of people from different agencies, statutory and voluntary, in the juvenile justice system and the vital importance of effective relationships between them (Cohen, 2005). Lord Kilbrandon proposed the establishment of 'social education' departments, arguing that academic education and 'social living' could not be separated (Cohen, 2005). His arguments, though not acted upon at the time, prefigured thinking about restructuring many years later and the 'whole child' approach to children's services, central to the launch of New Community Schools in Scotland (Cohen, 2005).

Some commentators have identified the Conservative administrations of the 1980s as a crucial phase in the recent history of interagency working (Percy-Smith, 2005). During the first administration under Margaret Thatcher there was increasing concern about economic inefficiency and the rising costs of the public sector. The welfare state was viewed as an inefficient bureaucracy with public services reflecting the priorities and interests of professional providers as much, if not more, than service users. The market was seen as a much more efficient vehicle than state ownership for providing services, and the government sought to 'open up' the public sector to competition and the economic disciplines of the marketplace; 'the role of identifying needs for services and planning to meet those needs could be separated from the role of delivering the services' (Percy-Smith, 2005, p. 9).

These ideas led to the 'contract culture' whereby local authorities were obliged to contract with a wide range of private and voluntary organisations, buying in services which they may previously have provided themselves. One of the results of this shake-up of the welfare state was to further increase the complexity of service delivery.

However, at the same time there was an increasing focus, at the highest level of government, on a range of problems that other government policies frequently exacerbated, such as urban regeneration, child abuse and neglect, the environment, community safety and social exclusion.

> These issues were characterised by their 'cross-cutting' nature. In other words, they did not fall clearly within the remit of any one single organisation. Furthermore, they were seen as beyond the ability of any single organisation working alone to solve ... As a result the 1990s saw the development of multilateral partnerships involving the public, private and voluntary sectors, in part stimulated by the availability of central government funding, especially in relation to regeneration.
>
> (Percy-Smith, 2005, p. 10)

When the government changed in 1997, concerns about the public sector remained. Labour thinking about public services centred on the need to modernise. Education, health and social care were thought of as being in dire need of reform, and a more rigorous, rational and 'scientific' approach to managing the public sector was introduced. This consisted of ensuring that public sector organisations were set clear targets and outcome measures as a means of evaluating how successful they were in achieving their stated objectives (Lister, 2005). The argument for this approach was partly about the efficient use of taxpayers' money, but also about the perceived need to drive up the quality of public services. An emphasis on joining up and working together was an explicit strand within this 'modernisation' agenda (Lister, 2005). The rationale of saving public money by investing strategically in early intervention in order to make savings later on was one of the key arguments used in making the case for the Sure Start programme.

Social exclusion and the work of the now disbanded Social Exclusion Unit played a central role in providing some of the theory underpinning this new approach to social policy.

> The principal driver of integration was, from the outset, the six cross-cutting reviews set up under the Labour Government's Comprehensive Spending Review initiated in 1997. The seeds of the children's cross-cutting review can be discerned earlier, in the

Labour manifesto pledge to set up Early Excellence Centres. Among its terms of reference was 'to consider whether the multiple causes of social exclusion affecting young people could be more effectively tackled at the family and community level by using a more integrated approach to service provision.' The Social Exclusion Unit was already highlighting the so-called 'wicked areas' of public provision: cracks through which too many young people were falling.

(Clode, 2003, pp. 4–5)

The drive to work together across different departments, sectors and professional groups to achieve agreed outcomes became the conventional wisdom. 'Joined up thinking and joined up working' was the mantra as partnership arrangements became the vehicle for achieving the aims of government social policy right across the spectrum of public policy, including health, teenage pregnancy, drugs and youth crime – areas emphasised by the work of the government's Social Exclusion Unit. The key problems of delivering a service with many agencies and practitioners involved was restated at the start of the process of introducing a far-reaching reform of children's services known as 'Every Child Matters' in England – including a recognition that some of the hurdles in the way of closer working together are caused by governments themselves:

Children may experience a range of professionals involved in their lives but little continuity and consistency of support. Organisations may disagree over who should pay for meeting a child's needs because their problems cut across organisational boundaries. Fragmentation locally is often driven by conflicting messages and competing priorities from central Government.

(DfES, 2003, pp. 21–22)

With the change of government in 2010, children's services were also encouraged to refocus on their core business, whether that was education, care or health. In England some key pieces of Labour policy were archived, such as Every Child Matters (2003), an overarching policy used across education, healthcare and social care settings, with major implications for working together. Governments in different parts of the UK continually try to reduce bureaucracy and this has the potential to impact on children's services in a number of ways. The Children's Workforce Development Council (CWDC), created to embed integrated working practices and processes across the children's workforce, perished in a drive to reduce what was perceived as bureaucratic, centralised control. The CWDC's final report regretted the 'lack of a clear government steer' on integrated working, suggesting that this would result in an 'uncoordinated approach across departments' (Lepper, 2012).

In England the regulation of education providers and early years sector providers was to be reduced and OFSTED inspections were refocused to concentrate more rigorously on the core business of schools. Revised agendas for education services emphasised the autonomy of schools (leading to Academy and Free Schools), strengthening leadership and quality of teaching and examining the rigour of external testing (DfE, 2011). The education systems of the UK remain a 'mixed market', and this continues to be seen as a way of shaking up perceived stagnation within the state sector. The Munro report (DfE, 2011) into child protection, commissioned by the Secretary of State for Education in England, advocated a retreat from a procedural and target-driven approach to working together to protect children, and argued that professionals should be allowed some space in which to operate in the best interests of the vulnerable children with whom they work. However, the drive towards integration started over a decade ago continues.

Examples of this are widespread. For example the current safeguarding guidance (at the time of writing) clearly states that 'Ultimately, effective safeguarding of children can only be achieved by putting children at the centre of the system, and by every individual and agency playing their full part, working together to meet the needs of our most vulnerable children' (HM Government, 2013, p. 8). Or, in another example, the Family Justice Review (2011) had identified as a priority reducing delay in care cases and speeding up the care planning process, making adoption easier and quicker for those children who cannot return to their birth parents, predicated on the children's workforce (including the legal profession) working together in an integrated and efficient way.

This is reflected in service development too: see Practice box 2.1.

Practice box 2.1

New integrated family centre for Powys

Thursday 22 September 2011

The Integrated Family Support Centre in Newtown will act as a one-stop shop for information, advice and support, as well as early years provision, health services, family support, parental education and other services.

The centre will also offer the Welsh Government's Flying Start programme that helps children up to the age of three in the most disadvantaged communities in Wales, including free quality part-time childcare and parenting programmes.

The First Minister said:

'This new centre is here to serve and help the local community and provides a one-stop-shop for many vital services, from childcare through to adult learning. It is a great example of the Welsh Government working with different parts of the public and third sectors to deliver services people rely on in a way that suits them.

'As a government we are focused on providing support for families and tackling child poverty. We are doing this through flagship programmes, and we have made a commitment to double Flying Start, as well as rolling out our Families First initiative, which focuses on new and better ways of supporting families, particularly those living in poverty. Together we will deliver on integrated and seamless services for families.

'I am delighted to see how Montgomeryshire Family Crisis Centre and Powys County Council have established an Integrated Family Centre here in Newtown through working together. It is essential that we all work together in developing our services for children and their families, and I am always greatly encouraged when I see work that is going on locally to address local needs.'

(Welsh Government, 2011)

Of course, working together for children could have become less a matter of principle and more a matter of pragmatic, economic necessity. The overriding preoccupation for policy makers, managers and practitioners working for children in the immediate future is likely to be how to work together in order to achieve more with fewer resources and how to combine or collaborate between, or integrate, different disciplines, professional bodies, organisations and agencies to achieve the best possible outcomes for children within a shrinking welfare state.

2.3 Partnerships

> Multi-agency working became a policy imperative when the Labour government fixed on 'partnerships' as an alternative ethos to the internal market and competition in services.
>
> (Alexander and MacDonald, 2001, cited in Abbott et al., 2005, p. 229)

Partnership, rather like community, is a very nebulous term meaning different things to different people.

Thinking point 2.2: What do you understand by partnership in work with children and families? What might be some of the strengths and weaknesses of a partnership?

In this context, partnership is used to describe the new strategic framework through which twenty-first century services were to be delivered. An early example of this was the Children's Fund in England in 2000, for children aged 5–13, which illustrated some of the key features of this approach:

> The programme aims to identify at an early stage children and young people at risk of social exclusion, and make sure they receive the help and support they need to achieve their potential.
>
> The Children's Fund provides a responsive approach to developing services that address the difficulties faced by some children and their families. It encourages voluntary organisations, community and faith groups to work in partnership with local statutory agencies, and children, young people and their families, to deliver high-quality preventative services to meet the needs of communities.
>
> (DfES, 2005)

The extract above reveals several things about the government's concerns with social exclusion and early intervention, but it is the summary of the way the service is to be developed that explains the nature of partnership. These developments were also frequently led by voluntary organisations rather than local authorities.

Strategic partnerships continued to be the way such service developments were taken forward in all areas of health and social care, in Scotland, Wales and Northern Ireland as well as England (Glaister and Glaister, 2005; Hudson, 2005). Hudson (2007) argued that these principles have been more explicitly pursued in Scotland, as in England they are complicated by the emphasis placed on the role of the market and competition in the provision of services.

Many local Children's Fund partnerships did succeed in involving small voluntary organisations with large statutory ones in a creative way, although the experience was variable. The voluntary and community sector can be a major player at the local level, but because the sector is so diverse, communication with the statutory services for children can be problematic. Whereas the larger children's charities such as Barnardo's and the NSPCC may have an influencing voice at the 'top table' where strategy is agreed, there are many other charities working for children whose voices are rarely heard. The contribution these smaller organisations can make, through community projects or family centres, for example, to the welfare of children can be significant. (For an example of smaller organisations' contributions to the welfare of children, see the material on the voluntary group 'Plus' in Chapter 1.) Those within faith communities, for example, play a significant but often overlooked role, having contact with many of the most vulnerable and, in some cases, socially isolated children in the UK. Some families turn to these smaller groups because of a mistrust of larger or more statutory organisations. It could therefore be important that they are included within partnerships working together for children.

Significantly, the extract above about the Children's Fund also refers to children, young people and their families as being part of these partnerships. This model was typical of new initiatives in its emphasis on consultation and representation on partnership boards. There was recognition that children and young people could actively engage in the development of policy. Government departments were starting on the process of 'learning to listen' (Children and Young People's Unit, 2001) and expecting everyone else to do the same. Subsequent policy initiatives have increasingly seen consultation, particularly e-consultations, becoming widespread; for example the Welsh Government regularly opens consultation periods. Websites (such as the Welsh Government site http://wales.gov.uk/consultations/?lang= en&status=open) make extensive consultation relatively easy.

Policy makers are now more likely to engage in consultation, particularly e-consultations.

Partnership is not just networks of professionals working together with children and families. It also refers to a style of working and an attitude towards working alongside others for the benefit of children. This attitude constantly questions power relationships 'with the lived experience of users, carers and students foregrounded, and the knowledge and status of "experts" challenged at all times' (Curran, 1997, in Taylor et al., 2006, p. 19).

An extensive body of literature around partnership working with children, parents and carers has appeared since a number of the studies reported in *Child Protection: Messages from Research* in 1995:

Wanting partnership is a step in the right direction but achieving it is difficult. A positive attitude to partnership needs to underpin action, a fact emphasised by their finding that partnership with parents tended to follow from involving the child in the process.

(DH, 1995, p. 37)

The finding that it is important for professionals to be seen to be working *with* families is key to creating the right atmosphere for partnership working and is equally applicable to all settings. Partnership relations can be complicated when there are issues of power, status and respect, parents seeing professionals as being gatekeepers to scarce and much needed resources (DH, 2001). Empowerment of children and families is therefore a central strategy for promoting greater equality in the relationship between the service user and the practitioner and the service they work for.

The continued centrality of partnership working to the Children Act 2004 in England and Wales can be seen very clearly in the following table.

Sections in the Children Act 2004 requiring partnership working	
Section	**Description**
Section 10: The duty to co-operate	A duty is placed on local authorities to make arrangements to promote co-operation between agencies in order to improve children's well-being defined by reference to the five outcomes, and a duty on key partners to take part in those arrangements. It also provides a new power to allow pooling of resources in support of these arrangements.
Section 11: The duty to safeguard and promote welfare	Creates a duty for the key agencies who work with children to put in place arrangements to make sure that they take account of the need to safeguard and promote the welfare of children when doing their jobs.

Section 12: Information sharing	Allows further secondary legislation and statutory guidance to be made with respect to setting up databases or indexes that contain basic information about children and young people and their families.
Sections 13–16: Local safeguarding children's boards (LSCBs)	Requires that local authorities set up statutory LSCBs, and that the key partners take part.
Section 17: The children and young person's plan	Establishes a single plan to replace a range of current statutory planning.
Sections 18–19: Director of children's services and lead member	To be appointed by local authorities, and to be responsible for, as a minimum, education and children's social services functions. Local authorities have discretion to add other relevant functions, such as leisure or housing, if they feel it is appropriate.
Sections 20–24: Integrated inspection	Require an integrated inspection framework to be established by the relevant inspectorates to inform future inspections of all services for children.

(Hudson, 2005, p. 9)

While partnerships appear to provide a participative and inclusive mechanism for the development of children's services and the tackling of social exclusion, Lister (2005) emphasised that the role of partnerships can also be seen as part of a changing model of governance. In effect they could represent a greater penetration of state power by drawing others into the government agenda:

> The spread of an official and legitimated discourse of partnership has the capacity to draw local stakeholders, from community groups to business organisations, into a more direct relationship with government and involve them in supporting and carrying out the government's agenda ... Labour's emphasis on holistic and joined-up government, and its use of partnerships as a means of delivering public policy, can be viewed as enhancing the state's

capacity to secure political objectives by sharing power with a range of actors, drawing them into the policy process.

(Newman, 2001, quoted in Lister, 2005, p. 450)

2.4 Early and effective intervention

Several policies discussed above have also stressed the importance of identifying '*at an early stage* children and young people at risk of social exclusion', and making sure 'they receive the help and support they need to achieve their potential' (DfES, 2005, our emphasis). This was another significant aspect of the development of early twenty-first century social policy. There had been a growing consensus around the possibility of research identifying risk factors associated with subsequent social exclusion (France and Utting, 2005). Complex and seemingly intractable social problems such as teenage pregnancy or juvenile crime were seen to have their roots in early childhood and the quality of care given to a child before they even get to school, therefore the arguments for intervening early on in a child's life seemed to be inescapable (France and Utting, 2005).

The certainty with which such 'risk' factors can be identified is controversial. Children could easily become labelled as potentially anti-social or proto-criminal from a very young age, while statistically this will be true for only a small percentage. However, while direct causation is impossible to predict, it was argued that reducing children's exposure to a range of risk factors would be a beneficial preventative strategy. This was supported by research indicating that where multiple overlapping factors are present in children's lives, 'the chances of later problems and problem behaviour increase disproportionately' (France and Utting, 2005, p. 79). This has been characterised as a paradigm that is preventative but also focused on risk:

> However, the underpinning paradigm can more accurately be described as 'risk and protection-focused prevention' since it embraces the concept of enhancing protective factors in children's lives as well as tackling risk. 'Protection' in this context is defined as something other than the opposite of risk. It refers, specifically, to factors that have been consistently associated with good

outcomes for children growing up in circumstances where they are, otherwise, heavily exposed to risk.

(France and Utting, 2005, p. 80)

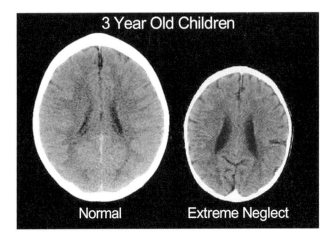

To many policy makers, early intervention remains the priority (from Allen Report, 2011)

Allen's (2011) review of early intervention demonstrated how mainstream this thinking on early intervention has become among policy makers. The report, which had all-party support, had two startling images on its front cover. One image was of the brain of a three-year-old child who experienced severe neglect and this was placed next to an image of a normal three-year-old child's brain. The neglected child's brain was small and shrunken compared to that of his or her neighbour. The message is blindingly obvious: poor-quality care in the early years stunts children's development and therefore early intervention is self-evidently necessary.

The thinking that underpins this kind of approach demonstrates the focus on interagency working. Tackling the multiple interlocking problems affecting children's development required multiple agencies engaged with children and families at an early stage, and this informed much of subsequent policy strategy.

The drive towards more integrated services for children in a range of differing configurations – extended schools, community schools, children's centres – sought to bring together co-located services and 'wrap-around' care. Any perceived barriers to communication between practitioners were to be dismantled by enabling shared assessment, the recognition of shared common skills, and the increased sharing of information.

Key points

1 Terminology in this area can be imprecise and confusing but there are some distinct and important differences in what terms describe. One perspective on the way agencies work together is to view their relationships on a continuum of partnership.
2 Interagency working has been a constant theme in policy developments over the last twenty years, particularly in relation to safeguarding children and overlaps with other key ideas such as public sector modernisation and the benefits of early intervention.
3 Partnerships have been a central feature of much interagency working, involving the development of policy as much as its implementation.

3 Boundaries and barriers

The previous sections have focused on the various arguments, rationales and drivers towards agencies and their practitioners working more closely together – even changing their roles and structures. The reality of practice has shown that this is often a complex task. Problems have been identified with more integrated approaches to working, but acknowledgement of the issues can contribute to finding solutions.

3.1 Thinking about professionalism

If you were to ask a cross-section of the public to identify which occupational groups constitute the 'professions', it is likely that most people would include those traditionally associated with the label such as doctors and lawyers. Some might also include teachers, nurses, health visitors and social workers if asked about professionals working with children. But what about nursery nurses, classroom assistants, play workers, early years workers, childminders and foster carers? The more you examine the various groups of people who work with children, the more blurred the boundaries become between professional and 'non-', 'semi-' or 'para-' professional groups. The situation is also complicated by change, as can be seen in the creation of new roles such as the 'early years professional' and early years teacher, as discussed in Chapter 1, or those with the word 'integrated' in the title.

Is professionalism about status and prestige or is it simply about economics? How important are expert knowledge, accountability, self-governance and professional ethics? Is professionalism related to the extent to which one is managed and regulated or autonomous? Is there a distinction between acting in a professional way and being a professional? To what extent is being a professional compatible with demonstrating care and compassion? Many of these distinctions are not particularly helpful in understanding what it is that people within the children's workforce actually do. However, some discussion of professionalism is relevant here. The key knowledge bases that must be 'worked across', as discussed earlier, have become closely associated with professional disciplines. The 'professional' label and its history also have significance for hierarchy and power relations – crucial issues given that we are essentially discussing effective working relationships.

Thinking point 2.3: How might different ideas about what constitutes being a professional affect interprofessional working?

The thinking and writing about professionalism which developed in the first half of the twentieth century focused on establishing characteristics or traits that professions were expected to hold. These traits included such things as altruism, trustworthiness, expert skills and knowledge, self-regulation, care and compassion, membership of a professional association and a code of ethics. Members of the professions were contrasted with other occupational groups by the altruistic and ethical way in which their expertise was applied. Most occupations were seen as driven by economic self-interest, whereas professionals were also motivated by 'higher things'. Other perspectives suggested that professionals carry out tasks that are typically characterised by a high level of complexity and uncertainty requiring an equally high level of education, judgement and skill. From this standpoint the tasks carried out by other occupations are less complex and can be more easily standardised, therefore they require less training. Professions have to exercise discretion and judgement, and therefore professional knowledge is seen as more than a set of rules and procedures (Finlay, 2000).

Finlay (2000) suggested that this idea of 'expert knowledge' has remained a very powerful factor in the public acceptance of professions. This in turn has influenced historically 'newer' groups such as nursing and social work to seek to establish an expert knowledge base of their own.

> Some kinds of knowledge are seen as more valid than others. In general, scientific knowledge carries more weight and respect than practical, experiential knowledge. In an effort to gain recognition of their professional status, many 'newer' professions in recent years have driven to establish a more expert knowledge base and increase their academic and scientific credibility ... 'semi-professionals' have campaigned to extend existing diploma training to degree level and replace on-the-job training with university-based study. Turning away from common-sense knowledge, they have struggled to develop their professional research base to show the worth and value of their work.
>
> (Finlay, 2000, p. 77)

Also crucial to the debate on the position of professionals is the question of power and control over particular areas of work (Hugman, 2005). This can be reinforced by the use of language through jargon and defining and labelling people's needs and problems – labelling a child as 'special needs', for example. Professional power can both reflect and reinforce the relatively privileged positions some groups hold in the social and economic hierarchy. If control over areas of work is central to the identity of a professional group, then it is easy to see how working with other agencies in a way that might involve sharing an area of work might be problematic. In addition to this, there is concern that a loss of professional autonomy can be profoundly damaging to effectiveness and accountability (DfE, 2011).

Power issues between groups of practitioners can also be seen in a variety of dimensions, notably class, ethnicity and gender. Finlay (2000) suggested that in relation to gender it is not just that women have been excluded from certain professions but also that those few professions dominated by women are defined in relation to those which are more traditionally male-oriented. Care is not accorded the same weight as the application of knowledge even though the latter may be dependent on the former. Some of the struggles between the relative professions of nurses and doctors can be perceived in this way (Finlay, 2000).

Professional power and status is also associated with issues such as gender, class and ethnicity

These critiques of professionalism have left many occupational groups working with children ambivalent about their professional status. On the one hand, they want to be seen as being 'professional' in the sense of having credibility (recognised by qualification), in terms of their specialised knowledge about children and their skills in working with children. On the other hand, it is obvious that elitism and professional language can act as a powerful barrier between the worker and the children and families with whom they are trying to build a relationship. Some practitioners have seen their role as forming radical alliances with people they work with, and have questioned why regulation and university-based education are essential to working in a professional way. Both social work and youth work, for example, have had anti-professional strands in their development (Banks, 2004). It might be argued that the difficulties faced by the social work profession in uniting around the College of Social Work, established in response to the government's social work reform board recommendations, could be seen in this light (McGregor, 2012).

Some of this questioning of the basis of being a professional has led to the idea that a new form of professionalism could emerge. It has been suggested that this could take the form of more democratic relationships with service users, reflecting the participatory style of practice discussed earlier. At the same time there is a recognition of the difficulties of actually achieving this in the modern, pressured, managerialised working environment (Banks, 2004). In an article about what she calls the 'new multi-agency working', Edwards (2004) outlined her view of what could be a way of working together for children. Rather than being led by the needs of the service providers, Edwards argued that the new multi-agency working for children should be geared around the needs of the child and family:

> The characteristics of the new professional practice include:
>
> - a focus on children and young people as whole people, ie not as specific 'needs'
> - following the child's trajectory
> - an ability to talk across professional boundaries
> - an understanding of what other practitioners are able to offer the responsive package of protection that is built around the child or young person
> - acknowledgement of the capacity of service users and their families to help to tailor the services they are receiving
> - an understanding that changing the trajectories of exclusion of children and young people involves not only building confidence and skills but also a reconfiguring of the opportunities available to them – ie systems-wide change.
>
> (Edwards, 2004, p. 5)

There is no intention here to reach a conclusion about who is a professional and who is not; definitions are diverse and changing, and may be of limited value. The whole concept of professionalism is a fluid one as established professionals find their position challenged and new roles emerge and become more qualified or claim new areas of expertise. Other practitioners may adopt elements of working in a 'professional way' even if not any formal label. Nevertheless, even if unresolved, differing views about expert knowledge, established cultures and hierarchies will inevitably be an issue as workers are asked to cross established boundaries. Hudson (2002) argued that the sociology of professionalism suggests that there are three major features of interprofessional working:

- professional identity: how professionals understand themselves and their role including the more informal and implicit aspects of professional cultures
- professional status: how different professional groups are variously distributed along the continuum of power and influence in society
- professional accountability: the extent to which different professional groups have the ability to exercise professional discretion and the way in which they are supervised and managed.

In research with a range of social care professionals (Banks, 2004), the most common themes that emerged from conversations with practitioners were perceived threats to professional identity, values and culture, a point illustrated by the following comment:

> 'I think you have to have a very good grounding in social work, as not just a profession, but as a value base, otherwise it is very easy to get sort of sucked into the dominant culture which social work is not in an integrated team.'
>
> (Manager in a CAMHS team, quoted in Banks, 2004, p. 135)

It may be that any actual difference in values is less important than the fact that workers say that their values are different in order to distinguish themselves, for example as social workers and not nurses, or vice versa (Banks, 2004). Banks also argued that this can be threatening because being, for example, a social worker 'may contribute to part of what an individual thinks about as the deepest and most enduring features of their unique selves' (Banks, 2004, p. 138). Similarly, elements of a personal identity can contribute to an individual's whole approach to their working life.

A theme emerging from interagency working, particularly within teams, is that it is a process that needs to be worked through, individually and collectively. It is at the problematic points of this 'working through' that references to culture and values seem to be stressed by practitioners. Rose's (2011) research on interprofessional teams working in different areas of children's services involved talking to groups of professionals about their experiences of working together. Through their focus on how they resolved dilemmas of interprofessional working, themes emerged which included professional identity, power, territory and expertise, all of which mean that working together in practice may not always be straightforward. The study concluded:

> The key contribution of this paper to the field, therefore, is to show that enacting collective preferences (the construction and co-ordinated pursuit of joint goals) may entail some kind of professional self-sacrifice, whether that is around identity, expertise, territory or power.
>
> (Rose, 2011, p. 161)

This professional self-sacrifice has some similarity, it might be argued, with the sort of sacrifice expected of parents in putting their children's needs above their own.

The drive towards increasingly integrated working therefore brings challenges to accepted professional boundaries and those that have worked within them. In multi-disciplinary teams, different specialisms, based on professional knowledge bases, can collide in uncomfortable ways:

> In multi-agency teamwork, professional knowledge boundaries can become blurred and professional identity can be challenged as roles and responsibilities change. Such changes can generate discomfort, anxiety, and anger in team members as they struggle to cope with the disintegration of one version of professional identity before a new version can be built. Moreover, the rapid pace of reform leaves little time for adjustment.
>
> (Frost et al., 2005, p. 188)

Thinking point 2.4: To what extent do you think 'learning together' might overcome the problems of working together?

3.2 Barriers to collaborative working

Children's services could increasingly embrace the third sector and involve more work with volunteers. This will raise more issues in relation to the notion of professionals and professionalism, particularly issues such as information sharing. Knowledge and status are crucial factors to be addressed in enabling collaborative working, along with numerous other interrelated individual and agency factors identified as potential obstacles. Salmon (2004) noted the importance of the differing governing policies of agencies, their guidelines, definitions, eligibility criteria, budgets, reporting cycles, supervisory structures, salaries and career development. Salaries can undoubtedly be a sensitive issue:

> Joined-up work often means different professionals doing the same work; for example, in the emerging children's teams many staff will be expected to use the common assessment framework. Where they are on different salary scales and service conditions they may resent this, and ask why they are not being paid as much as another profession doing the same work.
>
> (Frost and Lloyd, 2006, p. 13)

In a review of interprofessional collaboration between professionals working with children and families in areas of high social need, significant areas of disagreement were found to be:

- Differences of view over the nature of the intervention that was required
- Differences of view over who was responsible for carrying out the intervention
- Poor communication or a breakdown in communication where the different services were prioritising liaison/collaboration itself differently
- Different time scales for action between different services and agencies, though this may be seen as mainly a resource issue
- Differences in prioritising cases and in what constitutes a 'crisis'
- Differences in the way the services were organised.

(Easen et al., 2000, quoted in Salmon, 2004, p. 158)

A large-scale study of the implementation of Children's Trusts in England reported some early findings based on the Pathfinder Trusts (O'Brien et al., 2006). The authors concluded:

> Our findings suggest that whilst professional communities are
> embracing a commitment to the education, health and care of the
> 'whole' rather than the 'sectoral' child, differences between
> professional discourses and traditions remain, particularly in
> relation to threshold and intervention decisions.
>
> (O'Brien et al., 2006, p. 394)

The study made the point that a tension exists at the level of
philosophy and policy about the overall shape of children's services
around the balance between targeted and universal services.

A report commissioned by the Children's Commissioner for Scotland
(Lancaster, 2012) indicated that, in spite of Scotland's high-profile drive
to 'get it right for every child' mentioned earlier in this chapter, children
with a disability and their families in Scotland are still not always
consulted about the services they receive, and eligibility for social work
services varies from authority to authority. Another study carried out
over roughly the same time period as the O'Brien study looked at
practical issues around the implementation of the Common Assessment
Framework (CAF) and lead professional working (Brandon et al., 2006).
An evaluation of the early piloting of these initiatives in twelve English
local authorities found that there are a number of interlocking factors
that either help or hinder implementation. Where there was enthusiasm
for multi-agency working and a clear structure understood by
practitioners on the front line, the CAF and lead professional role were
helping agencies to come together much faster and enabling better
follow-up services. However, hindrances included the lack of a local
history of successful multi-agency working, breeding professional
mistrust and fuelling anxiety about change (Brandon et al., 2006).

Sometimes it appears that there are fundamental issues of structure and
philosophy that make desired change problematic. Cohen et al. (2004)
analysed the reorganisation of early years services in England and
Scotland to identify the success or otherwise of integrating the 'care'
and 'education' aspects of early years provision. These different aspects
of provision were developed in different departmental areas but were
brought together under the department responsible for education in the
late 1990s. The same integration occurred in Sweden, and the authors
used this as a point of comparison.

Integrating different philosophies into care and education in the early years can be problematic

The process of integration in England and Scotland had proved to be problematic from the most strategic level downwards. Amalgamating services under one department had not necessarily resulted in a service that could be described as integrated, particularly in terms of philosophy. There was, for example, a problem with 'services formerly in the welfare system –"childcare"– adopting education principles' (Cohen et al., 2004, p. 188). Different elements of provision in England and Scotland were increasingly 'linked' but could not be described as integrated where this is understood as 'merging or fusion'.

The relative success of this experience in Sweden highlighted some of the reasons why integration in the UK had proven so difficult. In England and to a lesser extent in Scotland, delivery of early years provision had become very fragmented after many years of a policy of a mixed economy of care. Drawing together these services here was always going to be much more complex than in Sweden, where the equivalent of the local authority was the main provider. Similarly, in the UK there is a history of a wide divergence between practitioners in the workforce of different aspects of early years work, for example in terms of training, pay and union membership; the differentiation between teachers and other early years workers is less marked in Sweden. Finally, the Swedish model is more focused on attaining a common view of children's learning and care (pedagogy being 'an integrating concept'), while in the UK the main drivers for change were concerns about solving long-standing social and economic problems. The employment agenda, for example, could be seen as 'a gravity field pulling childcare away from being fully integrated with education' (Cohen et al., 2004, p. 196).

There is no suggestion by Cohen and colleagues that the Swedish model can be easily copied; indeed, that would not be possible. Attempts to merge different services need to take account of their histories and cultures. The analysis of Cohen et al. (2004) provided a useful insight into why the stated desire for integration of services may not be achievable.

3.3 Communicating across boundaries

Worthy of specific consideration is the issue of communication. Communication is one of the most frequently reported problems of interagency and interprofessional work. Different groups of practitioners bring different terminology and meanings to any exchange, drawn from their specific training and worldviews. The most high-profile failings of communication are those repeated in numerous child protection inquiry reports. When such concerns were reflected again in the Victoria Climbié inquiry (Laming, 2003), Lord Laming argued for more strategies to be employed to enable clearer communication. His report recommended the amalgamation of current guidance into 'one simplified document' that enables a 'common language':

> It must establish a common language for use across all agencies to help those agencies to identify who they are concerned about, why they are concerned, who is best placed to respond to those concerns, and what outcome is being sought from any planned response.

> (Laming, 2003, p. 373)

The twin solutions for practitioners working more closely together were to increasingly co-locate them, moving towards integrated teams, and to enable this process through a commitment to sharing information and to developing a shared language. These are bold attempts to crack an important, recurrent and persistent issue. However, there have been questions raised about the logic of this approach. Does being physically in closer proximity automatically result in closer working relationships?

Just because practitioners are saying the same thing, do they mean the same thing?

White and Featherstone (2005) observed communication in a child health team (paediatrics, Child and Adolescent Mental Health Services (CAMHS), child and family social work) who had recently moved to an integrated centre. The co-location did not automatically break down different agency perceptions of the same case. In some instances the visibility of certain practices – for example the time some groups spent in meetings – served to sharpen rather than reduce prejudices between certain groups. Interactions occur with long-established and ritualised ways of working and ways of viewing practitioners from 'other' groups:

> professionals working at the multi-agency interface operate with robust social identities, which they take for granted as members of particular occupational groups, organizations or teams. Co-location does not straightforwardly lead to more or better communication. People cannot communicate with proper openness to the 'other' (professional) whilst the aspects of their professional narratives that maintain ritualized ways of working are underexplored.
>
> (White and Featherstone, 2005, p. 215)

In the child protection arena there have been numerous examples of poor communication in terms of sharing information with the right person (Laming, 2003). However, even where there is good practice in this respect, information received is not always interpreted in the way it was intended. Reder and Duncan (2003) argued for the need to focus less on a common language than on the actual process of communicating itself. They emphasise that communication is a sophisticated process that involves a great deal more than simply sharing information. A message has to be both given and received and then meaning attributed to it. In the complex and emotive area of child protection this process is highly problematic and there are lots of opportunities for messages to be distorted or lost in transition. Reder and Duncan (2003) pointed to numerous examples of such problems given in the evidence heard by the Victoria Climbié Inquiry (Laming, 2003):

'I cannot account for the way people interpreted what I said. It was not the way I would have liked it to have been interpreted.'

(Paediatrician quoted in Laming, 2003, p. 9)

These examples include conflicting versions of what was said:

To get a better understanding of the medical concerns, Ms Arthurworrey telephoned Dr Rossiter. Dr Rossiter remembered a conversation with Ms Arthurworrey occurring some time that week, but their recollections of what was said are rather different.

(Laming, 2003, p. 150)

Reder and Duncan's conclusion was that the focus of successful interagency working should be less on structural change and more on a commitment to change and on the skills level of communication itself:

Some have argued that communication between relevant professionals would improve if agency boundaries were dissolved and they all worked together within the same organizational structure. This call for reorganization fundamentally misses the point about the psychology of communication: that individuals and groups create and recreate their own boundaries based on beliefs, attitudes, work pressures, and so on. Furthermore, each episode of communication has an interpersonal dynamic of its own, and clarity of understanding will not necessarily be enhanced by different organizational structures. In our view, efforts to enhance professionals' capacity to think, and therefore to communicate, would be more rewarding.

(Reder and Duncan, 2003, p. 95)

Key points

1 The idea of the professional and professionalism still has an important influence on the effectiveness of practitioners working across their traditional boundaries

2 Research studies have highlighted a substantial range of issues that arise and must be understood when practitioners are asked to work in a more integrated way.

3 Communication is a particularly significant issue which may be partly enabled by closer integration of workers and the use of more common tools and language. Other aspects of this issue, however, may also need to be acknowledged, including practitioner skills in communication and their ability to reflect on practice.

Conclusion

In exploring a topic that necessarily focuses on the nature of relationships between agencies and practitioners, this chapter has attempted to reinforce the importance of starting with the views and rights of children and their families and the context of their lives. The increasing drive towards interagency, interprofessional and integrated working has created complex issues with a huge range of potential barriers and surrounded by confusing terminology. In highlighting some of the most significant issues we hope to start the process of unravelling whether it is working and what might enable practice to develop further.

References

Abbott, D., Watson, D. and Townsley, R. (2005) 'The proof of the pudding: what difference does multi-agency working make to families with disabled children with complex care needs?', *Child & Family Social Work*, vol. 10, no. 3, pp. 229–238.

Aldgate, J. (2006) 'Children, development and ecology' in Aldgate, J., Jones, D., Rose, W. and Jeffery, C. (eds) *The Developing World of the Child*, London, Jessica Kingsley.

Allen, G., MP (2011) *Early Intervention: The Next Steps: An Independent Report to Her Majesty's Government*, London, Cabinet Office.

Banks, S. (2004) *Ethics, Accountability and the Social Professions*, Basingstoke, Palgrave Macmillan.

Bichard, M. (2004) *The Bichard Inquiry Report*, London, The Stationery Office.

Blaenau Gwent County Borough Council (nd) *Team around the Child*, available online at <http://www.blaenau-gwent.gov.uk/education/12790.asp>, accessed 13 August 2013.

Brandon, M., Howe, A., Dagley, V., Salter, C. and Warren, C. (2006) 'What appears to be helping or hindering practitioners in implementing the Common Assessment Framework and lead professional working?', *Child Abuse Review*, vol. 15, no. 6, pp. 396–413.

Bronfenbrenner, U. (1979) *The Ecology of Human Development*, Cambridge, MA, Harvard University Press.

Children and Young People's Unit (2001) *Learning to Listen: Core Principles for the Involvement of Children and Young People*, London, DfES.

Clode, D. (2003) *Integrated Working and Children's Services – Structures, Outcomes and Reform: A Briefing Paper*, London, Integrated Care Network.

Cohen, B. (2005) 'Inter-agency collaboration in context: the "joining-up" agenda' in Glaister, A. and Glaister, B. (eds) *Inter-Agency Collaboration – Providing for Children*, Edinburgh, Dunedin Academic Press.

Cohen, B., Moss, P., Petrie, P. and Wallace, J. (2004) *A New Deal for Children? Re-forming Education and Care in England, Scotland and Sweden*, Bristol, The Policy Press.

Department for Education (DfE) (2011) *The Munro Review of Child Protection: Final Report – A Child Centred System*, London, The Stationery Office.

Department for Education and Skills (DfES) (2003) *Every Child Matters*, London, The Stationery Office.

Department for Education and Skills (DfES) (2004) *Every Child Matters: Change for Children*, London, The Stationery Office.

Department for Education and Skills (DfES) (2005) Every Child Matters: Children's Fund, available online at <http://www.everychildmatters.gov.uk/strategy/childrensfund>, accessed 24 April 2007.

Department for Education and Skills (DfES) (2007) *Care Matters: Consultation Responses*, London, DfES.

Department of Health (DH) (1989) *Working Together to Safeguard Children*, London, The Stationery Office.

Department of Health (DH) (1995) *Child Protection: Messages from Research*, London, The Stationery Office.

Department of Health (DH) (2001) *The Children Act Now: Messages from Research*, London, The Stationery Office.

Department of Health, Social Services and Public Safety (DHSSPS) (2003) Cooperating to Safeguard Children, available online at <http://www.dhsspsni.gov.uk/cooperating_to_safeguard_children>, accessed 11 April 2013.

Edwards, A. (2004) 'The new multi-agency working: collaborating to prevent the social exclusion of children and families', *Journal of Integrated Care*, vol. 12, no. 5, pp. 3–9.

Family Youth Justice Panel (2011) *Family Justice Review Final Report*, published on behalf of the Family Justice Review Panel by the Ministry of Justice, the Department for Education and the Welsh Government.

Fawcett, M. (2000) 'Early development: critical perspectives' in Boushel, M., Fawcett, M. and Selwyn, J. (eds) *Focus on Early Childhood: Principles and Realities*, Oxford, Blackwell, pp. 49–64.

Finlay, L. (2000) 'The challenge of professionalism' in Brechin, A., Brown, H. and Eby, M.A. (eds) *Critical Practice in Health and Social Care*, London, The Open University/Sage, pp. 73–95.

France, A. and Utting, D. (2005) 'The paradigm of "risk and protection-focused prevention" and its impact on services for children and families', *Children & Society*, vol. 19, no. 2, pp. 77–90.

Frost, N. (2005) *Professionalism, Partnership and Joined-up Thinking*, Dartington, Research in Practice.

Frost, N. and Lloyd, A. (2006) 'Implementing multi-disciplinary teamwork in the new child welfare policy environment', *Journal of Integrated Care*, vol. 14, no. 2, pp. 11–17.

Frost, N., Robinson, M. and Anning, A. (2005) 'Social workers in multidisciplinary teams: issues and dilemmas for professional practice', *Child & Family Social Work*, vol. 10, no. 3, pp. 187–196.

Glaister, A. and Glaister, B. (2005) 'Space for growth' in Glaister, A. and Glaister, B. (eds) *Inter-Agency Collaboration – Providing for Children*, Edinburgh, Dunedin Academic Press.

HM Government (2010) *Working Together to Safeguard Children: A Guide to Inter-agency Working to Safeguard and Promote the Welfare of Children*, London, The Stationery Office.

HM Government (2013) Working together to safeguard children: a guide to inter-agency working to safeguard and protect the welfare of children, available online at <http://media.education.gov.uk/assets/files/pdf/w/working%20together.pdf>, accessed 29 July 2013.

Hudson, B. (2002) 'Interprofessionality in health and social care: the Achilles' heel of partnership?', *Journal of Interprofessional Care*, vol. 16, no. 1, pp. 7–17.

Hudson, B. (2005) 'Partnership working and the children's services agenda: is it feasible?', *Journal of Integrated Care*, vol. 13, no. 2, pp. 7–12.

Hudson, B. (2007) 'Partnering through networks: can Scotland crack it?', *Journal of Integrated Care*, vol. 15, no. 1, pp. 3–13.

Hugman, R. (2005) *New Approaches in Ethics for the Caring Professions*, Basingstoke, Palgrave Macmillan.

Kilbrandon, Lord (1964) *The Kilbrandon Report: Children and Young Persons, Scotland*, Edinburgh, HMSO.

Laming, Lord (2003) *The Victoria Climbié Inquiry*, London, The Stationery Office.

Lancaster, B. (2012) *Social Work Services for Disabled Children and Young People and their Families: Assessment and Eligibility*, summary report, Edinburgh, Scotland's Commissioner for Children and Young People.

Lepper, J. (2012) 'CWDC issues warning to government ahead of closure', *Children and Young People Now* web page, available online at <http://www.cypnow.co.uk/cyp/news/1072578/cwdc-issues-warning-government-ahead-closure>, accessed 13 August 2013.

Lister, R. (2005) 'Investing in the citizen-workers of the future: transformations in citizenship and the state under New Labour' in Hendrick, H. (ed.) *Child Welfare and Social Policy*, Bristol, The Policy Press.

McGregor, K. (2012) *College of Social Work to receive £1m in govt funding this year*, available online at <http://www.communitycare.co.uk/articles/09/10/2012/118589/college-of-social-work-to-receive-1631m-in-govt-funding-this.htm>, accessed 24 April 2013.

Moss, P. and Petrie, P. (2002) *From Children's Services to Children's Spaces*, London, Routledge.

O'Brien, M., Bachmann, M., Husbands, C., Shreeve, A., Jones, N., Watson, J. and Shemilt, I. (2006) 'Integrating children's services to promote children's welfare: early findings from the implementation of Children's Trusts in England', *Child Abuse Review*, vol. 15, no. 6, pp. 377–395.

Percy-Smith, J. (2005) *What Works in Strategic Partnerships for Children?*, Ilford, Barnardo's.

Reder, P. and Duncan, S. (2003) 'Understanding communication in child protection networks', *Child Abuse Review*, vol. 12, no. 2, pp. 82–100.

Rose, J. (2011) 'Dilemmas of inter-professional collaboration: can they be resolved?', *Children & Society*, vol. 25, pp. 151–163.

Salmon, G. (2004) 'Multi-agency collaboration: the challenges for CAMHS', *Child and Adolescent Mental Health*, vol. 9, no. 4, pp. 156–161.

Scottish Government (2010) *National Guidance for Child Protection in Scotland*, Edinburgh, Scottish Government.

Scottish Government (2013) *Getting it right for every child*, available online at <http://www.scotland.gov.uk/Topics/People/Young-People/gettingitright>, accessed 7 May 2013.

Taylor, I., Sharland, E., Sebba, J., Leriche, P., Keep, E. and Orr, D. (2006) *The Learning, Teaching and Assessment of Partnership Working in Social Work Education*, London, SCIE.

Townsley, R., Abbott, D. and Watson, D. (2004) *Making a Difference?*, Bristol, The Policy Press.

Turner, C. (2003) *Are You Listening? What Disabled Children and Young People in Wales Think About the Services They Use*, Cardiff, Welsh Assembly.

Welsh Assembly Government (2006) *Safeguarding Children: Working Together under the Children Act 2004*, Cardiff, Welsh Assembly Government.

Welsh Government (2011) *New Integrated Family Centre for Powys*, available online at <http://wales.gov.uk/newsroom/firstminister/2011/110922integratedfamilycentre/?lang=en>,, accessed 7 May 2013.

White, S. and Featherstone, B. (2005) 'Communicating misunderstandings: multi-agency work as social practice', *Child & Family Social Work*, vol. 10, no. 3, pp. 207–216.

Chapter 3 Parenting, practice and politics

Stephen Leverett

Introduction

The chapters in this book have identified some of the ways that changes to systems, relationships and shared practices can promote and maintain children's health, education and safety. This includes the involvement of parents and family caregivers, the subject of this chapter. Throughout the twentieth century, the state progressively increased its level of support to, and its surveillance of, parents and carers (of children) with an emphasis on ensuring children were healthy, educated and safe. Although sometimes difficult to translate into practice, the ethos of working together with parents was usually maintained even in situations requiring more interventionist approaches such as child protection. This has continued into the twenty-first century when the expected outcomes for children from the perspective of governments have been more clearly defined and explicitly linked to the political and economic goals of the day (for example, children's attainment and wellbeing, social mobility, help for 'troubled families' and a competitive economy). There is always a constant shifting of the boundaries between the state, families and the voluntary and private sectors (Wasoff and Cunningham-Burley, 2005) in terms of responsibilities for education and childcare and the management of children's behaviour. Consequently the expectations and demands placed upon parents and carers are more clearly stated (and open to scrutiny), extending their responsibility to promote the wellbeing not only of their children but to some extent the wellbeing of society in general:

> Parenting has become one of the most charged political and cultural subjects of our age. As the evidence about the decisive impact that the quality of parenting has on children's outcomes continues to grow, parents have come to be seen not just as the cause of many [of] society's ills but also the key to unlocking positive change.
>
> (Rake et al., 2011, p. 13)

The willingness and ability of parents to fulfil these responsibilities can in some cases be affected by where they and their children are positioned, socially, economically or culturally. In response there has been a dramatic increase in interagency support initiatives for parents, some of which are built around existing universal services, whilst others target, or even coerce, specific parents into fulfilling these responsibilities. In some cases parents are even encouraged to take on further responsibility through active participation in the design and delivery of services for their children.

The purpose of this chapter is to examine how parents fulfil the changing expectations and make use of the support available to them. We introduce the theoretical concepts of economic, human, social and cultural capital, and consider ways in which the state can enhance these assets to support parenting.

Core questions

- Whom do children and professionals identify as parents and carers?
- What inhibits or enhances parenting capacity?
- In which political context does support for parents operate?
- What are the concepts of economic, human, social, and cultural capital, and how can they help to analyse parenting and parenting support?
- How do different types of capital influence changing social policies and practice initiatives designed to support parents?

1 Defining parents and parenting

Thinking point 3.1: Who are parents/carers and what do they do?

If we were to write a job description for the role of parent or carer it would surely present itself as a complex and challenging task, subject to high levels of scrutiny and anxiety. Despite this, significant numbers of people in all populations continue to derive great pleasure and satisfaction from doing it. Attention has been drawn to the way in which those directly involved in the day-to-day care of children can be supported by agencies and adults (both formal and informal) located in a wider network. The African proverb 'It takes a village to raise a child' is often cited to reinforce this point. In addition to formal childcare settings, working parents also rely on extended family and friends. One in three now involve grandparents as a source of childcare (Speight et al., 2009), a reality formalised in some policies, for example in the Scottish Charter for Grandchildren:

> Families come in all shapes and sizes. Grandparents, aunts, uncles and cousins can all play an important role in nurturing children. While parents are responsible for caring for children and ensuring their needs are met, the wider family can play a vital supporting role.
>
> (Scottish Executive, 2006, p. 1)

Scotland has introduced a charter for grandchildren acknowledging the important role of grandparents in some children's lives

It can be easy to overlook the wide diversity of relationships and cultures within which children are embedded, but children's own accounts reveal that they recognise the interconnectedness of the wider network of people who contribute in different ways to their wellbeing:

'People help little children – like teachers, dad, the bank, the big sister, mam, people, uncle, your grandma, grandpa, hospital, auntie.'

(Child quoted in Crowley and Vulliamy, 2003, p. 11)

Yet they also reveal that children 'hold differentiated views of key people in their networks, with parents (particularly mothers) and friends usually being the main confidants' (Hill, 2005, p. 81). As we will discuss later, it makes sense to identify and work alongside adults who are the most closely involved in children's day-to-day care.

Definitions of parenting appear to centre on people who take the most significant role in this set of interrelationships within a home or family context 'including biological parents, step-parents, foster parents, adoptive parents, grandparents or other relatives' (Moran et al., 2004, p. 6). In this chapter 'parents' has been used as shorthand to include 'mothers, fathers, carers and other adults with responsibility for caring for a child, including looked after children' (DfES, 2006, p. 3). Carers acknowledged in this definition can include siblings, other family members and neighbours, as well as statutory and voluntary care provided by foster carers and residential care staff.

A distinction can be made between people who have parental responsibility for a child and people who provide care for the child. These may or may not be the same person or people. Parental responsibility is a term used across the UK to describe the legal relationship between parents and children. It governs all the rights, duties, powers and responsibilities which by law a parent of a child has in relation to the child. People who have parental responsibility for a child can take decisions about a range of matters such as education, religion and consent to medical treatment for the child. Birth mothers automatically have parental responsibility, as do married fathers or unmarried fathers who either are named on their child's birth certificate or legally acquire responsibility. Others, including local authorities, can acquire or share parental responsibility if this is agreed by a court. All parties with parental responsibility have to cooperate in making decisions on behalf of the child, using the court as a last resort to resolve disagreements. It is important for professionals to identify and work with the people who have parental responsibility for a particular child. As the following case illustrates, this can be complicated for some children; however, it is still possible for adults to work in partnership in the best interests of the child.

Practice box 3.1

Teachers in a residential school for disabled children mostly discuss a student's day-to-day issues (homework and behaviour) with both the individual child and the school-based residential care workers. However, whenever teachers need to discuss broader curriculum issues (concerning religion, diet or sex education) they will consult with the child's parents. If one of the children is the subject of a care order, meaning parental responsibility is shared between the local authority and the child's parents, teachers have to liaise with both. All children in the Looked After care system have a regular statutory review, and through their attendance teachers can develop a good working relationship with the parents, the residential care staff and social workers. They are also able to contribute to the ongoing care plan.

Parenting is a multifaceted process requiring time, skills, knowledge and values. It often involves living with the child and performing discrete activities or physical tasks such as preparing food, buying and washing their clothes or liaising with health and education professionals. It also includes general behaviour such as being a role model, and providing encouragement and physical or emotional comfort. Underpinning all of these and making parenting unique, however, is mutual affection in an enduring, secure, trusting, responsive and loving relationship. The latter is particularly important; one young person's view on what will help you achieve your potential was:

> 'You need encouragement – someone behind you ... the love of your family, advice and help ... so you can believe you can do it.'
>
> (Quoted in Crowley and Vulliamy, 2003, p. 9)

There are several weaknesses in how parenting features in political and social debates and definitions. Frequently the gender and generational dimensions are down-played; the next section, for example, highlights how it is mainly women who are actively involved in parenting. But also the part played by children in parenting is overlooked, despite evidence that all children actively engage and contribute to the process of being parented. It could be argued that children make parents just as parents make children. The parent–child relationship is dynamic and parents can and do learn from their children and adjust their parenting style. In more specific situations involving parental incapacity on the part of an ill, disabled or drug-misusing relative, some children actively 'parent' their parents and directly perform tasks associated with parenting, but there are gradations, the child rarely taking over completely.

> **Key points**
>
> 1 Children are embedded in a range of networks and relationships that includes people with and without parental responsibility and these networks could be more visible, involved and supported.
> 2 Parenting is both a role and a process requiring a range of skills, knowledge and values.
> 3 Children are active social agents who contribute in many different ways to the role and process of parenting.

2 The politics of parenting

Parenting has variously been constructed within political discourses as a vehicle of socialisation, as the root of inequitable life chances and as a resource or source of strength for children, practitioners and service providers. Attention has been drawn to the differences between parents in relation to factors such as gender, generation and social class. The state has historically maintained a relatively **laissez faire** attitude to families and parenting, intervening only when necessary to ensure children's safety and wellbeing. However, over the last two decades the state has been more willing to intervene with a range of specific social and economic policy objectives related to anti-social behaviour, poverty, educational standards, job creation and the development of a free market. Attempts to restructure welfare have involved a shift of responsibility away from statutory services towards charities, the private sector and individual families (Taylor-Gooby and Stoker, 2011). All these developments directly involve or affect parents. In this section we briefly review some of the political debates that surround parenting and

Laissez faire is a French phrase meaning 'leave alone'. In English it has been adopted as a political term to describe minimal interference by the state in people's lives. It is the opposite of an interventionist (or 'nanny') state.

consider some of the implications for people working with children and families.

Policy and practice with children have been directly influenced by, or had to contend with, debates concerning the suitability (or otherwise) of specific groups of parents or carers (including lone parents, lesbian and gay parents, exclusively Black parents for Black 'looked after' children). Subsequently there has been a continuation of the belief in the early twenty-first century that families are the best environments in which to raise children as long as they are able to uphold the best interests of any individual child. Progress has been made in accepting the diverse ways families are structured and the way that parent–child or carer–child relationships are configured. For example, at the time of writing, legislation in England, Wales and Scotland (not in Northern Ireland) makes it possible for unmarried partners, including same-sex couples, to jointly adopt, giving them the same parenting rights as heterosexual couples. Acceptance of diversity, however, sits (sometimes uncomfortably) alongside expectations in which parents are constructed as responsible for ensuring that members of their families reproduce dominant social, cultural and economic values. For example, the UK government continues to state a belief 'that strong and stable families of all kinds are the bedrock of a strong and stable society' (HM Government, 2010). Two implications can be read from this statement. First, that parents through their actions share responsibility for the nation's economic and social wellbeing. Second, a need to ensure that practitioners overcome any preconceptions or prejudices and that services and agencies represent and seek to make welcome the rich diversity of parents and families.

Parenting is often presented as a gender-neutral practice despite the fact that the majority of childcare is carried out by women. Women rather than men are likely to spend more time with children and have direct contact with children's services such as GPs and schools. They are also likely to be the parents receiving more targeted provision: 'Currently 80% of parenting orders are handed down to mothers – even though in half of these cases the father is living with her and may even be in the court room at the time' (Williams, 2011, p. 68). 'Consequently, it is primarily mothers who bear the brunt of initiatives and sanctions designed to promote "good parenting"' (Gillies, 2005, p. 841), including the more coercive policies.

Whilst the term parent or parenting in social policy may highlight the similarities between men's and women's experience of bringing up children, 'it can obscure the need to pay attention to their differing positions' (Daniel et al., 2005, p. 1344).

Some commentators have argued that child welfare policies should promote or mainstream gender equality (Daniel et al., 2005) and that some policies designed to eradicate child poverty are unlikely to meet with total success unless gender inequality is fully addressed (Bradshaw et al., 2003). The UK government's failure to produce equalities impact statements has left it to others to point out that budget deficit reduction policies designed to cut welfare benefits and investment in the public sector disproportionately disadvantage women ahead of men:

> one-fifth of women's income comes from welfare transfers compared to one-tenth of men's; women are heavier users of public services for themselves or the people they care for; and 65 per cent of workers in the public sector are women.
>
> (Annesley, 2012, p. 19)

Lone-parent families, of whom the vast majority are headed by women, are predicted to be the biggest losers from cuts to spending on services and benefits (Sands, 2011). As a result many lone mothers are being pressurised into finding work just at the point where adequately paid jobs are becoming harder to get (Sands, 2011).

These figures are a reminder of the covert or hidden causes of women's poverty identified by Bradshaw et al. (2003), in particular the unequal allocation of time, money and other resources across the economy but also within the domestic sphere. Domestic inequalities can affect most income groups, a fact overlooked in the government's decision to withdraw child benefit payments from families where one partner's earnings exceed £50,000. Familial and social pressures that construct women as primarily child carers create conflicts for some mothers who at the same time are being encouraged, or coerced, by the government into paid employment.

Some people have argued for a more effective use of family and employment policy, including adequately paid paternity leave, to encourage men into sharing childcare responsibilities (Women's Budget Group, 2005). The 'low levels' of involvement (Lloyd et al., 2003) by fathers identified in the early Sure Start programmes appears to have endured into the era of children's centres. Even though the government has become less prescriptive about how local children's centres should conduct their work it has still issued guidance specifically earmarking fathers and grandfathers alongside 'disadvantaged families, minority ethnic groups and families of children with SEN and disabled children' as the groups whose involvement in children's centres needs to be increased (DfE, 2012). It remains to be seen whether ongoing cuts to services and funding will marginalise efforts to increase participation by these groups. Where resources are available the following ideas are still relevant ways of attracting and involving fathers:

- as direct care-givers to their children ...
- in understanding children's developmental needs ...
- in demonstrating their emotional attachment to their children ...
- in developing and maintaining a positive, co-operative relationship with the mother of their children ...
- in developing their own support networks ...
- finding work, training for work or learning opportunities to enable them to better support their families, and financial support for such learning ...
- help with benefits, child support responsibilities, and entitlements, including housing; and
- during times of exceptional stress, for example following separation or on arrival in the UK as a refugee.

(Sure Start, 2006, p. 82)

Thinking point 3.2: In what ways, if at all, do these aims to involve fathers highlight the ways in which men could be more involved in the care of children and the deep-seated reality that women rather than men look after children? What else could be done?

The guidance document in which these aims are listed devotes only one chapter (out of fourteen) specifically to fathers and fails to make any overt reference to gender equality. The guidance fails to address many of the factors considered by Daniel et al. (2005) that can impede work with men, such as:

- women practitioners' fear of violent men;
- lack of spaces within agencies to explore the fears and anxieties such work can engender;
- lack of a common belief system about what being a 'good' father means;
- different value systems in agencies and across user groups;
- the impact of social structures, and especially employment patterns.

(Daniel et al., 2005, p. 1351)

Some services actively encourage fathers to become more involved in caring for their children

Parenting is widely constructed as a form of social duty and an aspect of citizenship devoted to a greater good for society and the economy. Successive governments have chosen to emphasise that parenting involves responsibilities alongside rights or freedoms (PMSU, 2007; HM Government, 2010)) and spelled these out in relation to parental work, life balance and children's behaviour and education. The state is willing to invest in child and family welfare in return for parental investment in wider social and economic projects.

Therefore all UK governments since the late 1970s, it has been argued, developed policies consistent with a model of **neoliberalism** (Hall, 2011). Although attempts were made in the 1990s to equalise life chances and reduce child poverty, it was argued that the UK government also used welfare services to encourage and enable people 'to take up positions within a neoliberal workforce' (Garrett, 2006, p. 10). Neoliberal policies, it was claimed, also targeted spending cuts upon 'anyone associated with, relying or dependent on the state and public services' (Hall, 2011, p. 24) whilst making it easier for the private sector to profit from health, education and social care services.

One specific outcome of neoliberal policies has been the construction of a moral demarcation, reinforced most recently in some sections of the popular media as 'strivers versus scroungers'. The former are hard working tax payers and customers who can make personalised choices within a free market (Hall, 2011). A 'scrounger' on the other hand is a loosely applied stereotype applied to people who (regardless of circumstances) do not work yet receive statutory support. Parents in particular may find themselves judged in relation to these simplistic stereotypes. Consequently they may feel compelled (in addition to other responsibilities) to demonstrate the self-reliance, knowledge and skills that are prerequisite in a free market economy.

This also adds to the anxieties for parents who find themselves seeking a sometimes impossible balance between work and childcare responsibilities. Although UK governments have shown more sensitivity in this area by making the parental leave system more flexible and increasing the availability of part-time free childcare for three- and four-year-olds, parental decision making is still dependent upon individual circumstances and how they relate to market conditions and policy changes.

The expansion of government funding of part-time free childcare has led to growth in the numbers of childminders and nurseries but the supply of free childcare places could not meet the demands and choices of parents seeking childcare. This was evident in comments gathered from parents by Ball and Vincent (2005) in London:

> 'couldn't find a nursery place – waiting lists'
> 'There just aren't many childminders, they are difficult to find'

Neoliberalism is 'a theory of political economic practices that proposes that human well-being can best be advanced by liberating individual entrepreneurial freedoms and skills within an institutional framework characterized by strong private property rights, free markets, and free trade. The role of the state is to create and preserve an institutional framework appropriate to such practices' (Harvey, 2005, p. 2).

'I was in the market too late at 6mths pregnant'
'sounds like a lot of choice but there isn't'

(Parents quoted in Ball and Vincent, 2005, p. 561)

However, during an economic recession childcare providers found it necessary to increase fees and cut staff wages to offset a downturn in demand (Evans, 2010). Childminders and nursery managers subsequently reported concerns that many parents were struggling to afford their fees (BBC, 2012).

Investment in childcare by the UK government, in the interests of incentivising parents (specifically mothers) into work, helped reduce the cost to most families of childcare as a percentage of disposable income. Despite this the childcare costs to UK families remained higher compared to families in other OECD countries (Alakeson and Hurrell, 2012). Attempts to target support through means testing combined with a universal entitlement to free part-time childcare increased variation in childcare costs for families across the income ladder. Dual middle-income families and higher-income single parent families were particularly hard hit (Alakeson and Hurrell, 2012), highlighting the complex ways in which childcare costs serve to help or hinder parents' abilities to find or remain in paid employment.

> Reducing the percentage of disposable income families spend on childcare even to very low levels may not be enough to make work pay because of the negative interaction between childcare costs and means-tested childcare support provided through the tax credit system. Second earners in low to middle income families already lose a significant amount of each additional pound they earn. As they earn more, they lose benefits and tax credits and start to pay taxes. Add to this the costs of childcare and they can face deduction rates of close to 100 percent which means that they are no better off from working an additional hour.
>
> (Alakeson and Hurrell, 2012, p. 22)

Whether in the interests of helping parents fulfil the expectations and responsibilities bestowed upon them by neoliberalism or in order to overcome inequalities that prevent mothers (and some fathers) from balancing paid work and childcare responsibilities, the provision of an affordable childcare system continues as a key political issue affecting the economy, parents and children.

Thinking point 3.3: In your view is the success of families, first and foremost, down to the commitment and behaviour of those within them?

The politics of childcare illustrate how choices made by parents that impact on children's lives can be fully understood only by considering the wider context in which they are formed and enacted. Politicians sometimes find it expedient to be seen to be tough on particular behaviours and choices without consideration of the wider social context:

> 'Society needs to condemn a little more and understand a little less.'
>
> (British Prime Minister John Major in an interview in the Mail on Sunday, 21 February 1993)

Butler and Drakeford (2001) remarked that:

> there are some citizens who, through their behaviour, demonstrate their capacity to respond to the investment which the state might make in them and in their conditions. Then there are those whose behaviour demonstrates the opposite. To the first group, New Labour turns its generosity. To the second, it turns the stony face of authoritarianism.
>
> (Butler and Drakeford, 2001, p. 11)

> 'That thing, "You must stay together for the kids", is out of fashion but is right. It's not arguing parents that children don't like, it is having one parent.'
>
> (Iain Duncan Smith, BBC, 2005)

Williams (2004, p. 419) suggested that the emphasis in education and welfare policy towards a 'responsibilisation of parents' is unnecessary as 'most parents are acutely aware of their responsibilities to their children, even though they may differ in the ways they carry these out'. Other commentators are concerned that policy has become too focused on what it considers to be inadequate behaviour by parents (specifically mothers) whilst ignoring wider 'material factors' (Clarke, 2006, p. 718). Attempts were made for example through the Troubled Families Programme to identify parents whose behaviour was considered to be of concern (see below).

In addition to individual causes of childhood morbidity and mortality there are wider social and environmental causes including poor housing conditions

Concern has been expressed by some commentators at the way inadequate parenting has always been seen as a moral issue closely linked, particularly within policies on social exclusion, to poverty, low aspiration and anti social behaviour. 'Policy literature commonly cites the "condition" of exclusion referring to a disconnection from mainstream values and aspirations, as opposed to marginalization from material resources' (Gillies, 2006, p. 283). It is common to hear politicians reinforcing discourses such as that of the 'striver/scrounger' by praising 'hard working families' or encouraging parents through 'welfare to work' policies that 'work pays'. This implies that families where people do not work are in some way failing in their responsibilities as parents and as citizens. As Williams (2004, p. 420) noted, these concepts are simplistic and contingent on wider social and geographical factors. Work does not always pay, for example 'because jobs, especially jobs open to mothers, are low-paid and insecure', or 'terms and conditions of local employment undermine their capacity to carry out their responsibilities in relation to the education of their children'. Sometimes children are paying the price of their parents' hard work.

As we shall discuss later, service providers and practitioners can help parents and provide them with support based on analysis of the wider familial, social, economic and political context. Practitioners can also reflect upon the negative impact of parental stereotypes and expectations promoted within the media and popular culture. Despite pressures to the contrary, it is important that practitioners position themselves as enablers rather than enforcers. As Williams (2004, p. 419) remarked: 'What parents need is time and support to follow their responsibilities through rather than reminders to carry them out.'

Key points

1   The quality of parenting is considered more important than the configuration of family forms, but who judges this remains debatable.
2   Although parenting is presented as gender neutral, it is mainly mothers and female carers who access services and support which is predominantly provided by a female workforce.
3   Attempts to actively involve fathers in parenting cannot be considered separately from issues associated with gender equality.
4   Supporting parents can best be understood in relation to the wider social, cultural, environmental and economic context.

3 Using theory to conceptualise parenting

As we have already discussed, parenting cannot be understood without reference to each individual's wider context, which in turn implies that parents are different from each other. This section will introduce some theoretical concepts that help us understand the different resources (referred to here as different types of capital, under four main headings) that parents may or may not possess. These concepts will then be applied later in the chapter to what we understand as parenting capacity and the different ways of providing parenting support.

Thinking point 3.4: In what ways can a child's success be influenced by parental wealth, social contacts, skills or knowledge?

3.1 Economic capital

This generally relates to financial physical and material resources available to parents that can be utilised to promote children's wellbeing. Within a capitalist society it is accepted that economic capital can be transformed into services and products. In terms of parenting this may involve obtaining a good education, good health or leisure for children. In a departure from previous welfare approaches, recent social policy has looked to support parents to generate economic capital for their children through work and saving rather than being provided directly with benefits. This change potentially affects the role, function and interrelationships of practitioners and services working with children and families.

3.2 Human capital

This describes the skills and knowledge possessed by people usually associated with education or work. At the national level, investment by government in people (through, for example, promoting 'soft skills' within the education system) can result in economic returns (such as a skilled workforce who will contribute to a more competitive economy). Human capital can also refer to skills and knowledge acquired at the level of the individual. Parents can invest time in developing their child's human capital, perhaps through supporting them with learning and helping them negotiate the education system. Practitioners and services for children and families may find themselves involved directly or indirectly in supporting parents with this task.

3.3 Social capital

This refers to the level of connectivity and reciprocity between individuals, through networks and within social groups. It consists of and helps maintain shared norms and levels of trust. It is multi-dimensional and can bring benefits at many ecological levels, particularly within the family, the community or society as a whole.

Coleman (1991, 1997) identified social capital as a resource that can be generated and employed within the family through parent–child relations and outside of the family through relationships within the local community. Social capital is utilised by some parents who wish to develop their children's human capital and educational achievement: 'Where you live and whom you know – the social capital you can draw on – helps to define who you are and thus to determine your fate' (Putnam, 1994, p. 14).

Bourdieu (1986) interpreted this in a different way, highlighting how forms of capital represent resources and power which in turn are unequally distributed amongst a population. The possession of one form of capital can be used as an investment to acquire other forms of capital. The ability of some parents, but not others, to invest their financial capital in purchasing social capital (that is, access to new social networks for their children, including membership of sport and leisure clubs, and private education) results in some children receiving opportunities ahead of others.

Coleman (1997) identified how obligations and expectations are built up and reciprocated over time within social groups. Families where members look after each other have social capital, as do groups of parents who might take turns to baby-sit or transport each other's children to school. These social interactions can enable the sharing and acquisition of knowledge. Knowledge acquisition also occurs where parents come together informally (for example at the school gate) or deliberately (for example through participation in antenatal classes or parent and toddler groups). The types of knowledge related to their role as parents may include where the best deals are for buying children's clothing, what the most beneficial after- schools activities in the area are, and how to manage children's health and behaviour. Such relationships also help construct socially acceptable and unacceptable behaviour and norms. In some families this may involve prioritising children's education and the enhancement of their human capital above anything else. Parents may also learn prevailing norms and expectations through interaction with other parents in the community, for example encouraging them to volunteer to support their children's after-school clubs or discouraging them from leaving their children at home alone. Because social capital is unequally distributed amongst groups of parents, the consequences for individual children vary considerably.

Three components of social capital have been identified (Woolcock, 2001). *Bonding social capital*, such as within families, helps create a sense of belonging and understanding. The importance of family interconnectedness and resource sharing was evident in a study by Bayat (2007) of families with autistic children. It suggested that adversity can promote bonding between family members, which in turn can build resilience:

> 'My son's autism has made our family life tougher, emotionally and financially. Each member has to devote additional time and effort to help him, and learn how to live peacefully in such [an] environment.
>
> Through working together, we all learned how to help my son together. In some sense, this also makes our family closer, because an individual cannot handle the toughness alone.'

> (Mother quoted in Bayat, 2007, p. 709)

Yet in order for this not to become too insular or detached it also requires bridging social capital or interactions of an outward character, such as with other families, which in turn help generate social norms and trust. Some parents find it helpful to join or develop support groups for this purpose. Positive outcomes including mutual sharing of experiences and support, personal empowerment and a sense of identity were found in one evaluation to be associated with peer groups of parents who have children with chronic disabling conditions (PenCRU, 2012). This is also true for disabled parents:

> 'One of the really great things I get out of my involvement and work with Disabled Parents Network is the support and contact with other disabled parents ... Other disabled parents can really

understand so many of the issues, and offer empathy and emotional and practical support.'

(Parent quoted in Baker, 2006, p. 1)

The final component is linking social capital, which involves connections outside of the community enabling access to resources and opportunities, for example, formal parental support. This is evident in accounts given by disabled children and their families about support provided through Children's Fund projects (Pinnock and Evans, 2007). In particular they highlighted the importance of individually tailored, flexible, reliable and sustainable relationships with practitioners and service providers:

'If you have a problem ... if you tell them they can help you deal with it. And then if you want more help from, like, someone professional, they will give you numbers and stuff. And they will phone and take you there if you really want to.'

(Disabled child quoted in Pinnock and Evans, 2007, p. 7)

'I still have contact with [the project worker] ... they don't just help you and leave you, they're there all the time ... I know that I've only got to say to [the project worker] I need help and I know that help is there.'

(Parent of a disabled child quoted in Pinnock and Evans, 2007, p. 9)

One of the advantages of social capital as a concept within the context of interagency working with children is that it embraces the multi-layered formal and informal networks around and through which support for children is provided. Furthermore, it is a loose enough concept around which it may be possible to unify the energies of practitioners from different agencies and disciplines. The idea that social capital can serve the interests of the public good has proven particularly popular with policy makers, particularly as it has been linked to solutions to problems including social exclusion and community regeneration. The Scottish Executive, for example, clearly intended to make sure 'that individuals and communities have the social capital –

the skills, confidence, support networks and resources – to take advantage of and increase the opportunities open to them' (Scottish Executive, 2002, p. 6).

Both Coleman (1988) and Putnam (1994) expressed concern that social capital is a quality that over time has been eroded. Some commentators take issue with this view of social capital. But Morrow (1999) suggested that the concept harks back to a glorious past that cannot be supported with historical evidence. By placing a strong positive emphasis on social connections, it glosses over the fact that although family and friends can be a source of support to parents, they are sometimes a source of stress (Quinton, 2004). It also fails to acknowledge gender, in particular the work of women in creating or sustaining social networks in relation to parenting (Morrow, 1999). Also, children's agency and ability to develop social capital is largely ignored, in particular by Coleman, who dismissed children's rights as a contributory factor in the decline of social capital by apparently reducing 'the strength of the parental role' (Coleman, 1988, p. 401).

Bourdieu (1986) suggested that like other forms of power, social capital is transmitted from one generation to another and leads to the reproduction of existing class inequalities. In other words social capital is something that you are more likely to inherit through existing social networks than anything offered through government social policies.

Thinking point 3.5: Do you agree that social capital is declining, or does it contribute to the reproduction of inequality from one generation to the next? Can children's services do anything to dissipate the impact of such self-sustaining inequality ?

3.4 Cultural capital

Two competing causal theories have emerged in academic literature to explain the ways that parents from different social strata raise their children (Chin and Philips, 2004). Firstly, parents differ in the aspirations and expectations that they have for their children. Secondly, inequalities of time and other material resources mean that some parents are more able than others to fulfil their own or wider society's expectations (Chin and Phillips, 2004). Bourdieu's concept of cultural capital goes some way to bringing together these different theories. As we have seen, social capital is knowing who can help parents achieve their goals to raise children; in contrast, cultural capital is knowing how to use these assets and other qualities to achieve goals (St Clair, 2005).

According to Bourdieu (Jenkins, 2002), cultural capital is a form of **legitimate knowledge** that individuals and families can use to secure some form of advantage. As we have seen above, knowledge and norms are often developed via social capital or contact with a particular social group. Of course, many parents are knowledgeable about many different things; in some cases this knowledge can be traded in to secure advantage for their children, yet in other cases it may appear to have no value. Knowledge has to be of a legitimate form in order to become cultural capital and secure advantage. This begs the question of who or what decides what kind of knowledge is legitimate. Bourdieu helps us understand how this works through the use of two further concepts which he refers to as *habitus* and *field*.

Habitus refers to the dispositions an individual has to feel, think, behave or understand the world in a particular way (Jenkins, 2002). '[T]he dispositions that make up habitus are ... so embodied in the individual that they can be identified in appearance, speech, behaviour, manners and tastes' (Tomanović, 2004, p. 343). Habitus is closely linked to the concept of habit, a way of behaving that is often learned through socialisation and experience and occurs without much prior thought. Certain dispositions found amongst some parents and not amongst others could potentially be explained through the use of habitus. A woman's intention to breastfeed, for example, appears to be influenced by social relationships and prolonged participation (to at least age 18) in full-time education (Hamlyn et al., 2002; Bolling, 2005).

According to Bourdieu, a *field* is 'a social arena within which struggles or manoeuvres take place over specific resources or stakes and access to them' (Jenkins, 2002, p. 84). Fields vary in terms of how specific or concrete they are, and can include housing, education, land, prestige, life style or any other arena in which a person might wish to have a stake (Jenkins, 2002). In order to access or gain advantage within a particular field, it is necessary to have legitimate knowledge (cultural capital) specific to that field. The formation of habitus brings with it the possibility of inheriting, primarily through their family (Reay, 2000), cultural capital or knowledge about a particular field. 'When an individual's habitus is consistent with the field in which he or she is operating, that is, when the field is familiar to and understood by the individual, he or she enjoys a social advantage' (Lee and Bowen, 2006, p. 197). One way of thinking about the field is as a game or sport. As with any game, some people have a better understanding of the rules and tactics (the habitus) and therefore have an advantage. The concept

Legitimate knowledge is knowledge that is valued and useful within one context but not necessarily another. For example, an educational psychologist has a very good understanding of the Special Educational Needs Code of Practice. Outside of her employment this knowledge may have little relevance. However, if her son was having difficulty learning at school this knowledge might prove valuable. A parent without this form of legitimate knowledge may be relatively disadvantaged.

of cultural capital has been utilised in explaining inequalities within the education system. Grenfell and James (1998) drew a comparison between cultural capital being used by some parents to enhance their children's education just as they might use their economic capital as power to purchase products. Although the parents in the following example have financial capital, it is insufficient to secure private education for all their children. But they do have legitimate knowledge (cultural capital) of school catchment areas that they employ in the interests of securing maximum educational advantage for their child.

> Katherine Bailey and her husband, Nicholas, are prepared to pay an extra £70,000 to move their young family a few miles south, into the heart of the catchment area for Henlow Middle School in Bedfordshire.
>
> 'We would have sent one child to private school but can't afford to send both, so this is the next best thing,' said Bailey. 'We have been absolutely rigorous about it: we have had long discussions with the local education authority and have got local gazetteer lists that show exactly which road is in which catchment area.'
>
> (Hill, 2004, webpage)

Thinking point 3.6: What are some of the advantages and disadvantages, linked to the different types of capital, for both the parents and children in making their house move?

Neoliberalism can construct parents simplistically as either 'strivers or scroungers' and promotes the idea that advantage and success are down to individual effort and that disadvantage is the result of failure by individuals to take the opportunities open to all. Bourdieu's application of both social and cultural capital challenges this and helps us understand that institutions and processes essential to providing children with opportunities (such as education) are more accessible to particular parents than others, and often without realising it they reproduce rather than help eradicate social inequality. It was a reminder that parents' capacity to provide for their children cannot be reduced to a simplistic label or explanation; instead it needs to be understood in relation to the wider social, economic and political context.

Key points

1   Human and social capital are concepts that have been interpreted as beneficial to society, as well as individuals, and therefore have been influential in the design of children's services and the role and working relationships of practitioners.

2   Economic, human, social and cultural capital are concepts that enable us to understand resources unequally possessed by parents and unequally provided by parenting support.

3   The possession of one form of capital can be used as an investment to acquire other forms of capital.

4 Parenting capacity

All practitioners within the children's workforce are responsible for children staying safe, and this involves holistic assessment of children's lives including the capacity of their parents or the carers who look after them. In England the dimensions of parenting capacity were laid out in the Framework for Assessment of Children in Need and their Families (DH et al., 2000). In Scotland, areas for assessment of the people who look after children were contained within the Getting it Right for Every Child Framework (Scottish Government, 2013).

Contemporary assessment frameworks across the four nations now consider the wider ecological context in which the parent and child are located. In doing so they replace historic parenting models that, it has been argued, were constructed around the values of a dominant white middle class culture (Azar et al., 1998). Children's services as a result are now much better positioned to assess parents fairly without discrimination linked to factors such as age, sexuality, health status, social class or ethnic background. It is also recognised that the capacity of parents can be enhanced or undermined by factors and experiences, sometimes within their control sometimes not, located in family and wider social networks or created by the cultural, social, political and economic environment.

> Unfortunately, the social networks of parents and children, and the social capital of the areas in which they live, tend to reflect individual and area levels of disadvantage, often leaving those most in need of additional help with the most restricted social support resources.
>
> (Jack, 2006, p. 339)

Assessing parenting capacity within an ecological context helps practitioners understand and attribute explanations for parents' behaviour and attitudes, particularly where an act of omission or commission appears to be undermining a child's wellbeing. Thus concerns about a child coming to school hungry because they have had no breakfast, after investigation may reveal a parent who starts work early and leaves their child to get their own breakfast. On the other hand it may reveal a parent neglecting their child's needs as a result of a dependency on drugs or alcohol. Either case may be the result of a parent lacking sufficient social or cultural capital to recognise the problem or access, or negotiate access to, possible sources of support.

Thinking point 3.7: In what way can children's services help develop social and cultural capital to support parenting capacity?

The misuse of drugs and/or alcohol is a good example to consider here.

> The majority of parents using alcohol or drugs will present no increased risk of harm to their children. Most (but by no means all) of the harm which is caused to children will be the result of problematic drug or alcohol use. Problems will not only be caused by the quantity of drugs and alcohol consumed but also by the types of drugs and the pattern of use.
>
> (Cleaver et al., 2011, p. 36)

Children's accounts reveal the nature of their relationships with parents who abuse drugs and alcohol:

'My parents started giving me alcohol when I was 1 (year old) to put me to sleep. I got taken into hospital to have my stomach pumped.'

(Child quoted in Ayrshire and Arran NHS Board, 2002, cited in Scottish Executive, 2003, p. 15)

'I used to get really embarrassed at school when mum turned up drunk to collect me. I knew that I would have to make the tea when I got in.'

(Child quoted in Ayrshire and Arran NHS Board, 2002, cited in Scottish Executive, 2003, p. 15)

Other studies with children revealed that they often feel responsible for caring for a parent who misuses alcohol or drugs, possibly staying home from school in an attempt to stop parents from taking drugs (Barnard, 2007). Children can become torn between love for their parent and dislike of the same parent's behaviour. In some cases children said that they would like to be involved in finding solutions to the problems (Aldridge and Becker, 2003). A number of protective factors are known to support children facing these and similar difficulties, including regular school attendance and social networks outside of the family including peer and positive adult relationships (Cleaver et al., 2011).

Holistic assessment of parenting capacity entails gathering information about the influence of formal and informal support networks, access to education, childcare, and transport, housing and employment (CWDC, 2007). This information, along with knowledge of the child's own capital resources (Chin and Phillips, 2004) including resilience, self-care skills and willingness to work with others, is a good foundation for putting together a plan with the family. Attention would be paid to the kind of linking social capital already at the disposal of members of a family. For example, it may be possible to involve existing social networks such as the child's school (it may have extended provision) or introduce the family to a local children's centre or specialist services. In the following example, a plan is developed that involves exploring the potential use of bonding social capital within the extended family as well as linking social capital with a range of agencies.

Practice box 3.2

A 20-year-old woman presented to hospital maternity services 12–16 weeks pregnant. She was injecting heroin and using diazepam, financed by prostitution. Her GP had been prescribing methadone but her behaviour in the surgery led to her removal from the practice list. Her partner, the baby's father, deals and uses heroin. They live in bed-and-breakfast accommodation. The specialist maternity service for pregnant women with substance misuse carried out other routine investigations and assessed her and the baby's father. She was prescribed methadone and her partner referred to a local community-based drugs project who provided an appointment within two days. A hospital social worker referred the couple to the area team for allocation. At 18 weeks the woman was admitted to hospital to manage detoxification from benzodiazepines. She was admitted again at 29 weeks having relapsed. The maternity service hosted a pre-bir th case conference at 32 weeks' gestation, which recommended that the baby be placed on the Child Protection Register when born. Thereafter the mother used only prescribed methadone until her baby was born. She gave birth to a healthy but low birth-weight baby boy who developed withdrawal symptoms. He remained in the neonatal unit for treatment, and nursing staff carefully assessed how his mother was managing his care. She seemed to do well in the first few days but left the hospital with her partner and did not return for several days. When she returned she appeared drunk and when worried nursing staff refused to let her take her son home she assaulted a nurse and was arrested. The local authority sought a Child Protection Order and placed the baby with emergency foster carers. The local authority is now carrying out an inter-agency assessment and supervising the mother's contact with the baby in a family centre to see whether he can go home. Concurrently the social worker is assessing whether the maternal grandmother may look after the baby in the medium term. Drug treatment services are working with the mother to stabilise her emerging chaotic substance misuse.

(Scottish Executive, 2003, p. 39)

The challenges presented in the above practice box illustrate the complexities of providing adequate and ongoing support for children and drug-misusing parents. It could be particularly difficult for the various individual practitioners who become involved, some of whom may be unfamiliar with the practice skills and theoretical knowledge necessary to provide holistic support. It highlights the need for clear communication and information sharing between agencies and practitioners.

Sometimes basing practitioners from different disciplines and agencies together in teams or particular settings can enhance the effectiveness of support. Closer working proximity would enable individual practitioners to appreciate and develop a clearer understanding of each other's roles and working methods. The practice box below illustrates an innovative healthcare project involving cooperation between different agencies to provide holistic support to parents of preschool children. As well as promoting general issues such as healthy diets and exercise, it was also well placed to provide support with more complex issues, including where parents misuse drugs. Although it was based within a universal service, it enabled the development of linking social capital with specialist agencies. The emphasis on community capacity-building suggests the development of bridging social capital, and the educational emphasis was an opportunity for participants to develop cultural capital.

Practice box 3.3

The Health Promotion Nursery is a pilot project funded by the North Hamilton Blantyre Social Inclusion Partnership. The project consists of a multi disciplinary team from the partnership agencies: Health Promotion, Education and Social Work Resources. It is based within the Whitehill Parent and Child Centre and St Paul's Primary School and it focuses on the health and well-being of children, parents and professionals on the campus. The project is based upon the Pacific Institute Training: Steps to Excellence and consists of a rolling programme of training for staff, parents and children. The training has a strong community capacity-building theme. It concentrates on the promotion of health through building confidence and self-esteem, raising awareness and healthy lifestyles. This project is complemented by the Integrated Family Support Strategy and the multi-disciplinary team at Whitehill Family Centre who offer a range of family support groups at the nursery and school. This project

> supports children whose parents misuse drugs along with children with other problems.
>
> (Scottish Executive, 2003, pp. 27–28)

From a re-analysis of data from earlier studies, Cleaver et al. (2011) identified that 25 per cent of children under five years and 41 per cent of children aged five to nine who were living with parental substance misuse experienced severe unmet needs (i.e. social workers identified developmental needs in three or more of the following five dimensions: health, education, emotional and behavioural development, identity and social development and family and social relationships). Alcohol and/or drugs misuse is only one of many potential impacts on parenting capacity, including mental health, disability, domestic violence or previous history of abuse (Cleaver, 2006). It is important to acknowledge that none of these are absolute indicators of inadequate parenting, yet they do alert people working with children to potential situations where support may be needed. Poverty is a further factor affecting parenting capacity. Access to financial capital, whether through regular employment, savings, benefits or tax credits, is a central factor for most parents and carers, in particular when related to the potential costs involved in bringing up children.

Quinton (2004, p. 181) argued that formal services should see themselves as part of the ecology of parenting: 'inter-agency working needs to be part of an effort to understand the whole of parenting ecology – not just a desire to see agencies work together better'. This is illustrated when one considers that some of the cost of bringing up children is forced upon parents by statutory agencies themselves. Education, even when provided by the state, is particularly expensive for parents in terms of transport, lunches and clothing, and may have a negative impact on children whose parents cannot afford it.

> 'People don't claim free school meals out of embarrassment. I would let people with money go ahead of me in the queue so they wouldn't see.'
>
> (Boy quoted in Crowley and Vulliamy, 2003, p. 15)

'Poor children can't buy the proper kit and if they didn't have the proper kit some people in the school were meanies and kept saying they haven't got the proper uniform, and they haven't got enough money to get sandwiches either.'

(Boy quoted in Crowley and Vulliamy, 2003, p. 15)

'They bully you in school and go ha! ha! you can't go on the school trip and all that.'

(Boy quoted in Crowley and Vulliamy, 2003, p. 16)

As the above accounts illustrated, the stigma associated with receiving free school dinners or not being able to afford the correct uniform, school trips or essential learning tools such as pens or calculators can impact negatively on children's experience and motivation within school (Children in Wales, 2006). Yet, as another account from Crowley and Vulliamy's research indicated, where schools are prepared to extend themselves even in very small ways, they can positively enhance parenting capacity amongst poorer and marginalised families. In the following account, a school ensures that a mother can develop cultural capital enabling her to stimulate and support her child's learning:

'My mum helps me to do the spellings, coz she's got a dictionary and she's Arabic but she doesn't know much English so we got an English dictionary from school and she borrowed it.'

(Boy quoted in Crowley and Vulliamy, 2003, p. 15)

This idea of schools extending their provision to support families is popular across the UK as a vehicle for breaking cycles of deprivation. An evaluation of twenty schools offering extended activities in Northern Ireland found evidence that they indirectly improved some children's educational performance and wellbeing by helping their parents 're-engage with education following their own, often poor, experiences and perceptions of schools' (DfE, 2010, p. 4). Although such initiatives are still evolving, they demonstrate the potential role of schools as a form of social capital and as part of the ecology of parenting.

> **Key points**
>
> 1 Parenting capacity is a useful concept for assessing parent–child relationships and should be understood within an ecological context.
> 2 Different forms of capital may affect individuals' parenting capacity.
> 3 Children's services can strengthen parenting capacity through developing social capital between practitioners, agencies and families.

5 Parenting support

Our discussion on parenting capacity has inevitably led us to explore some of the ways in which parents are supported. We will now look more closely at parenting support in terms of how it is used and structured within social policy, in particular the distinction between universal services (open to anyone regardless of need) and targeted services (open to eligible people with an assessed need). One definition of parenting support describes 'any intervention for parents or carers aimed at reducing risks and/or promoting protective factors for their children, in relation to their social, physical and emotional well-being' (Moran et al., 2004, p. 6). The idea of supporting parents has endured maybe because it is viewed as a vehicle for social change (Henricson, 2008) but also because many parents appear to want it. 75 per cent of parents say there are times in their lives when they would like more advice and support in their parenting role (Social Exclusion Unit, 2000).

A number of independent reviews (Allen, 2011; Munro, 2011; Field, 2010) have indicated that good parenting can support good outcomes for children. Consequently governments have invested time and money in finding suitable ways of ensuring that parents get the support that they need. Universal support, for example via community-based children's centres, was widely adopted. Parenting support available to all parents who want it has the advantage of lacking stigma and being available to people who are at risk yet who have not been identified. Despite its popularity and successes this type of support was found not to necessarily reach the parents with the greatest need. Evidence exists from Sure Start evaluation that vulnerable families may be reluctant to use services dominated by 'affluent, assertive and confident parents' (Tunstill et al., 2007, p. 140)

The expense and identified failings of universal parenting support has led to an interest in cost-effective models receiving favourable evaluations (DfE, 2011) like Family Intervention Projects (FIPs) that targeted support towards specific groups of parents. It was claimed that the intensive approach of these programmes could 'prevent anti-social behaviour' and 'keep children out of care' (Tickell, 2011, p. 102). Here families with multiple problems such as low incomes and levels of educational attainment, health problems and poor housing were targeted. The projects involved action planning with whole families and provided a 'persistent, assertive and challenging approach'. Each family was offered its own dedicated worker and practical hands-on support. One of the problems with this was the ease with which targeted families became negatively labelled and targeted support was constructed as punishment:

> 'Family intervention projects work. They change lives, they make our communities safer and they crack down on those who're going off the rails.
>
> Starting now and right across the next Parliament every one of the 50,000 most chaotic families will be part of a family intervention project – with clear rules, and clear punishments if they don't stick to them.'
>
> (Prime Minister Gordon Brown, Labour Party Conference, 2009)

Intensive targeted support was seen as a potential solution to a series of riots in England during 2011, which were blamed by some politicians upon a rise in bad parenting. This view was expressed despite an extensive body of research indicating that the involvement and expectations of many contemporary parents towards their children were greater at this time than that found in earlier generations (Rake et al., 2011). The riots fitted with a general concern about anti-social behaviour caused by families that (in the words of Prime Minister David Cameron, 2011) 'some people call "problem", others call "troubled".' One consequence was the development of a specific department and a series of strategies designed to target 120,000 'troubled families' across England. Eligibility for support involved meeting three of the following four criteria:

- Are involved in youth crime or anti-social behaviour
- Have children who are regularly truanting or not in school
- Have an adult on out of work benefits
- Cause high costs to the taxpayer.

(Department for Communities and Local Government, 2012, p. 3)

The emphasis on targeted support deflects attention from some of the preventative, early-intervention and non-stigmatic benefits of universal support. Children's centres and other universal services provide support that potentially prevents a drift into crisis and the creation of families that are eligible for targeted services. Although many parents seek support, they do so from a position of wanting to maintain their independence and retain control over how they deal with problems (Quinton, 2004). Parents showed a preference for being provided with information to solve their own problems, and where this is not possible, to be provided with specialist advice (Quinton, 2004). Some parents prefer peer learning, particularly within the context of classes that provide parents with opportunities to develop cultural and social capital:

'Frankness and, um, the bond that we reached between the parents. We were not afraid to express our particular problems or issues and were there for each other and give advice and take advice. So, you know it is give and take.'

(Parent discussing parenting programme in Barlow and Stewart-Brown, 2001, p. 121)

Parents can form groups for mutual support

Some forms of parenting support are also compulsory. Three levels of parenting support have been identified:

> primary ... intervening to prevent the onset of problems ... secondary ... intervening with high risk groups or where problems have begun but are not yet strongly entrenched ... tertiary ... when problems are already strongly present and require active treatment

> (Moran et al., 2004, p. 6)

The first two levels are very much preventative forms of support, whereas although the third level may try to prevent further problems, it is also helping people overcome or put right existing problems. This relates closely to the tiers of need model (PricewaterhouseCoopers LLP, 2006). In this model a fourth tier is included to represent the type of support being undertaken with children mostly within the Looked After care system, enabling them to return to live with their birth parent (s). Most support in tiers 1 and 2 is received on a voluntary basis by parents. At tiers 3 and 4, support may be provided on a compulsory basis, following a professional referral.

It is easy to assume that support is given and received willingly, yet it cannot be divorced from the power relationships in which it operates. Service providers and practitioners are endowed with power enabling them to gate-keep resources and make judgements about parenting capacity. Parents are sometimes disempowered by poverty, lack of information or discrimination. In some cases what is presented as support may be unwanted or experienced as an intrusion; on other occasions it may be inadequate. In some cases something 'may need to be done against one person's wishes in order to support the needs of another' (Quinton, 2004, p. 179). This was illustrated in Practice box 3.2 where a nurse rightly made a judgement in refusing to let a mother who appeared drunk take her child home. Even though 'providers still prefer to work with parents who are ultimately willing to receive their help' (PricewaterhouseCoopers LLP, 2006, p. 6), on occasions which involve prioritising the best interests of the child, hard and unpopular decisions may need to be made. The nurse in the Practice box example was assaulted by the mother, an event that illustrates that practitioners need empowerment in the form of adequate resources and support when making these difficult decisions.

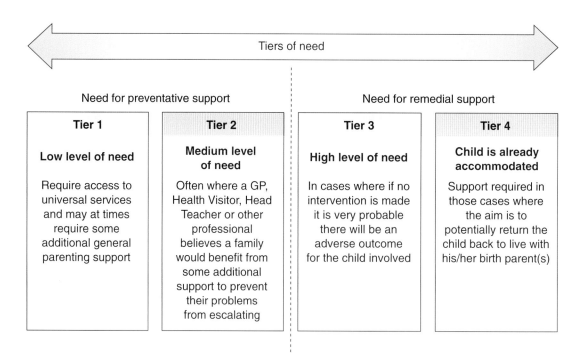

Tiers of need (PricewaterhouseCoopers LLP, 2006, p. 6)

The terrain over which parents must pass in order to seek and find support can be difficult to negotiate. Seeking and requesting support may require aspects of cultural capital not available to all parents. In a government- funded piece of research, a wide variety of poorly coordinated parental support was identified, provided by statutory agencies, community groups, private providers and individuals (PricewaterhouseCoopers LLP, 2006). The following chart maps the type of provider against the four tiers of parenting support described above.

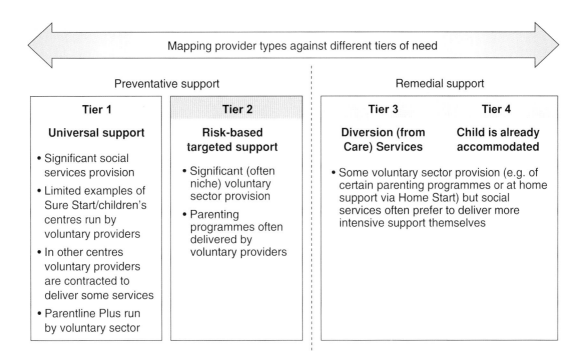

Mapping provider types against different tiers of need
(PricewaterhouseCoopers LLP, 2006, p. 9)

The types of service available to support parents in the community are sometimes diverse and disconnected from each other, and may exist only for as long as funding is available. This has resulted in services that protect their boundaries and restrict activity to their own area of expertise (Quinton, 2004). Furthermore, 'what is available locally is not always known to professionals who meet parents and children in their day to day work' (Royal College of Paediatrics and Child Health (RCPCH), 2002, p. 22). Quinton (2004) suggested that there was a lack of cooperation between services providing support to parents, and where there was cooperation it could usually be attributed to energetic individuals rather than effective systems or structures. It could be argued that service providers need to develop their own social capital.

A distinction has been made between formal support (usually from statutory or mainstream services) semi-formal support (community or voluntary groups) and informal support (provided by family and friends) (Quinton, 2004). Sometimes a contrast is made between the capacity of formal services to provide specialist help and the capacity of informal networks to provide comfort and emotional and practical support. Parents appeared to judge services not only on what is made available but how it is offered (Quinton, 2004). The key issue for success in providing support for parents was the quality of relationship developed by those providing the service; in some cases parents indicated that they feel not listened to or talked down to (RCPCH, 2002).

Thinking point 3.8: Who, if anyone, should be targeted for parenting support?

In a situation where resources are scarce, support targeted on people with the greatest need would appear to be the most efficient system. However, 'it is difficult to identify families at highest risk – there are no screening programmes with a high sensitivity and specificity'.

Consequently: 'there will always be parents who could benefit from services but do not receive them' (RCPCH, 2002, p. 23). As discussed above, targeting parents experiencing specific difficulties forms the basis of some intensive family programmes. Targeting also happens in relation to particular communities (for example, poor neighbourhoods), particular children (for example, disabled children) or parents at particular points in the life course (for example, very young or first-time parents). However, situations requiring support do not always follow clearly defined patterns of distribution (for example, domestic violence) and therefore make targeting difficult to achieve.

The idea of targeting particular groups of parents at particular points has some disadvantages. Feinstein (2003) was concerned that the prioritising of early years intervention ignores the importance of providing support into and beyond middle childhood. There was also evidence that targeted interventions fail to reach their intended subjects. One evaluation (Sure Start, 2005, p. 8) concluded that 'parents/families with greater human capital were better able to take advantage of [Sure

Start] services and resources than those with less human capital
(i.e. teen parents, lone parents, workless households)'. It has also been
shown in research that some groups of parents within a target
population were particularly hard to work with, including Looked After
teenage parents, imprisoned fathers and emotionally abusing or rejecting
parents (Quinton, 2004). In some cases, the barriers to engagement may
be the result of differences in cultural capital between service providers
and potential service users. In 2007 the NHS issued guidelines to staff
on engaging with all fathers rather than those possessing a particular
form of cultural capital. In support, the chief executive of Fathers
Direct said: 'Staff are often good at engaging fathers if they are polite,
articulate and middle class. But, if they are young or from an ethnic
minority, they are regarded as too much trouble' (Carvel, 2007).

Communities develop their own ways of keeping safe by developing Home
Zones in conjunction with statutory and voluntary agencies

An alternative to targeted sources of support was where parents and
communities were encouraged to identify their own needs or priorities
and construct appropriate solutions with the help of different agencies.
This was evident in the Home Zone initiative imported from the
Netherlands and Germany and piloted in England, Wales and Scotland.
It sought to create spaces in local neighbourhoods where children can
play free from traffic. Although funding was targeted, communities had
to apply to a funding body. Consequently it relied on parents and other
community members having sufficient cultural capital to be able to put
together successful bids. However, such schemes, it has been claimed,

encourage community cooperation and 'can reduce barriers to the development of bonding and bridging social capital between neighbours' (Aldridge et al., 2002).

Practice box 3.4

Cavell Way is a residential area consisting of family houses and low-rise blocks of flats. 85 per cent of households receive Housing Benefit. It has a high child density, with over half the children aged under eleven. Children make use of streets and open spaces for play. However, a number of traffic hazards exist including a lack of pavement in one area and roadways that fail to discourage speeding. The key organisations (Moat Housing Society, the Residents Association and Swale Borough Council) worked together enabling Cavell Way to become one of the country's first Home Zone pilot sites. Local people including children and parents were attracted into the project by holding a street party, and a visit was made to see similar projects in the Netherlands. This was followed by a period of consultation and the drawing up of a plan of action for the estate, including traffic calming measures and the creation of a ball game space for children.

(Source: Field, 2000, webpage)

A related policy approach more closely aligned to the free market ideology of neoliberalism adopted in England allowed self-selecting groups of parents (as well as community, charity and religious organisations and businesses) to organise their own schools. Like Home Zones, these policies emphasise a departure in that parents are not only seen as in need of support services but have been reconstructed as a resource for providing services for their children. The Free Schools initiative was particularly relevant to parents who possessed certain forms of cultural and social capital. An account of how a Free School was organised by parents in conjunction with teachers and people with business experience is shown in Practice box 3.5.

Practice box 3.5

Free Schools: Cramlington Village Primary School

Free schools are funded directly by the DfE [Department for Education], based on how many pupils enrol, and are independent of the local authority but operated as charitable trusts. They are non-fee-paying and non-selective and can set pay and conditions for staff, pick and choose from the national curriculum, and decide on the length of the school day and term. New free schools can be established by businesses, parents, teachers, charities, faith groups, universities, private schools and not-for profits. However, school governors can contract private companies to manage a school for a fee.

The first 24 free schools opened in 2011. The school that we're establishing with a dozen like-minded parents and teachers will be one of 72 opening in this academic year. A third wave of 102 has been approved for 2013.

The government's intent, based on American and Swedish experience, is to give parents more choice, to encourage innovation and to raise standards by promoting competition. But it also wants to wrest control from local authorities and power from teaching unions.

That's the government's agenda. We have our own. We want simply to create a small school for the children of Cramlington that focuses on their individual needs and interests. We'll integrate those into an engaging curriculum with aspirational targets, delivered in a flexible way that suits each child.

Children at our school will have much more scope to choose where they learn on a daily basis. There won't be much whole-class teaching in the early years. For example, in reception and year one, they'll be able to choose to learn either indoors or outside for part of their day. They'll have access to iPads and iPod Touches, and a secure IT system will allow parents to share in their children's learning and achievements from home.

We've recruited a head chef, who will help children learn and understand more about cooking and healthy living. We're including cookery spaces in every classroom and an innovative IT space with an interactive floor and images projected onto walls to create 'immersive spaces'.

> Each child will also have the chance to attend an extra-curricular activity free of charge every day after school.
>
> (Wylie, 2012)

Thinking point 3.9: What kinds of capital are needed by parents who wish to become involved in setting up free schools and community Home Zones?

Free Schools are one of many policy initiatives (like the City Technology Colleges and Academies programme) that sought to raise educational standards while reducing inequalities (Hatcher, 2011). Educational achievement had become a key concern for creating human capital suited to the changing economy and employment market. Research, however, revealed that equality of opportunity within education for children appeared to be heavily influenced by parental background. Children in the Looked After care system compared to other children underachieved in the education system (Social Exclusion Unit, 2003). An influential study by Feinstein (2003) showed that at an age as early as twenty-two months, distinct differences in cognitive development can be observed, with children from more advantaged backgrounds performing better than those from disadvantaged backgrounds. Significantly, these early scores can be used to predict (although not determine) final educational attainment. The research showed that the education system is better at promoting upward mobility for children from advantaged backgrounds than for children from less advantaged backgrounds.

One way to explain this is by attributing success to middle class parents' cultural and social capital enabling them to 'provide their children with the skills needed to perform well at school and ... use their social contacts for the benefit of their children's education' (Gewirtz, 2001, p. 376). Similarly Lee and Bowen reported: 'The finding that parent involvement at school and high educational expectations, which were most common among parents from dominant groups, showed the strongest associations with achievement suggests the better fit of these parents' habitus to the field of education' (Lee and Bowen, 2006, p. 213). Furthermore, accounts of parents setting up Free Schools (Wylie 2012, and see Practice box 3.5) indicate a process in which only parents with particular skills and forms of cultural and social capital are the most likely to benefit.

Free Schools draw upon a similar model adopted in some parts of Sweden and the Charter School movement in the USA. Even though these models have been extensively researched, a review of the evidence claiming that Free Schools will raise standards and reduce educational inequality suggested they are 'unlikely to be more effective in this respect than comparable mainstream schools, and some may increase social segregation, on grounds of social class, ethnicity or religion' (Hatcher, 2011, p. 500).

Key points

1   Parenting support is presented in social policy as a solution to a range of diverse policy goals.
2   Parenting support can be understood in relation to human, social and cultural capital.
3   Parenting support operates at different levels and can be formal or informal, universal or targeted.
4   Models designed to involve parents in supporting their children can lead to stigma and reinforce inequalities.

Conclusion

This chapter has encouraged practitioners to reflect on the political context in which parenting support operates. It is evident that most parents take their parenting responsibilities seriously and are willing to receive support. Parental involvement, whether targeted, universal or parent-led, may work for some families yet for others it may also lead to alienation, stigma and the reproduction of pre-existing inequalities. Intensive support if presented as enablement rather than enforcement appears to have a chance of succeeding. Practitioners who provide support should be willing to positively embrace the wide diversity of family forms and understand parenting capacity within an ecological context. This chapter has demonstrated how theoretical knowledge can play a part alongside research and evaluation in improving services for children. The concepts of social and cultural capital are useful thinking tools when supporting parents through social networking or when constructing fair, accessible and equitable services.

References

Alakeson , V and Hurrell, A. (2012) *Counting the Costs of Childcare*, Resolution Foundation, available online at <http://www.resolutionfoundation.org/media/media/downloads/Counting_the_costs_of_childcare_2.pdf>, accessed 22 May 2013.

Aldridge, J. and Becker, S. (2003) *Children Who Care: Inside the World of Young Carers*, Loughborough, Department of Social Sciences, Loughborough University.

Aldridge, S. and Halpern, D. with Fitzpatrick, S. (2002) *Social Capital: A Discussion Paper*, London, Performance and Innovation Unit.

Allen, G. (2011) *Early Intervention: The Next Steps*, London, The Stationery Office.

Annesley,C. (2012) 'Campaigning against the cuts: gender equality movements in tough times', *The Political Quarterly,* vol. 83, no. 1 (Jan – March), pp. 19–23.

Ayrshire and Arran NHS Board (2002) *Needs Assessment of Alcohol and Drug Usage within Ayrshire,* Kilmarnock, Ayrshire and Arran NHS Board.

Azar, S.T., Lauretti, A.F. and Loding, B.V. (1998) 'The evaluation of parental fitness in termination of parental rights cases: a functional-contextual perspective', *Clinical Child and Family Psychology Review,* vol. 1, no. 2, pp. 77–100.

Baker, S. (2006) *Why I Volunteer*, available online at <http://www.disabledparentsnetwork. org.uk/cgi-bin/site/site.cgi?page=site/why_i_volunteer>, accessed 20 January 2008.

Ball, S.J. and Vincent, C. (2005) 'The "childcare champion"? New Labour, social justice and the childcare market', *British Educational Research Journal*, vol. 31, no. 5, pp. 557–570.

Barlow, J. and Stewart-Brown, S. (2001) 'Understanding parenting programmes: parents views', *Primary Health Care Research and Development*, vol. 2, pp. 117–130.

Barnard, M. (2007) *Drug Addiction and Families*, London, Jessica Kingsley Publishers.

Bayat, M. (2007) 'Evidence of resilience in families of children with autism', *Journal of Intellectual Disability Research*, vol. 51, no. 9, pp. 702–714.

BBC (2005) *Quote unquote: Iain Duncan Smith*, available online at <http://news.bbc.co.uk/hi/english/static/in_depth/uk_politics/2001/tory_leadership/iain_duncan_smith/quote.stm>, accessed 22 May 2013.

BBC News (2012) *Childcare: One in four providers 'make loss'*, available online at <http://www.bbc.co.uk/news/education-18300026> accessed 3 March 2012.

Bolling, K. (2005) *Infant Feeding Survey 2005: Early Results*, London, Information Centre for Health and Social Care.

Bourdieu, P. (1986) 'The forms of capital' in Richardson, J.G. (ed.) *Handbook of Theory and Research for the Sociology of Education*, New York, Greenwood Press.

Bradshaw, J., Finch, N., Kemp, P.A., Mayhew, E. and Williams, J. (2003) *Gender and Poverty in Britain*, Manchester, Equal Opportunities Commission.

Brown, G. (2009) 'Brown's conference speech: the full text', *The Independent*, 29 September, available online at <http://www.independent.co.uk/news/uk/politics/browns-conference-speech-the-full-text-1794938.html>, accessed 10 June 2013.

Butler, I. and Drakeford, M. (2001) 'Which Blair project? Communitarianism, social authoritarianism and social work', *Journal of Social Work*, vol. 1, no. 1, pp. 7–19.

Cameron, D. (2011) 'Speech on the fight-back after the riots', *New Statesman*, 15 August, available online at <http://www.newstatesman.com/politics/2011/08/society-fight-work-rights>, accessed 22 May 2013.

Carvel, J. (2007) 'Maternity services urged to include fathers', *Guardian*, 4 June, available online at <http://www.guardian.co.uk/medicine/story/0,2095080,00.html>, accessed 7 September 2007.

Children in Wales (2006) *Tackling Child Poverty in Wales: A Good Practice Guide for Schools*, available online at <http://www.childreninwales.org.uk/publications/genpubdownloads/index.html>, accessed 4 September 2007.

Children's Workforce Development Council (CWDC) (2007) *The Common Assessment Framework for Children and Young People: Practitioners' Guide: Integrated Working to Improve Outcomes for Children and Young People*, Leeds, CWDC, available online at <http://www.everychildmatters.gov.uk/_files/0C734C7BC2984FA94F5ED0D500B7EF02.pdf>, accessed 20 January 2008.

Chin, T. and Phillips, M. (2004) 'Social reproduction and child-rearing practices: social class, children's agency, and the summer activity gap', *Sociology of Education*, vol. 77, July, pp. 185–210.

Clarke, K. (2006) 'Childhood, parenting and early intervention: a critical examination of the Sure Start national programme', *Critical Social Policy*, vol. 26, no. 4, pp. 699–721.

Cleaver, H. (2006) 'The influence of parenting and other family relationships' in Aldgate, J., Jones, D., Rose, W. and Jeffery, C. (eds) *The Developing World of the Child*, London, Jessica Kingsley, pp. 122–140.

Cleaver, H., Unell, I. and Aldgate, J. (2011) *Children's Needs – Parenting Capacity: Child Abuse: Parental Mental Illness, Learning Disability, Substance Misuse, and Domestic Violence*, second edition, London, The Stationery Office.

Coleman, J.S. (1988) 'Social capital in the creation of human capital', *American Journal of Sociology*, vol. 94, Supplement, pp. S95–S120.

Coleman, J.S. (1991) 'Prologue: constructed social organisation' in Bourdieu, P. and Coleman, J.S. (eds) *Social Theory for a Changing Society*, Oxford, Westview Press.

Coleman, J.S. (1997) 'Social capital in the creation of human capital' in Halsey, A.H., Lauder, H., Brown, P. and Wells, A.S. (eds) *Education: Culture, Economy and Society*, Oxford, Oxford University Press, pp. 80–95.

Crowley, A. and Vulliamy, C. (2003) *Listen Up! Children and Young People Talk: About Poverty*, London, Save the Children.

Daniel, B., Featherstone, B., Hooper, C.-A. and Scourfield, J. (2005) 'Why gender matters for Every Child Matters', *British Journal of Social Work*, vol. 35, no. 8, pp. 1343–1355.

Department for Communities and Local Government (2012) *The Troubled Families Programme: Financial Framework for the Troubled Families Programme's Payment-by-Results Scheme for Local Authorities*, available online at <https://www.gov.uk/government/uploads/system/uploads/attachment_data/file/11469/2117840.pdf>, accessed 22 May 2013.

Department for Education (DfE) (2010) *Extended Schools – Building on Good Practice*, circular number 2010/21, available online at <http://www.deni.gov.uk/extended_schools_circular_2010.pdf>, accessed 10 June 2013.

Department for Education (DfE) (2012) *Foundation Years – Sure Start Children's Centres*, written evidence submitted by the Department for Education, available online at <http://www.publications.parliament.uk/pa/cm201213/cmselect/cmeduc/writev/surestart/m22.htm>, accessed 22 May 2013.

Department for Education and Skills (DfES) (2006) *Parenting Support: Guidance for Local Authorities in England*, London, DfES.

Department of Health, Department for Education and Employment, Home Office (2000) *Framework for Assessment of Children in Need and their Families*, London, The Stationery Office, available online at <http://www.dh.gov.uk/en/Publicationsandstatistics/Publications/PublicationsPolicyAndGuidance/DH_4003256>, accessed 20 January 2008.

Evans, M. (2010) 'Analysis: Providers wait for mists to clear on early years landscape', *Nursery World*, available online at <http://www.nurseryworld.co.uk/news/1006925/Analysis-Providers-wait-mists-clear-early-years-landscape/>, accessed 22 May 2013.

Feinstein, L. (2003) 'Not just the early years: the need for developmental perspective for equality of opportunity', *New Economy*, vol. 10, no. 4, pp. 213–218.

Field, C. (2000) *Cavell Way – A Planning Zone*, available online at <http://www.homezones.org/homeZUKCavellWay.html>, accessed 4 September 2007.

Field, F. (2010) *The Foundation Years: Preventing Poor Children Becoming Poor Adults*, London, Cabinet Office.

Garrett, P.M. (2006) 'How to be modern: New Labour's neoliberal modernity and the *Change for Children* programme', *British Journal of Social Work*, available online at <http://bjsw.oxfordjournals.org/cgi/reprint/bcl345v1>, accessed 10 September 2007.

Gewirtz, S. (2001) 'Cloning the Blairs: New Labour's programme for the re-socialization of working-class parents', *Journal of Education Policy*, vol. 16, no. 4, pp. 365–378.

Gillies, V. (2005) 'Raising the "meritocracy": parenting and the individualization of social class', *Sociology*, vol. 39, no. 5, pp. 835–853.

Gillies, V. (2006) 'Working class mothers and school life: exploring the role of emotional capital', *Gender and Education*, vol. 18, no. 3, pp. 281–293.

Grenfell, M. and James, D. (1998) *Bourdieu and Education: Acts of Practical Theory*, Bristol, PA, Falmer.

Hall, S. (2011) 'The neoliberal revolution: Thatcher, Blair, Cameron – the long march of neoliberalism continues', *Soundings*, no. 48 (July).

Hamlyn, B., Brooker, S., Oleinikova, K. and Wands, S. (2002) *Infant Feeding 2000*, Norwich, The Stationery Office.

Harvey, D. (2005) *A Brief History of Neoliberalism*, Oxford, Oxford University Press.

Hatcher, R. (2011) 'The Conservative–Liberal Democrat Coalition government's "free schools" in England', *Educational Review*, vol. 63, no. 4, November, pp. 485–503.

Henricson, C. (2008) Foreword, in Klett-Davies, M., Skaliotis, E. and Wollny, I. (eds) *Mapping and Analysis of Parenting Services in England*, London, Family and Parenting Institute.

Hill, A. (2004) '£42,000: what parents pay for a place in a top state school', *Observer*, available online at <http://education.guardian.co.uk/schools/story/0,1376960,00.html>, accessed 4 September 2007.

Hill, M. (2005) 'Children's boundaries: within and beyond families' in McKie, L. and Cunningham-Burley, S. (eds) *Families in Society: Boundaries and Relationships*, Bristol, The Policy Press, pp. 77–94.

HM Government (2010) *The Coalition: Our Programme for Government: Freedom, Fairness, Responsibility*, London, Cabinet Office.

Jack, G. (2006) 'The area and community components of children's well-being', *Children & Society*, vol. 20, no. 5, pp. 334–347.

Jenkins, R. (2002) *Pierre Bourdieu*, London, Routledge.

Lee, J.-S. and Bowen, N.K. (2006) 'Parent involvement, cultural capital, and the achievement gap among elementary school children', *American Educational Research Journal*, vol. 43, no. 2, pp. 193–218.

Lloyd, N., O'Brien, M. and Lewis, C. (2003) *National evaluation summary: Fathers in Sure Start local programmes*, available online at <http://www.ness.bbk.ac.uk/documents/activities/implementation/160.pdf>, accessed 4 September 2007.

Mail on Sunday (1993) 'Interview with British Prime Minister John Major', 21 February.

Moran, P., Ghate, D. and van der Merwe, A. (2004) *What Works in Parenting Support? A Review of the International Evidence*, available online at <http://www.dfes.gov.uk/research/data/uploadfiles/RR574.pdf>, accessed 4 September 2007.

Morrow, V. (1999) 'Conceptualising social capital in relation to the well-being of children and young people: a critical review', *Sociological Review*, vol. 47, no. 4, pp. 744–765.

Munro, E. (2011) *Munro Review of Child Protection: Final Report: a Child-Centred System*, Department for Education, London, the Stationery Office.

Peninsula Cerebra Research Unit (PenCRU) (2012) *Parent-to-Parent Support – Does It Help?*, available online at <https://wombat.pcmd.ac.uk/document_manager/documents/Peer_Plain_English_summary.pdf>, accessed 24 April 2013.

Pinnock, K. and Evans, R. (2007) 'Developing responsive preventative practices: key messages from children's and families' experiences of the Children's Fund', *Children & Society*, available online at <http://www.blackwell-synergy.com/doi/full/10.1111/j.1099–0860.2007.00081.x >, accessed 26 October 2007.

PricewaterhouseCoopers LLP (2006) *DfES Children's Services: The Market for Parental and Family Support Services*, London, PricewaterhouseCoopers LLP.

Prime Minister's Strategy Unit (PMSU) (2007) *Building on Progress: Families*, Policy Review, London, Cabinet Office.

Putnam, R. (1994) 'Social capital and public affairs', *Bulletin of the American Academy of Arts and Sciences*, vol. 47, no. 8, pp. 5–19.

Quinton, D. (2004) *Supporting Parents: Messages from Research*, London, Jessica Kingsley.

Rake K., Grigg, P. and Hannon, C. (2011) 'Parenting under the microscope', in Family and Parenting Institute, *Where Now For Parenting: Perspectives on Parenting, Policy and Practice,* London, Family and Parenting Institute, pp. 13–19.

Reay, D. (2000) 'A useful extension of Bourdieu's conceptual framework?: emotional capital as a way of understanding mothers' involvement in their children's education', *Sociological Review*, vol. 48, no. 4, pp. 568–585.

Royal College of Paediatrics and Child Health (RCPCH) (2002) *Helpful Parenting*, London, RCPCH, also available online at <http://www.rcpch. ac.uk/doc.aspx?id_Resource=1761>, accessed 11 September 2007.

Sands, D. (2011) 'Summary: the impact of 2010–15 tax and benefit changes on women and men', in *Single Mothers Singled Out,* The Fawcett Society, available online at <http://www.fawcettsociety.org.uk/ documents/Single%20MothersSingled%20Out%20The%20impact%20of %202010-15%20tax%20and%20benefit%20changes%20on%20women% 20and%20men.pdf>, accessed 27 February 2013.

Scottish Executive (2002*) Better Communities in Scotland: Closing the Gap: The Scottish Executive's Community Regeneration Statement*, Edinburgh, Scottish Executive.

Scottish Executive (2003) *Getting Our Priorities Right: Good Practice Guidance for Working with Children and Families Affected by Substance Misuse*, Edinburgh, Scottish Executive.

Scottish Executive (2006) *Family Matters: Charter for Grandchildren*, available online at <http://www.scotland.gov.uk/Resource/Doc/ 112493/0027333.pdf>, accessed 4 September 2007.

Scottish Government (2013) *Getting it right for every child*, available online at <http://www.scotland.gov.uk/Topics/People/Young-People/ gettingitright>, accessed 7 May 2013.

Social Exclusion Unit (SEU) (2000) *Employment and the Policy Action Team 12: Report on Young People*, available online at <http://archive. cabinetoffice.gov.uk/seu/page864c. html?id=418>, accessed 7 September 2007.

Social Exclusion Unit (SEU) (2003) *A Better Education for Children in Care*, available online at <http://archive.cabinetoffice.gov.uk/seu/ downloaddocdac1.pdf?id=32&pId=398>, accessed 20 January 2008.

Speight, S., Smith, R., Valle I., Schneider, V. and Perry J. (2009) *Childcare and Early Years: Survey of Parents 2008,* research report no. DCSF-RR136, London, Department for Children, Schools and Families.

St Clair, R. (2005) *Working Paper 1: Introduction to Social Capital*, available online at <http://www.gla.ac.uk/centres/cradall/docs/01workingpaper. pdf>, accessed 4 September 2007.

Sure Start (2005) *Early Impacts of Sure Start Local Programmes on Children and Families: Report of the Cross-Sectional Study of 9- and 36-Month Old Children and their Families*, London, DFES.

Sure Start (2006) *Sure Start Children's Centres: Practice Guidance*, London, DfES.

Taylor-Gooby, P. and Stoker, G. (2011) 'The Coalition programme: a new vision for Britain or politics as usual?' *The Political Quarterly*, vol. 82, no. 1, pp. 4–15.

Tickell, C. (2011) 'Building on what we know to break the cycle', in Family and Parenting Institute, *Where Now For Parenting: Perspectives on Parenting, Policy and Practice,* London, Family and Parenting Institute, pp. 102–104.

Tomanović, S. (2004) 'Family habitus as the cultural context for childhood', *Childhood*, vol. 11, no. 3, pp. 339–360.

Tunstill, J., Aldgate, J. and Hughes, M. (2007) *Improving Children's Services Networks: Lessons from Family Centres*, London, Jessica Kingsley.

Wasoff, F. and Cunningham-Burley, S. (2005) 'Perspectives on social policies and families' in McKie, L. and Cunningham-Burley, S. (eds) *Families in Society: Boundaries and Relationships*, Bristol, The Policy Press, pp. 261–270.

Williams, F. (2004) 'What matters is who works: why every child matters to New Labour. Commentary on the DfES Green Paper *Every Child Matters*', *Critical Social Policy*, vol. 24, no. 3, pp. 406–427.

Williams, R. (2011) 'If we want fathers to change their ways, we need to first change ours', in Family and Parenting Institute, *Where Now For Parenting: Perspectives on Parenting, Policy and Practice*, London, Family and Parenting Institute, pp. 68–70.

Women's Budget Group (2005) *Response to 'Choice for parents, the best start for children: a ten year strategy for childcare*, available online at <ht1p://www.wbg.org.uk/ documents!WBGResponsetoChildcareStrategy.pdf>, accessed 4 September 2007.

Woolcock, M. (2001) 'The place of social capital in understanding social and economic outcomes', *Isuma: Canadian Journal of Policy Research*, vol. 2, no. 1, pp. 1–17.

Wylie, I. (2012) 'How we started our own free school', *Management Today*, 1 September, pp. 38–40.

Chapter 4 Interagency working with children and families: what works and what makes a difference?

Nick Frost

Introduction

In recent years interagency working has become an increasingly dominant method of working with children and young people. This chapter explores the evidence we have in relation to both the process and outcomes of such interagency working. The chapter attempts to address an overarching question: 'what works' in interagency practice with children and young people? and closes with a focus on the challenges and its possible future.

Core questions

- What are the contexts and forms of interagency working?
- 'What works' in interagency working and what are the different perspectives, or kinds of evidence, that we can use for its evaluation?
- What are the challenges in implementing interagency working?
- What Might the future of interagency working look like?

1 Interagency working with children and families

Across many countries there has been an increased focus on interagency working – an issue which is addressed throughout this book. This growth of interest reflects a number of factors: the persistence of complex social problems and inequalities which some thought 'the welfare state' and increasing wealth generation might address; the development of information technology that has made 'networking' more possible; and the realisation that 'silo' professions cannot be effective in isolation (Skidmore, 2004). Today the lexicon of child welfare regularly features phrases such as 'interagency working', 'multi-professional hubs', 'co-location' and 'information sharing', all of which reflect this profound shift in the delivery of services to children and young people. Even where professions are working separately there will be talk of 'networking', 'coordination' and 'working together' – all forms of interagency working (Anning et al., 2010). The challenges of such terminology are discussed in Chapter 2. The origins of this focus on interagency working seemed to lie in faith that such approaches will work, rather than on actual evidence. For example, in 2002 the then English Secretary of State for Health, Alan Milburn, stated that:

> The old style public service monoliths cannot meet modern challenges. They need to be broken up. In their place we can forge new local partnerships that specialize in tackling particular problems local communities face.
>
> (Quoted in Anning et al., 2010, p. 4)

Interagency working with children and young people now takes place in many settings: schools, children's centres, youth offending teams and family support teams, to name but a few. In fact it is becoming increasingly difficult to name pure 'single' profession sites. Interagency working is taken to be an accepted positive: it is assumed to improve working life for professionals and both process and outcomes for service users.

We should also be aware that, as Skidmore points out, the growing number of forms of networking has spread well beyond child welfare:

> The institutional landscape of modern society is being ripped up. Be they companies or public agencies, individual organisations are finding that the only way to satisfy the changing demands and expectations of customers and citizens is to be embedded in networks of organisations able to stitch together different products, services, resources and skills in flexible combinations and deliver them when and where they are most needed. Splendid isolation is out. Collaboration is in.
>
> (Skidmore, 2004, p. 91)

Thus interagency working and networking are certainly key features of twenty-first century ways of working in general, and of child welfare specifically. These developments partly recognise the reality of the lives of children, young people and their families. Real children and young people do not live in 'silos' – their education, development, health and welfare do not exist in separate arenas. In fact, the social professions of the post-Second World War period often treated children as if they existed in such separate arenas. Children may have seen the midwife, the childcare officer, the teacher and sometimes the doctor with little 'information sharing' taking place. This may well be rooted in the fact that professions are trained separately and tend to develop distinct professional identities. The momentous early child death inquiries highlighted the lack of communication; the report on the death of Maria Colwell (Secretary of State for Social Services, 1974), for example, showed the lack of communication between teachers and social workers. In England in 1968 the Seebohm Report pointed out the absurdity of the welfare officer, the childcare officer and the housing officer visiting the same family without being fully aware of each other's roles (Seebohm, 1968).

A childcare officer in the early 1960s

There were then probably irresistible forces working towards interagency working: but the key underpinning issue remains – what difference does this way of working make for children, young people and their families?

Key points

1 Interagency working with children and young people has become an increasingly common way of working.
2 Initially there has been a 'leap of faith' that interagency working would be effective, without a strong evidence base.

2 What works? Evaluating interagency working

An exploration of 'what works' in interagency working will be undertaken throughout the remainder of this chapter. Research that addresses the 'what works' question will be outlined and analysed through a focus on service users and their voices and professionals and their organisations. Contemporary national and international research findings will be utilised to illustrate the main points. The research on these issues is not plentiful but we will explore some of the limited research that exists and perhaps by the end of the section we may be able to assess whether or not interagency working does indeed 'work'.

The evidence for the success of interagency working has been sparse and researchers have often made statements along the lines of the following:

> There appears to be a dearth of evidence to support the notion that multi-agency working in practice brings about benefits to children and families.
>
> (Abbott et al., 2005, p. 229)

> Primary research in the areas of early intervention and of integrated working are in their infancy, and there is, therefore, limited direct evidence.
>
> (Wolstenholme et al., 2008, p. 3)

> More research is needed on the long-term impact of inter-agency collaboration in particular for non-profit childcare centres.
>
> (Coleman Selden et al., 2006, p. 421)

The first two quotes come from a British context and the third from the United States.

Along similar lines, a senior operations manager in Birmingham, England, has stated that from a practitioner viewpoint:

> 'Because we couldn't find any evidence on cost effectiveness of early interventions in this country we went overseas.'
>
> (Practitioner, quoted in Cooper, 2010, p.18)

How can we find out if interagency working is effective? It can be argued that there are four perspectives on interagency working that can be analysed to establish whether it can be said to work:

1 Interagency working can work in improving 'outcomes' for children and families: that is, helping them achieve better health, be safer, be happier, be better educated and economically more secure, for example. In theory these are measurable – we should be able to tell, with carefully designed research studies, if interagency working is improving outcomes, or not. This is often known as the 'what works' question. We will refer to this as 'outcome evidence'.

2 Interagency working can work in the sense of improving the process for children, young people and their families. By 'process' we mean their experience of professional interventions. For example, families may feel that it is positive that they do not have to repeat their story to a range of professionals. They may appreciate that professionals can cooperate and work more effectively together. We will refer to this as 'service user process evidence'.

3 Interagency working can also work in the sense of improving the working processes of professions: they may feel that it is easier to share information, easier to speak to each other and easier to mobilise each other's skills and resources. We will refer to this as 'professional process evidence'.

4 The final sense in which interagency working can be said to 'work' is if it is more efficient in terms of resources. It may well make better

use of resources through sharing offices, meetings, skills and so forth. It may save future expenditure if family problems grow worse. We will refer to this as 'efficiency evidence'.

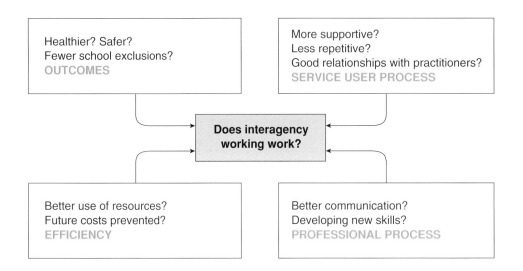

Approaches to evaluating interagency working

Thinking point 4.1: Think about any experience of interagency working you have had as a practitioner or service user. How do you think its effectiveness should be evaluated?

2.1 The outcome evidence

As we have seen, there has been an increasing emphasis on interagency working in recent policy and practice developments. While interagency working has become very popular, there remain fundamental questions about whether we can measure how effective it is in terms of outcomes and making a real difference.

Some of the earliest evidence was gathered by two researchers in the United States – A. Glisson and C. Hemmelgarn (1998). They used a 'quasi-experimental' method where there are two groups of participants, one of which is examined to explore the impact of a change or service (an intervention group) and the other which is not (a control group). We can then tell if the intervention has made a real difference. Their key findings are reported below.

Glisson and Hemmelgarn's quasi-experimental, longitudinal study assessed the effects of increasing inter-organisational services coordination in American public children's services agencies. The research team collected both qualitative and quantitative data over a three-year period, describing the services provided to 250 children by thirty-two public children's service offices in twenty-four counties in the state of Tennessee. The researchers focus on what they identify as 'organisational climate'. This concept attempts to capture the motivation and support for individual workers. The researchers used low levels of conflict, high levels of cooperation, the existence of role clarity, and staff being able to exercise personal discretion as measures of a positive organisational climate. They also measured outcomes for children and inter-organisational coordination. Inter-organisational coordination was measured using the concepts of authorisation, responsibility and monitoring.

Authorisation was measured as the number of separate authorisations required for a child to receive services from multiple sources. The fewer required, the greater the coordination.

Responsibility was measured as the number of individuals responsible for ensuring that the services needed were delivered to a child. The lower the number, the greater the coordination, professionalism, partnership and joined-up thinking.

Monitoring was measured as the proportion of those monitoring services for each child that also provided a service to the child. (Because coordination requires a separation of these responsibilities, lower proportions represent greater coordination).

The very complex data gathered by Glisson and Hemelgarn suggests that organisational climate was 'the primary predictor of positive service outcomes (the children's improved psychosocial functioning) and a significant predictor of service quality. In contrast, inter-organisational coordination had a negative effect on service quality and no effect on outcomes.' They therefore conclude that:

> Efforts to improve children's services systems should focus on positive organisational climates rather than on increasing inter-organisational services co-ordination. This is important because many large-scale efforts to improve children's services systems

> have focused on inter-organisational co-ordination with little success and none to date have focused on organisational climate.

> (Quoted in Frost, 2005)

This important and sophisticated study is negative in its assessment of the impact of interagency working. However, the research study raises many issues for us: it is after all now quite dated; the US findings may not translate to different cultural settings and environments; it is specifically about youth justice; and there are many different forms of interagency coordination; so perhaps it was just this one intervention that did not seem to work?

Having noted this study, we move on to explore what more recent, British studies tell us about the impact of interagency working. This is much more optimistic.

The most important studies regarding the outcomes of interagency working are undoubtedly those undertaken by LARC (the Local Authority Research Consortium) in English local authorities. This was in relation to the use of a multi-professional assessment method (which was known in England as the Common Assessment Framework (CAF)) for early intervention and interagency working. There are four studies, which we will discuss in some detail.

1 Lord, P., Kinder, K., Wilkin, A., Atkinson, M. and Harland, J. (2008) *Evaluating the Early Impact of Integrated Children's Services: Round 1 Final Report*, Slough, NFER.
2 Easton, C., Morris, M. and Gee, G. (2010) *LARC2: Integrated Children's Services and the CAF Process*, Slough, NFER.
3 Easton, C., Gee, G., Durbin, B., and Teeman, D (2011) *Early Intervention, Using the CAF Process, and its Cost Effectiveness: Findings from LARC3*, Slough, NFER.
4 Easton, C., Featherstone G., Poet, H., Aston, H., Gee, G. and Durbin, B. (2012) *Supporting Families with Complex Needs: Findings from LARC 4*, Slough, NFER.

We shall refer to these studies in turn as LARC 1, LARC 2, LARC 3 and LARC 4.

LARC 1

LARC 1 aimed to identify the early impact of integrated children's services and the features that promote or hinder success in improving outcomes for children and young people. The research operated in varied localities within the fourteen participating areas, with one locality being chosen as the focus within each area. Children, young people and parents in this study report a range of improvements in outcomes as a result of the support they currently receive. The most commonly noted are: getting on well with school work, feeling safer and feeling happier. Parents also frequently report their child's enhanced confidence or self-esteem. The report argues that it would seem important for leadership teams to give early attention to the development of robust and comparable measures of children's emotional health and wellbeing.

LARC 2

LARC 2 reported on findings supplied by twenty-four local authorities using the Common Assessment Framework. LARC 2 suggests that 'the CAF process appears to be supporting improved outcomes for children, young people and families' and notes that more needs to be done to embed the framework as a tool to support early intervention and prevention.

Three areas are suggested as requiring action:

- clear commitment and action from the Children's Trust Board to support the effective operation of the CAF process across all partner agencies…
- a clear policy for how the Lead Professional role is allocated and supported (including the possibility of a new cadre of professionals dedicated to this role).
- absolute clarity on what the CAF is, who it is for, and how it relates to other formal assessments undertaken by LAs [local authorities] and partner agencies.

(Easton et al., 2010)

These requirements for action suggest that there is a need for assessment practitioners to develop further professional expertise, that guidance and thresholds of needs can be problematic to apply, and that assessment practitioners may not fully understand that any other formal assessment undertaken for a child can be incorporated within the CAF assessment, thus creating a single, working document that reduces bureaucracy and would provide a holistic picture of the child and the child's world.

LARC 3

LARC 3 documented local research projects covering twenty-one local authorities. The study found that 'the costs invested in assessments and interventions identified in the LARC cases are consistently and significantly lower than the future costs avoided'. This is an important positive finding in today's context of limited or no increases to the government grants that are provided to local authorities, and should secure the future of CAF and its process as a tool for practice, within future government guidance.

LARC 4

In this chapter we will focus in more detail on the most recent study, LARC 4: *Supporting Families with Complex Needs: Findings from LARC* (Easton et al., 2012). This study presents findings from twelve local authorities, using thirty-nine case studies.

The authors of LARC 4 outline their methodology as follows:

> Eleven of the twelve LARC 4 local authorities carried out their own qualitative case study research projects within an overall agreed framework developed by the LAs and NFER [National Foundation for Educational Research]. Each case study involved interviews with LA practitioners, parents and (where appropriate) children and young people. In all, the LAs conducted around 80 interviews across 39 case studies between spring and autumn 2011. Each case study looked at whether the common assessment process is a cost effective way to support improved outcomes and avoid costly, negative outcomes for families later on.
>
> (Easton et al., 2012, Summary)

They also explored how to assess the costs and/or savings of implementing the assessment framework:

> To calculate a difference in costs (i.e. an indicative 'saving'), LARC adopted the adapted 'futures methodology' used during LARC3. Futures methodologies are increasingly being used within research and evaluation to ascertain what might happen if, for example, an intervention had not been implemented. LARC4 LAs asked practitioners, parents and, where appropriate, children/young people for their perceptions on what the life course of a child/family might have been had the CAF process not been initiated.
>
> (Easton et al., 2012, Summary; see also Helmer, 1983, on future methodologies)

The main areas of work undertaken in the cases explored were to:

- enhance parenting strategies (31 families)
- develop emotional health and resilience (22 families)
- improve engagement in education (18 families)
- engage in positive activities (13 families)
- promote physical health management (11 families).

(Easton et al., 2012, p. 8)

The key findings of the LARC 4 study are summarised in the report Foreword, as shown in Research box 4.1.

Research box 4.1

- Outcomes for children, young people and their families experiencing problems can be improved – and in some cases very dramatically - by appropriate interventions planned and managed by services working effectively together
- The Common Assessment Framework (CAF) process encourages, and provides a good basis for, such integrated planning and intervention
- There are five key success factors for early intervention, all of which should be present

---

> - The costs of working and intervening in this joined up way are likely to be repaid many times over by the avoidance of greater costs later in the life of the child or family (although not all of the savings will accrue at the local service level).
>
> (Easton et al., 2012, Foreword)

The third point in the box refers to 'five key success factors', which are as follows:

- engaging children, young people and families as equal partners in the process
- ensuring consistency of the lead professional support, which helped families and professionals work together better
- integrating all of the elements of the CAF process, from holistic assessment, TAC (Team Around the Child) model and meetings, lead professional role, action planning and reviews
- ensuring multi-agency working and information sharing, which improved understanding of need and service provision
- developing a better understanding of children and young people's needs at the earliest possible stage.

(Easton et al., 2012, p. 21)

In all cases it was reported that the families' situation had improved to some extent. More concretely, they explain the 'future' scenarios that the assessment intervention may have avoided from a total of thirty-nine cases:

Overwhelmingly, both practitioners and families felt that without the support put in place through the common assessment, the situation for the family would have deteriorated hugely. Examples of possible futures scenarios avoided as a result of the common assessment process included:

- social care intervention (22 families, including seven cases of a child being looked after)
- poor educational outcomes (21 families)
- police involvement or criminal prosecution (17 families)

- someone getting physically hurt following violent or aggressive outbursts (13 families)
- school exclusion (12 families)
- decline of parent's or children's mental health issues (12 families).

(Easton et al., 2012, p. 12).

How do we evaluate the impact of a family support worker on outcomes for children?

These four English studies, with our focus here mainly being on the most recent report LARC 4, are much more optimistic than the US study reported earlier. There are similar studies, for example, from Scotland, where a summary of family support research concludes:

Project staff assessed 81% of families as being at reduced risk of homelessness/eviction by the time their cases were closed. Complaints of anti-social behaviour had, at this point, been reduced in 94% of cases.

(Pawson, 2009, p. 84)

In this instance family support workers were drawn from a variety of professional backgrounds including housing, nursing, drug and alcohol services and the projects overseen by a multi-agency steering group.

These studies suggest that there are positive outcomes to be gained from interagency working. Having explored some material on outcomes, we now move on to explore other forms of change that interagency work may bring about.

2.2 'Service user process' evidence

In recent years professionals have grown used to dealing with outcomes: measuring and assessing the results of their actions. While this is very helpful, it could be argued that we have lost a focus on 'process' – that is, how we do things. Children and families often refer to 'being listened to' and 'being treated with respect' as something they value – this refers to 'process' rather than 'outcomes'. Such process issues are explored in this section.

In a sense 'process' studies are more straightforward than 'outcome' studies. We can simply ask service users what they thought about the services they have received and get their perspective on how they felt about the process, whereas outcome measures, as we have seen, are quite complex. However, process studies are not totally straightforward. For example, can service users compare single agency 'silo' approaches with 'interagency' responses? Keeping these issues in mind, we do have some evidence about service users' perspectives.

Process issues need to be explored from a child's point of view

A Leeds-based research team asked service users from a range of settings about their views of working with a wide range of interagency services (Brock et al., 2009). This is known as the TIPS (Towards Interprofessional Partnerships) study.

The TIPS service users identifed a 'supportive culture' as very important and they were very positive about the support received. Several service users commented on their levels of distress when initially accessing the services and how team members had been warm, welcoming and friendly. For the current author this is a reminder of a children's centre user saying to him: 'I used to cry alone but now I have many shoulders to cry on.'

A key aspect of the support offered was feeling that their individual voices had been listened to and that their needs had been taken into account. As a result of this the service users felt that effective services were put into place, such as support through transitions from Home Start:

> 'The support that went in was unbelievable … We hit crisis point a long time ago and it is only the support and working together that has made this kid still with me, still in school and still progressing, without that she wouldn't be where she is.'
>
> (Foster carer, quoted in Brock et al., 2009, p. 31)

Relationships that were built upon trust were considered to be very important and that trust was essential for people who are often in real need at the point of accessing services. Several service users commented on how the professionals in the settings felt like 'friends', of the closeness they felt and the warmth and easy access making the settings feel welcoming. These are key aspects of the 'process' issues that we discussed earlier, although these service user comments also highlight that their experience is a combination of the service and the skills and attributes of the individual worker. One service user stated how she felt her culture and religion was respected and there were several responses such as:

'They were friendly and helpful when I was in a bad position.'

'I feel at home here. They can tell if you are sad and they help you.'

(Mothers quoted in Brock et al., 2009, p. 11)

Some of the service users commented how they felt respected and sometimes perceived as having a professional standing. Mutual respect was therefore important:

'I think it is also mutual support isn't it? It is not just everybody get involved with that child, but it is mutual support for each other as well.'

'We are all involved in the same meetings. We have reviews and things with CAMHS, with schools, with all sorts of different professions really.'

(Practitioners quoted in Brock et al., 2009, p. 11)

There were many positive comments praising the level of support received from the settings.

Clear communication was also extremely important for the service users and they felt that this occurred not only when accessing services on site, but also through telephone and written communication. Information sharing between the staff of the settings was considered to be essential. Service users really valued that they did not have to keep repeating issues 'over and over again' because the staff communicated with each other very effectively. Knowing that staff do disseminate knowledge and issues about individual needs and progress promoted confidence and prevented stress for the service users:

'It has been seamless. They write and talk to each other.' (Mother)

'The staff are great. They write notes about us and actually read them and listen to each other.' (Mother)

'I know they have regular meetings and talk about all the patients.'
(Service user)

(Quoted in Brock et al., 2009, p.13)

Evaluation of key worker services for disabled children has revealed a mixed
picture of success

The service users believed provision worked well because of the
information sharing within a team, when a setting provided a 'wrap-
around' service. They commented on the multi-agency work and the
effectiveness of working in partnership with other people so that users
feel supported and that their needs are met. They felt they were
informed about health, social services and education and that these
services worked together:

'I also think there have been times when the school has had to
contact CAMHS [Child and Adolescent Mental Health Services] or
somebody like that with regards to one of my children and they
have then phoned me and let me know they have contacted

> CAMHS and let me know why and all the rest, so you know we all work together for that child.'

(Foster carer, quoted in Brock et al., 2009, p. 13)

The service users appreciated that there were policies, procedures and guidelines in place so that whoever was approached could deal with a problem, enabling appropriate expertise to be provided. The service users were also pleased with the facilities and at one children's centre they commented on the breadth of provision, that included day care, the parent and toddlers' group, toy library, coffee morning; and the job centre:

> 'It is a great resource for our children and I suppose for me too.'

(Mother, quoted in Brock et al., 2009, p. 11)

We can see from the TIPS study that process issues are highlighted by parents and carers. They are positive about information sharing within interagency teams – something that professionals are often wary of.

The general direction of the TIPS findings is supported by the LARC 4 study that we explored earlier:

> Reported benefits of the common assessment process included reducing duplication of effort and ensuring the family needed to tell their story only once; harnessing shared accountability and decision making between services; and longevity of the CAF process in giving families and professionals a chance to get to know one another, evaluate progress at regular points in time, and help to build an environment of trust and empowerment and resilience.

(Easton et al., 2012, Summary)

Positive service user attitudes are summarised as follows:

While some families were apprehensive at the start of the process, most welcomed the common assessment process and felt that the multi-agency practitioners who offered help had a good understanding of their needs.

(Easton et al., 2012, Summary)

Another study, of the experiences of parents of children with disabilities, quotes a service user as follows:

'I was spending so much time on the phone, I would be chasing up changed appointments ... so yes that cuts down on oodles of phone calls.'

(Mother, quoted in Abbott et al., 2005, p. 235)

We can see that service users seem to be generally positive about the 'process' aspects of interagency working. We now move on to explore professional perspectives on process from their perspective.

2.3 'Professional process' evidence

There is a relatively strong evidence base for professional process in interagency working. For example, the current author has undertaken two studies that have addressed this issue (Anning et al., 2010; Brock et al., 2009). The evidence here is powerful: professionals report learning new skills, enjoying enhanced information sharing, and feeling more effective in their interventions.

The evidence from a professional perspective suggests that:

'It cuts down a huge amount of duplication when other professionals are there. Sometimes we can short cut 'out patients' – go straight to the consultant for an opinion. It cuts down on phone calls. Makes things more efficient and easier.'

(Practitioner, quoted in Townsley et al., 2004, p. 29)

A US study suggests that interagency working is beneficial for professionals, as:

> It appears that working across policy domains does benefit staff through management processes.
>
> (Coleman Selden et al., 2006, p. 421)

In the TIPS research (Brock et al., 2009), five key themes for successful working were identified by professionals who were working specifically in interagency team settings:

Theme 1: communication

Theme 2: assertive leadership

Theme 3: a supportive culture

Theme 4: individual qualities

Theme 5: organisational issues

Each theme is discussed below with illustrative quotes from the focus groups which were held for participants.

Theme 1: communication

The need for regular and clear communication within multi-agency teams was seen to include the need to clarify the scope and limitations of the professional roles and context of team members. The importance of team meetings and away days was stressed as one mechanism for 'getting people to talk together' alongside the effective use of email. More informal communication and social networking was also recognised as valuable. One participant referred to the importance of being able 'to pull up a chair and chat', while another said that 'walking round the office getting ideas off people' was seen as important. Participants emphasised the value of clarity and the avoidance of jargon, recognising that there may be reasons why people use jargon and that it may be helpful to identify and address these. For example, individual team members may not feel confident or recognised within the team and maintain the use of profession-specific language in an attempt to bolster their position. It was suggested that ground rules regarding the use of jargon should be established and regularly revisited by the team so that 'everyone shares the same language' and there is an agreement that there is no jargon in either verbal or written communication. One participant talked about 'being challenged in a friendly manner' particularly in relation to the use of jargon. The sharing of information about roles and responsibilities and their scope and limitations was seen to be essential, with one participant reporting that whenever someone joined their team, they were asked to fully explain this so that everyone was aware. These findings are consistent with those of Anning et al., where one respondent stated:

> 'You get a young person coming through the system and you want to go and chat to someone about him or her and say "I've got this person and what do you think?" They might even know them.'

> (Practitioner, quoted in Anning et al., 2010, p. 79)

Research is identifying some of the key themes that can contribute to successful integrated working

Theme 2: assertive leadership

Leadership was seen as essential in the process of establishing a healthy team with a strong, shared value base that would enable a team to act promptly and effectively.

Participants referred to the importance of team members feeling secure and the value of a no-blame culture. A particular element that was recognised was the need to work to flatten hierarchies and ensure that everyone in a team feels valued and respected. There was a sense that the team leader needs to promote the view that everyone in a diverse team is essential to delivering the service: at times this might require pointing out to those who were more status conscious. There is a constant need to offer recognition and praise to everyone, with the team leader playing an important part in modelling this behaviour. Building relationships within and across the team and recognising the various dynamics involved in team formation and maintenance was seen to involve identifying difficulties and addressing them, often *'behind the scenes'*, as in supporting the new team member in adapting to the new environment. Leaders were also seen to be important in helping to negotiate and establish a clear vision and goals for the team.

Theme 3: a supportive culture

Participants referred to the importance of a team philosophy and vision which are continually generated through building relationships that share practice and values, and mutual respect and empathy towards each other and the needs of the service user. It was suggested that a supportive culture is underpinned by respectful relationships where everyone is valued for their contribution. Issues of trust and relationship building were seen as central while the need for 'rejuvenating and revisiting' team relationships was acknowledged. For teams working with vulnerable individuals or groups of people the need to have a secure team base was seen as vital if factions are to be avoided. It was recognised that there are particular challenges associated with incorporating part-time or sessional team members. One of the participants who had experienced this commented that:

> 'I don't always catch up with what is happening – you feel you don't belong anywhere.'
>
> (Practitioner, quoted in Brock et al., 2009, p. 10)

Again, this is consistent with findings from Anning et al., where a potentially marginal team member comments:

'I think that because it's very rare that I have opinions because I am usually quite quiet but at least when I have an opinion it is usually acknowledged.'

(Practitioner, quoted in Anning et al., 2010, p. 74)

Issues such as this require flexibility from everyone in the team to ensure that individuals feel supported and included, with one participant saying: 'We work round and fit in how we can.' A further complication was seen to arise if a number of staff were required to 'hot desk'. A sense of humour and team understanding were seen as necessary to make this work well, supported by effective communication systems including a communication book and minutes of meetings. The sense of culture also needs to incorporate and support change. There was a sense that 'people can resist change' and there can be difficulties associated with 'institutional practice and people who have been there too long'. However it was recognised that change is essential for the creation of an integrated team.

Theme 4: individual qualities

In the TIPS study it was recognised that each member of the team needs to sustain personal confidence in their own professional identity to ensure commitment to emotional and political ownership and investment in the shared values. On occasions this might be compromised because of how any one individual had joined the team and the extent to which they had made a personal choice about this, as opposed to an organisational decision being made to 'send' or second someone. The issue of personal 'readiness' was also explored, in recognition that it might not be the right time for any one individual to join an inter-professional team. One of the participants referred to someone who initially did not feel ready to join the team but who, several years later, was able to apply more confidently. One participant summed up that people in an inter-professional team:

'have to be strong confident and secure in themselves … you have to have confidence in yourself before you can have confidence in others.'

(Practitioner, quoted in Brock et al., 2009, p. 18)

The following quote also illustrates the need for individuals to have the capacity to manage uncertainty:

> 'We know what the end product should be, but there are so many people that need to be involved so sometimes to start with, it can feel a bit messy and as you start you don't know what is going to happen and then when it all falls into place, you need everyone to do their bit.'
>
> (Practitioner, quoted in Brock et al., 2009, p. 20)

Another participant referred to the need to 're-educate' people, getting them 'to think differently'. Case discussions were seen as offering an opportunity to see what others were thinking and to explore complex issues. In one team there had been experience of a split between members with very different views leading to some people moving on. This again is consistent with evidence from Anning et al. (2010):

> 'We're all independent ... because people all have their own roles to play and they're playing them together, that makes the team operate as a team.'
>
> (Practitioner, quoted in Anning et al., 2010, p. 82)

Theme 5: organisational issues

The ways in which teams are structured and resourced were seen to be an important influence on how a team operates. This includes the numbers of different staff from different agencies or professional backgrounds and the way in which they are recruited. The extent to which team members owe a primary allegiance to the inter-professional team was recognised and the balance that may have to be managed between belonging to the inter-professional team and another uni-professional team. This seemed to be more marked when team members were part-time or sessional and carried different roles and responsibilities elsewhere.

The way in which teams were constructed from willing volunteers or conscripts also seemed to make a difference.

It was recognised that there were many issues that teams did not have control over, including protocols for different services, organisational and strategic demands and differences in pay and conditions. It was acknowledged that 'services have different expectations' and that 'you don't have control over these'. For teams it was then a question of how these differences were managed and this required clarity regarding roles, responsibilities and accountability and a transparency about these, enabling everyone to understand and work together. With positive handling it is possible for everyone to 'value each other's contributions' (see Anning et al., 2010).

The question of generic and integrated roles was also explored, with participants clarifying that a generic role was one where the professional identity was seen as secondary to the particular requirements of the team. For example, someone might be a care coordinator rather than being known as an occupational therapist or a nurse. By comparison, an integrated role was used to describe how different professionals explicitly maintained their professional identity and philosophy but worked 'in partnership and liaison with other members of the team'. It was recognised that without organisational clarity and support individuals could feel insecure and perceive the loss of their professional identity.

Anning et al.'s findings include the following reflection:

> 'Our styles can be quite different. We end up complementing each other but also sometimes I have to think, OK, where are each other's perspectives? And how do we dovetail them?'
>
> (Practitioner, quoted in Anning et al., 2010, p. 69)

We can see from the TIPS findings, as supplemented by Anning et al. (2010), that working in multi-professional team settings can be both complex and challenging. We can also see that creative professionals can come up with ways of addressing challenges.

The lessons are similar, although of course the emphasis differs, when professionals work together across organisational boundaries. Researchers in the LARC team have uncovered some of the challenges to be addressed, for example: knowing at what point families should be referred on for social care assessment and support; understanding each other's roles; and managing parents' expectations (Easton et al., 2012, Summary).

2.4 'Efficiency' evidence

Intuition would suggest that interagency working is effective in terms of resources. It is easy to assume that joint premises, ease of access to colleagues, and sharing ideas and information will be efficient economically and in terms of resources. In this section we will explore the evidence that can inform our discussion of this issue so that we can move beyond intuition.

For interagency work to be effective there is a need for leadership and coordination at the highest level. Children's Trusts in England were the primary high-level local partnerships bringing together the organisations responsible for services for children, young people and families. An Ofsted study of multi-agency leadership offered through Children's Trusts found:

> In all six local authorities visited, the Children's Trust provided the focal point for strategic work across the services that come into contact with children and young people. The Children's Trusts strongly influenced arrangements for networking at all levels, evidenced by good co-operation, integrated services and joint commissioning and planning.
>
> (Ofsted, 2010, p. 5)

This finding is reinforced as follows:

> The leadership skills of the members of the Children's Trust Board were paramount in tackling a complex agenda, driving forward change and combining efforts to deliver better outcomes for children and young people.
>
> Ofsted, 2010, p. 6)

This basic underpinning of effectiveness is shared by an American study:

1   Network effectiveness is enhanced when the organisations are integrated through a control authority.

2   Networks that must respond to a single source of direct fiscal control are more effective.

3   All else being equal, network effectiveness will be enhanced by system stability, although stability alone is not sufficient for effectiveness.

4   In resource-scarce environments, networks are unable to be effective.

(Milward and Provan, 2000, quoted in Coleman Selden et al., 2006, p. 413)

Where effective leadership is in place the Ofsted study argues that interagency work is effective in terms of resources. The study cites a number of examples where it has proved to be effective, for example this one from Derby where co-located front-line teams are seen as having contributed to:

Fewer children needing a second child protection plan.

More teenagers in education, employment and training.

A lower incidence of child obesity.

Improved school attendance.

Wider participation by young people in positive activities.

(Ofsted, 2010, p. 19)

Again, the US evidence seems to back this up, demonstrating the link between outcomes and resource efficiency:

a study of maternity care coordination for Medicaid recipients in North Carolina found that case management reduced the number of low-birth-weight babies, decreased infant mortality and lowered the cost of medical care.

(Coleman Selden et al., 2006, p. 414)

The Scottish study of 'intensive family support' noted above also reaches optimistic conclusions:

> in exactly half of all cases the assessed risk of family breakup had been reduced by the point of case closure, with this figure rising to almost two thirds (63%) among those who had completed support programmes.
>
> (Pawson, 2009, p. 84)

The US researchers also suggest that there is a 'synergy' effect – where interagency work leads to attracting extra resources, an experience which may be familiar to many readers:

> Engaging in collaboration that brings in pre-school and/or Head Start funding can provide centres with additional services.
>
> (Coleman Selden et al., 2006, p. 420)

An English study of the Sure Start programme reaches a similar conclusion:

> There is some evidence that offering a combination of services within one programme has added to the value of all services.
>
> (Hannon et al., 2005, p. 254)

The most sophisticated study in an English context comes from the LARC 4 study discussed earlier. The research team measured the cost of the actual intervention and assessed this against potential 'future scenarios' that had been prevented, thus being able to confirm the economic effectiveness of the CAF. Their key findings are presented in the Research box 4.2.

Research box 4.2

LARC 4 found that:

For most cases, the cost of **the entire CAF process** fell by between £1,000 and £5,000 [per child]. Common assessments with greater costs generally had an increased number of professionals supporting a family and a larger number of TAC meetings were held.

The **costs of support interventions** varied considerably, ranging from just under £600 to almost £17,000. In most cases the cost of interventions was between £1,000 and £3,600. The costs of the interventions for these families with complex needs are therefore relatively low.

Looking at future scenarios, around half of the cases resulted in no financial saving to the authority and local services in the short term. The figures ranged from a 'loss' of £14,000 to a saving of £44,500. However, for the same cases, in the longer term the **potential savings** ranged from a 'loss' of £6,800 to a saving of over £415,000.

(Easton et al., 2012, Summary)

The researchers estimate that the 'potential future outcome costs' of the cases they explored were between £400 and £420,000. The cost of undertaking the 'CAF and the intervention costs' were between £1,500 and £27,000. It is argued that 'potential savings' range from £6,800 and £415,000. This evidence suggests that this form of early intervention is cost effective.

(Easton et al., p. 18)

This is significant evidence of the impact of interagency working. However, while this is the most powerful British evidence in the field, the US research discussed below undertook an exceptional forty-year follow-up!

The starting point for many early intervention debates is the US High/Scope Perry Preschool Program. The US programmes run in a context of a minimal 'universal' welfare state but where there are many intervention projects. The Perry project ran in an inner city area of

Michigan in the 1960s and involved an intervention with a group of African-American three-to-five-year-olds, and a non-intervention group which acted as a control. There were 58 children in the intervention group and 63 in the control – the attrition rate is remarkably low, with the researchers being in contact with about 90 per cent of the group at the fortieth birthday follow-up. The intervention was two and a half hours of day care for the children during the week, drawing on an active learning and child-centred model. The day care took place alongside a home visiting programme, and so was an interagency process. There was an extensive research programme which followed up the children at 15, 19 and 27 years of age and, finally at 40.

The High/Scope Perry Preschool Program from the 1960s

Heckman and colleagues undertook a secondary analysis of the statistics, which is critical of some of the original research methods, but they nevertheless conclude that 'crime reduction is a major benefit of this program' (Heckman et al., 2009, p. 11).

Bellfield et al. undertook an overall cost benefit analysis of the programme and estimated that $12.90 was saved from public costs for every $1 invested. They argue that 'program gains come mainly from reduced crime by males' (Bellfield et al., 2009, p. 2).

Cunha and Heckman, drawing from this High/Scope Perry Pre-School Program data and other programmes, argue that 'the most effective supplements supply family resources to young children from disadvantaged environments' (2006, p. 60).

Most commentators, including Cunha and Heckman, argue the social gains are related to education so that, in American terms, 'completing high school is a major crime prevention strategy' (Cunha and Heckman, 2006, p. 60).

This is because those completing high school are more likely to gain employment and less likely to be involved in crime. Unfortunately such a longitudinal study as the High/Scope Perry is not available in the British context; the LARC 4 team commented:

> While this study has looked in detail at family circumstances over a relatively short period of time, we are not aware of any good quality longitudinal data relating to CAF episodes and their medium and long term outcomes. At regional or national level such data would help to provide much more robust evidence of effective commissioning and intervention approaches – critical to judgements about longer-term cost-effectiveness and best use of limited local resources.
>
> (Easton et al., 2012, Foreword)

We can end our review of the evidence on an optimistic note from a US study, as Selden et al. state that their study did demonstrate a positive impact:

> In conclusion this study has demonstrated that inter-agency collaboration has clear impacts on the management, program and client outcomes of organisations engaged in collaborative relationships.
>
> (Coleman Selden et al., 2006, p. 423)

Thinking point 4.2: Think about any experience of working in an interagency setting you have had as a practitioner or service user. How effective do you think it is in terms of: outcomes for service users; process for service users; process for professionals; efficiency.
What sort of evidence might you look for in each of these four categories?

Key points

1 There are a number of different perspectives from which the effectiveness of interagency working can be evaluated.
2 The strength of research evidence for these different measures of effectiveness varies but overall there is an increasing body of evidence about 'what works' in interagency working.
3 More research is required – in particular in relation to the medium and long-term impact of interagency working.

3 Challenges of interagency working

We have seen that interagency working is often seen as a solution to complex social problems but is itself complex and demanding. This section will explore how professionals can address some 'real life' difficulties and dilemmas gathered from interagency professionals. By addressing these dilemmas we may see an improvement in the process and outcome issues we have explored above.

All workplaces contain stresses and dilemmas and it is argued in this section that these issues take a particular form in the case of inter-agency work, particularly where professionals are co-located. The author of this chapter has worked with many groups of co-located, multi-agency professionals and has worked with them in producing a series of vignettes: short scenarios which draw on real life situations. These vignettes can be utilised in training events to assist professionals in thinking about dilemmas in a safe environment and prepare them to think about how they would tackle similar situations in the workplace.

Vignette 1

An integrated, co-located team is working with children and young people and their families on a deprived estate with high levels of unemployment. Most of the team agree that the major issue is poverty. A new member of staff has joined and keeps talking about people 'who can't manage their money' and who 'spend all their money on fags and Sky TV'.

What is the issue here?

- Is there a shared value base in this team?
- Does every team need a shared value base?
- How does a team address differences and conflict?
- How should the team address this?

What is the wider point for multi-agency and multi-professional working?

Vignette 2

A multi-agency co-located team is working with children, young people and families. The members of the team are seconded into the team from various agencies and are paid on different scales. At a Saturday morning 'drop-in centre' the lower-paid members of the team say that they feel resentful about working on a Saturday and demoralised – the team is all doing similar work but are paid differently.

What is the issue here?

- To what extent does working together mean shared working conditions?
- To what extent does working in a co-located, integrated team mean a loss of separate roles and identities?
- Should team members take action to address this perceived injustice?

What is the wider point for multi-agency and multi-professional working?

Vignette 3

An integrated multi-agency team is working with families with relationship problems. The new team psychologist is a nice person and works well with the rest of the team but he persists in using very specialised psychology jargon which many others in the team do not understand. He has been challenged in a friendly and humorous manner but he still speaks using too much jargon.

What are the issues here?

- Is there a shared language in the team?
- Is it possible to address this kind of problem in a friendly and humorous way?
- Do you use jargon yourself?
- Would you feel comfortable asking for a translation of jargon?

What is the wider point for multi-agency and multi-professional working?

There are no easy answers to the dilemmas outlined above: that is why they are dilemmas! It can be seen that there are many dilemmas in working together in interagency settings. There are many more dilemmas, some of which are unpredictable, that we have not mentioned above. Below, however, we outline some of the issues raised in each vignette.

Vignette 1

Positive working relationships and positive organisational climates depend on such differences, issues and conflicts being discussed openly and used as an opportunity to move forward and improve service delivery.

Vignette 2

As more practitioners and agencies work together in children's services, such issues of service conditions may become more frequent. Extensive strategic and day-to-day work needs to be undertaken when establishing effective multi-professional and integrated agency working. Policies and procedures need to address such issues as funding, accommodation, information sharing and professional supervision, for example. However it remains important to respect professional identity and difference. Teams can be strengthened rather than weakened by a range of perspectives, knowledge and skills.

Vignette 3

Language is an important issue for multi-professional and interagency working. It is important not to use unnecessary jargon, to communicate openly and to develop a shared and mutually understood language.

It may be necessary to make sure there is plenty of time for communication. Well-organised team meetings, away days and case discussions are all important ways in which multi professional working can develop.

> **Key point**
>
> Enhancing the effectiveness of different forms of more integrated working requires challenges to be recognised and worked through.

4 A future for interagency working

As is illustrated through this book, interagency work has become established as a 'mainstream' method of working with children and young people. This tendency developed rapidly during the late 1990s and the early part of the twenty-first century in many industrialised countries. In this section we will examine the likely future of interagency working and how sustainable this shift towards interagency working is. I suggested earlier in the chapter that there were a number of forces contributing to the growth of interagency working. These factors included: the persistence of complex social problems, the availability of information and communication technology (ICT) and the recognition of the social and financial costs of poor cooperation, particularly in the case of high-profile child deaths. We will examine complex social problems, the role of ICT and issues around costs and efficiency in turn.

First of all, complex social problems are likely to continue to be with us and perhaps become more complex, extensive and intractable during a period of austerity. Government, experts and professionals alike have recognised that complex social problems require multi-dimensional approaches. For example, if we consider an issue such as youth crime, a single element approach – for example a 'law and order' approach – is unlikely to be successful. If we took a police-led approach which focused on arrests then it is likely that youth crime would not be addressed and that reoffending rates would increase. Thus the British New Labour government, in the Criminal Justice Act 1998, introduced Youth Offending Teams, including social workers, police officers, health and education professionals. Social problems across health, education, social care and crime are deemed to be best tackled through the use of interagency approaches.

Second, it is likely that the remarkably rapid growth and development of ICT will continue. This underpins the growth of interagency work through the gathering of data, the enhancement of real-time communication and the sharing of records. The eminent sociologist Manuel Castells (1996) refers to these developments as moving towards what he calls 'the network society'. Castells argues that 'the network' is as important to society today as agriculture or industry was in the past.

Third, the role of the state is under growing economic and social pressure, meaning that professionals will have to address increasing social problems with increasingly restricted resources. In this environment governments will attempt to utilise limited resources as efficiently and effectively as possible. There is likely to be a constant search for coordination, avoiding waste and duplication, ensuring the efficient use of resources – all of which point towards a continuing emphasis on interagency working, underpinned by research on its process and outcomes.

If our analysis is correct here, then interagency working with children and young people (and indeed in many other social policy fields) is likely to grow and continue. The 'acid test' of success will be provided by studies that explore the outcome and process issues discussed throughout this chapter.

Key points

1 The drivers towards interagency working – the persistence of complex social problems, the spread of ICT and the recognition of the costs of poor coordination – are likely to remain for the foreseeable future.
2 Like other components of health and social care, children's services will need to continue to try and overcome the barriers to interagency and interprofessional working that still exist.

Conclusion

Many of the most difficult issues in relation to children's wellbeing are inextricably linked to issues such as social deprivation and disadvantage. Within this bigger picture however it is important that services are organised in the best possible way for achieving positive outcomes for children and their families. In this chapter we have explored the growing body of evidence that exists on interagency working. We have suggested that this be seen as existing in four different categories: outcome evidence, service user process evidence, professional process evidence and efficiency evidence. We have seen that the data is often complex and sometimes contradictory. However we can reach some relatively well-evidenced conclusions:

- Interagency working is a growing phenomenon and is attracting increasing research attention.
- There is emerging evidence that interagency working can have a positive impact on outcomes for children and young people.
- There is some evidence that service users seem to appreciate that interagency working improves service user experiences of professional services.

- There is now strong evidence that professionals find the process of interagency working effective and that they can devise innovative methods of addressing the dilemmas that arise.

- There is some evidence of efficiency and effectiveness arising from interagency working.

References

Abbott, D., Watson, D. and Townsley, R. (2005) 'The proof of the pudding: What difference does multi-agency working make to families with disabled children with complex health care needs?', *Child and Family Social Work*, vol. 10, no. 3, pp. 229–238.

Anning, A., Cottrell, D., Frost, N., Green, J. and Robinson, M. (2010) *Developing Multi-professional Teamwork for Integrated Children's Services*, 2nd edn, Open University Press, Maidenhead.

Bellfield, C.R., Noves, M. and, Barrett, W.S., (2009) *High/Scope Perry Pre-School Program: Cost Benefit Analysis Uusing Ddata from the Aage 40 Yyear Ffollow Uup*, NIEER, New Brunswick, NJ.

Brock, A., Frost, N., Karban, K. and Smith, S. (2009) *Towards Interprofessional Partnerships [TIPS]: a Resource Pack*, Leeds, Leeds Metropolitan University.

Castells, M. (1996) *The Network Society*, Oxford, Blackwell.

Coleman Selden, S., Sowa, J. and Sandfort, J. (2006) 'The impact of non-profit collaboration in early childcare and education on management and program outcomes', *Public Administration Review*, May/June, pp. 412–425.

Cooper, J. (2010) 'Can preventive services survive?', *Community Care*, 3 June, pp. 3–5.

Cunha, F. and Heckman, J. (2006) *Investing in our Young People*, Chicago, University of Chicago.

Easton, C., Morris, M. and Gee, G. (2010) *LARC 2: Integrated Children's Services and the CAF Process*, Slough, NFER.

Easton, C., Gee, G., Durbin, B. and Teeman, D. (2011) *Early Intervention, Using the CAF Process, and its Cost Effectiveness: Findings from LARC 3*, Slough, NFER.

Easton, C., Featherstone G., Poet, H., Aston, H., Gee, G. and Durbin, B. (2012) *Supporting Families with Complex Needs: Findings from LARC 4*, Slough, NFER.

Frost, N. (2005) *Professionalism, partnership and joined-up thinking*, Totnes, Research in Practice.

Glisson, A. and Hemmelgarn, C. (1998) 'The effects of organisational climate and interorganizational coordination on the quality and outcomes of children's services systems', *Child Abuse and Neglect*, vol. 22, no. 5, pp. 410–422.

Hannon, P., Pickstone, C., Weinberger, J. and Fox, L. (2005) 'Looking to the future', in Weinberger, J., Pickstone, C. and Hannon, P., *Learning from Sure Start*, Maidenhead, OUP.

Heckman, J., Moon, S.H., Pinto, R. and Savelyev, P. (2009) 'The rate of return of the High/Scope Perry Pre-School Program', Discussion Paper 4533, IZA, Bonn.

Helmer, O. (1983) *Looking Forward: a Guide to Futures Research*, London, Sage Publications.

Lord, P., Kinder, K., Wilkin, A., Atkinson, M. and Harland, J. (2008) *Evaluating the Early Impact of Integrated Children's Services: Round 1 Final Report*, Slough, NFER.

Ofsted (2010) *Improving Outcomes for Children and Young People Through Partnership in Children's Trusts*, London, Ofsted.

Pawson, H. (2009) *Evaluation of Intensive Family Support Services in Scotland*, Edinburgh, Scottish Assembly.

Secretary of State for Social Services (1974) *Report of the Inquiry into the Care and Supervision in Relation to Maria Colwell*, London, HMSO.

Seebohm, F. (1968) *Report of the Committee on Local Authority and Allied Social Services*, London, HMSO.

Skidmore, P. (2004) *Leading Between Leadership and Trust in a Network Society*, London, Demos.

Townsley, R., Abbott, D. and Watson, D. (2004) *Making a Difference? Exploring the Impact of Multi-agency Working on Disabled Children with Complex Health Care Needs, their Families and the Professionals who Support them*, Policy Press, Bristol.

Wolstenholme, D., Boylan, J. and Roberts, D. (2008) 'Factors that assist early identification of children in need in integrated or inter-agency settings', Research Briefing 27, London, SCIE.

Chapter 5 Learning together

Andy Rixon

Introduction

Improving the level of skills and qualifications across the workforce has been a central part of the drive to change and modernise children's services. Many practitioners will have had the experience of the knowledge and skills prescribed for their specific role being periodically revisited and revised. There have even been attempts to define the skills that it is essential that all practitioners share. As the composition of the workforce changes and new practice roles emerge, so key knowledge bases are woven together in new ways. The emphasis on learning is also now not just for a particular job but as a continuous, 'lifelong' activity.

Several chapters in this book examine the increasingly integrated ways in which practitioners are expected to work, and many of the potentially problematic elements – agency structures, practitioner identities, power and hierarchy, divergent knowledge bases, cultures and values. The arena of learning holds the potential for at least some of these issues to be addressed. It is frequently argued that opportunities for practitioners to come together, share their knowledge, and gain insight into the world of other practitioners can contribute to overcoming barriers and blocks. This sharing can also give rise to new understandings and ways of working – learning how to work together.

As we will discuss, this learning does not necessarily have to take place in formal teaching or training situations but can also happen in the workplace both formally and informally. Practitioners should also recognise other sources of knowledge including that which children, parents and carers have and which can make an important contribution. It is these sources of knowledge, theories of learning, and experiences of practitioners that this chapter intends to explore.

> **Core questions**
>
> - What models are available to analyse the ways practitioners can learn, particularly across agency and professional boundaries?
> - What role can children and families play in enhancing the learning of practitioners?

- What can the theory of communities of practice and other theories of social learning contribute to our understanding of how professionals learn?
- What is the role of reflection in learning 'for' practice?

1 Learning

Any separation between what constitutes formal learning and that which occurs in more informal or social ways is ultimately artificial. Different elements have been separated out in this chapter for the sake of simplifying analysis and evaluation, but in the end practitioners have to bring them back together again to apply within their work. The experience of most practitioners will be of learning new things in the workplace from trial and error and through interactions with children, their families, and other colleagues. This learning is likely to build on some initial qualifying course and be supplemented by subsequent opportunities to undertake courses or attend training days. Practitioners have to blend together what they learn from 'theory' and 'practice' in the workplace and perhaps different forms of knowledge, what Eraut (1994) has described as 'codified' knowledge (for example, theory derived from textbooks) and 'personal' knowledge (for example, what is learnt from the workplace and what they themselves bring to practice). It has been increasingly argued in training and qualifying training across most groups of practitioners that reflective practice is a key mechanism through which practitioners can synthesise these different elements of their learning: the opportunity to stand back and review critically how their learning has been applied to practice and what in turn they have learnt from practice. There are different variations and degrees of complexity on this basic principle, and after exploring different elements of learning we will return to reflection in the final section.

With the growing expectations of continual professional development (CPD), these 'subsequent opportunities' may be both required and substantial. Many practitioners – for example, nurses, midwives and social workers – will be encouraged to take post-qualifying awards and higher degrees as well as having to demonstrate that they are keeping themselves up to date with new developments in their field. This is an issue for all staff but has particular resonance with the discussion in other chapters in this book on the meaning of being a professional in an era when professional status is under attack. The pace of change ensures that initial training that was received five or more years ago can no longer be seen as current. If the status of professionals in the eyes of the public is maintained by expert knowledge, then they also need to constantly renew these claims for expertise by the acquisition of new knowledge (Frost, 2001).

This section examines some examples of more formal approaches to learning. Although the importance of more informal learning is recognised, it is also important to stress the value of formal qualifications, and not just in terms of knowledge and skills. Research in the past by Davies and Bynner (1999) found that the certification of learning had an important impact on individuals, increasing their sense of achievement and their belief that it improved the quality of their work. It also has an important role to play in providing career opportunities and providing further opportunities for learning even if career pathways are less than clear in the constantly changing structure of the children's workforce.

Recognising the value of formal learning

Much of the move to modernise local government and the health services can be viewed in the wider context of an emphasis, particularly in government policy, on the increasing importance of knowledge in a global society. The demand for 'continuous improvement', discussed in Chapter 1, can therefore be seen to be underpinned by the continuous integration of new knowledge. Jarvis (2007) argues that while lifelong learning and the learning society are important for a wide range of reasons such as 'citizenship', 'social inclusion' and 'personal fulfilment', the needs of advanced capitalism are actually the driving force behind their development (Jarvis, 2007, p. 195).

The chapter does not set out to tackle the complex issue of the nature of knowledge, although the importance of this debate is highlighted at various points. Similarly, while 'training' and 'education' are often seen as very different forms of learning, here it is argued that training does not necessarily equate to the acquisition of 'technical' knowledge but can equip practitioners with the skills of critical thinking and reflection, just as education does not need to be abstract theory unrelated to practice.

Thinking point 5.1: Thinking back to when you last attended a work-related course, can you identify some examples of things you learnt that were useful when back in work? What were they – a new way of doing things, a piece of research, a new contact? How do you think you learnt them – through a talk/lecture, a group discussion, chatting in the coffee break, or perhaps just thinking about it later?

1.1 Training together to safeguard children

In the search for successful interagency working, the importance of practitioners training together is one of the most frequently cited key contributory factors. However, just as the view that working together is inevitably the solution to a range of social issues (see Chapter 4 for an analysis of this), so the reality of learning together needs to be viewed critically.

One particularly high-profile area of interagency working has been that required for protecting or safeguarding children. The success, or otherwise, of these working relationships has always been a subject of close scrutiny when there have been instances of children being seriously harmed. Over many years nearly all inquiries and reviews of serious cases have recommended to some degree the need for improvement in communication or working practices between the range of agencies involved, citing interagency training as one key way of achieving them.

Joint training will assist in the development of nationally recognised procedures and enhance the relationship between the agencies when they require to work together.

(Report of the Inquiry into the Removal of Children from Orkney in February 1991, Clyde, 1992, p. 337)

Almost all of the professional witnesses identified child protection training as a major requirement before services could be improved. Many expressed the view that it will have to be mandatory at all levels.

(Report of the Caleb Ness Inquiry, O'Brien, 2003, p. 8)

There were a number of recommendations, addressed to a variety of agencies and organisations in both the statutory and voluntary sectors, which called for greater clarity about staff roles and responsibilities within and across agencies. Overall, this issue was to be improved through the usual recourse to the establishment of guidelines and procedures, and more training.

(New Learning from Serious Case Reviews: a Two Year Report for 2009–2011, Brandon et al., 2012, p.121)

These conclusions have been reflected in policy terms by interagency training becoming a cornerstone of government guidance for improving 'Working Together' between practitioners in the area of child protection (HM Government, 2010; Scottish Government, 2010; Welsh Assembly Government, 2008; DHSSPSNI, 2003). For example:

multi-agency learning and development has a key role in building a common understanding and fostering good working relationships between people in different agencies, which are vital to effective child protection. Workers from all agencies who come into contact with children and young people, or other family members, in the course of their work should be actively encouraged not only to work together, but to learn together.

(Scottish Government, 2012, p. 26)

More specifically such training is claimed to promote 'improved communication', 'sound child-focussed assessments and decision-making' and 'more effective and integrated services' (HM Government, 2010, p. 113).

Interagency training repeatedly stresses the value of helping different practitioners to develop a shared understanding of practice and procedure in child protection work. The Laming Report (Laming, 2003) on the circumstances leading to the death of Victoria Climbié suggested that increased commonality was the answer, raising the possibility of a 'common language', common assessment, common referral forms, and 'common elements' in training (Laming, 2003, p. 352). This trend was subsequently reflected in the development of common qualification frameworks across practice groups (see for example Scottish Government, 2010).

Most interagency training focuses on enabling practitioners from different agencies and disciplines to work more closely together. However, following the Laming Report, when the nature of education and training for interagency work was again the subject of investigation, there was also an interesting emphasis on the role of training in enabling practitioners to challenge each other's views, such as in this recommendation to the police:

Training for child protection officers must equip them with the confidence to question the views of professionals in other agencies, including doctors, no matter how eminent those professionals appear to be.

(Laming, 2003, p. 321)

Interagency training, then, is positioned as an opportunity not just to help to develop a common knowledge base but also to consider, question and address other important dimensions to interagency working – such as power and hierarchy.

Of course, not all staff groups are equally likely to engage in training, relating primarily to whether they see this as a core part of their role. Re-emphasising that safeguarding children is everyone's responsibility sits alongside other changes, such as the focus on early identification and prevention, where all practitioners have been expected to become more involved in work with families and the wider community.

Actual responses to the value of training tend to be favourable, not just because of knowledge and skills gained but because of the value of personal contacts, which might tend to reinforce the view that one of the keys to interagency and interprofessional working is the ability to form and sustain working relationships. The success of local working arrangements may depend ultimately on interpersonal skill as much as interprofessional understanding. The more informal gains of training events, such as this development of personal contacts, should not be underestimated. As we will discuss later, these can provide a valuable contribution to groups of workers developing shared aims and continuing to develop their knowledge once they have returned to their day-to-day practice.

The most significant element of training that could succeed in improving practice is a matter of debate. It has been argued that the communication issues highlighted in Chapter 2 and the need for practitioners to focus on communication skills could be one valuable area to be addressed:

> interagency communication would improve if all professionals concerned acquired a 'communication mindset' as part of their core skills. It is, admittedly, a well-rehearsed recommendation that training is the key to such improvements: but it is true.
>
> (Reder and Duncan, 2003, p. 96)

Reder and Duncan (2003) argue that this emphasis should be in pre- and post-qualifying training as well as being addressed in an interprofessional learning environment.

In fact, surprisingly, considering that the value of interagency training in this field is almost universally accepted, its effectiveness in achieving its assumed ends is poorly researched. A review of evaluation of training in relation to child protection for the Scottish Institute for Excellence in Social Work Education concluded:

> recommendations in respect to the importance of and perceived need for training and education appear to be founded upon an untested hypothesis that training and education makes a difference – the arguments may be persuasive but evidence that it works remains elusive.

> (Ogilvie-Whyte, 2006, p. 7)

A review of the literature by Charles and Horwath (2009) also suggests assumptions about interagency training are 'mainly an act of faith' since despite a growing consensus about its content and value 'the underpinning evidence base stems from experiences and reflections rather than rigorous evaluation about interagency training's impact on practice' (Charles and Horwath, 2009, p. 372). A rare example found evidence that interagency training is highly effective in helping professionals understand their respective roles and responsibilities and the procedure of each agency involved in safeguarding children, and in developing a shared understanding of assessment and decision-making practices (Carpenter, cited in HM Government, 2010).

1.2 What works?

Thinking point 5.2: To what extent do you think practice in children's services is informed by research?

But what exactly is it that practitioners should be learning? The right sort of knowledge is a contested area. Macdonald (2001), while recognising the importance of the law, policy, values and 'practice wisdom' in shaping what it is that practitioners do, asserts that they also have 'an ethical responsibility', when making decisions to intervene in the lives of children, to also be informed by the best available research evidence; research which itself should be conducted to explicit standards.

> Evidence-based practice indicates an approach to decision-making which is transparent, accountable, and based on a careful consideration of the most compelling evidence we have about the

effects of particular interventions on the welfare of individuals, groups and communities.

(Macdonald, 2001, p. xviii)

Consequently, training for practitioners related to, for example, safeguarding children should make them aware of not just their responsibilities and procedures, but also what works in relation to contributing to a protective environment for children and when assessing and intervening in the lives of families. Macdonald reviewed the evidence for the consequences of child abuse and for which interventions are most successful, both at the level of broader primary prevention as well as secondary and tertiary work (Macdonald, 2001). Central to this 'knowing' is applying a rigorous approach to research evidence – systematically reviewing it, making explicit the methodology used, and placing more weight on the outcomes of research studies with experimental designs using, for example, control groups. This in turn focuses attention on the need for practitioners to be able to interpret and evaluate research and use it to inform their practice.

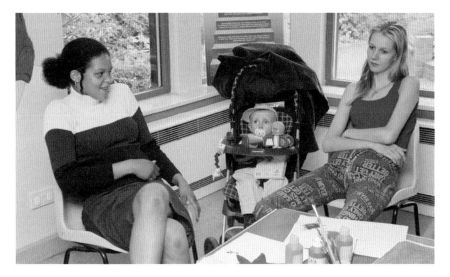

Is good practice with families shaped by knowledge of 'what works'?

The importance of utilising strategies that are shown to be 'successful' became a major strand in government thinking as confidence grew in identifying risk factors in families and communities that can be linked to later problems (France and Utting, 2005). This has underpinned the agenda of early intervention, as discussed in Chapter 2, and helped shape the nature of outcome targets that children's services are set to achieve.

Already well established in the education and professional development of health practitioners, evidence-based practice now features more prominently within social care, for example with the development of the Social Care Institute for Excellence (SCIE). The audit of child protection by the Scottish Executive was typical in its emphasis on wanting to identify 'links between research and knowledge and staff education and training and how this can be consolidated' (Scottish Executive, 2002, p. 14). There is little clear evidence of how much research is used overall by practitioners, especially those without professional qualifications (SCIE, 2004). Various strategies have been employed by social care organisations to address this, for example investment in resources like Research in Practice (see Practice box 5.1) and The Institute for Research and Innovation in Social Services (see Practice box 5.2), which can provide easily digestible summaries of current research. Certainly there is a debate as to the extent that agencies need to facilitate access to research and the responsibility of practitioners to become 'research minded' or 'evidence-informed'.

Practice box 5.1

Research in Practice (RiP)

Our mission is to build the capacity for evidence-informed practice in children's services. We support our network of Partners to move forward together, fostering a lasting culture shift in using evidence-informed practice to improve the lives of children, young people and families. Our work is about bringing together practitioner expertise with formal research evidence – creating new knowledge, new skills and a new energy to improve outcomes for children, young people and their families. We support your people, your priorities and your performance.

(RIP, n.d.)

Practice box 5.2

Early Years Evidence

Reviewing the evidence and effectiveness of preventative approaches

There is a body of evidence emphasising the importance of the early years of a child's life and the impact these years have on later life.

[...]

This project will provide a comprehensive and accessible review of the early years evidence base and in particular evidence relating to the effectiveness of preventative approaches undertaken in social services. This would seek to synthesise the range of material that has been produced across health, education, social services and other relevant disciplines. It will also seek to surface the challenges of working in the areas of early years and to share effective practice across the social services sector. The project will also include the development of a **special collection of resources related to the Early Years in the Learning Exchange**.

(IRISS, 2013)

The increasing focus on evidence-based practice is not without its critics. It has been seen as overemphasising positivistic approaches above other sorts of knowledge and as minimising the complexity of engagements with families. Evidence from different settings and different countries may also be difficult to apply in new contexts. The rise of evidence-based practice has also been linked to our increasing preoccupation with risk (Trinder, 2000) and the search for 'a level of certainty in highly uncertain times' (Turney, 2007, p. 58). However, it is clearly an important element in the debate about the nature of education, knowledge and, given the interdisciplinary nature of our discussion here, what it is that we should be 'learning together'.

1.3 Structured learning in the workplace

Learning within the workplace can be a complex process with a variety of different elements, the more informal aspects of which will be explored in more detail later. It is worth noting, however, that formal, more structured mechanisms can provide a valuable starting point for promoting continued sharing of knowledge and enhancing interprofessional understanding.

Thinking point 5.3: What strategies could teams in the same workplace use to encourage learning from each other?

Anning et al. (2010), in their research with a number of integrated teams, found that a range of mechanisms for learning and exchange of knowledge, often based around the team meeting structure, were being employed. This could involve using team meetings as points for discussion of particular cases or inviting experts to give presentations to the team. Learning also emerged from undertaking joint activities:

> 'If you do it together, you get it together. And so actually going on home visits and doing things in people's front rooms with colleagues is what really binds the system. Because you're actually trusting each other and you're seeing each other doing it.'
>
> (Psychologist quoted in Anning et al., 2010, p. 81)

In some teams these mechanisms were well developed. A child development team had used video to enable reflective discussions about specific sessions that had been undertaken with a family – professional exposure requiring a high degree of trust, and, as practitioners reported, humour. (The importance of being able to build in structured opportunities for reflection is discussed further below.) Similarly, a consultant observing a physiotherapist and occupational therapist working with a child provided a shared picture of the treatment required. Another example was the use of the key worker role to pull together information on and advocate for a particular child or client group – acting as a particular source of knowledge for the team (Anning et al., 2010).

However, the research also noted that while these positive strategies for sharing knowledge were valued by the teams, part-time members, who were not always able to attend team meetings, were inevitably not benefiting from the learning to the same extent. This was important in terms of some practitioners potentially feeling excluded from the shared understandings emerging in the team.

Team meetings can play an important role in developing learning

One conclusion that Anning et al. (2010) draw from their research is the potential value of structured discussions within teams that reflect on the very nature of the team itself and directly confront some of the well-known issues and barriers to integrated working. They propose a series of checklists that practitioners complete individually and which are then used as the basis of team discussion. These checklists range across structural, ideological, procedural, and interprofessional issues – see one example in Practice box 5.3.

Although co-location has been identified as a potentially important contribution to interagency working, it is likely that even some highly integrated teams will be dispersed geographically. While not replacing the value of face-to-face meetings, other communication technologies – conferencing, email discussion mechanisms, websites – may play a key role in supporting teams in a virtual environment and supplement more traditional ways of structuring learning.

Practice box 5.3

Multi-agency team checklist

Domain 2: Ideological – sharing and redistributing knowledge/ skills/ beliefs	Strongly disagree/ never	Disagree/ sometimes	Agree/ often	Strongly agree/ always
Different theoretical models are respected within the team				
Different professional groups are accorded equal respect within the team				
Supervision of work is attuned to the needs of the individuals within the team and their various professional backgrounds				
The team encourages members to share skills and ideas with each other				
The team has an awareness of the potential impact of multi-agency working on both professional identity and service users				

(Anning et al., 2010, p. 131)

1.4 Interprofessional education

Practitioners, perhaps particularly those with established 'professional' training, tend to be socialised into a particular worldview with an established frame of reference. A key task, and a key difficulty, for interagency training is to try to enable practitioners to question these perspectives, consider the way that knowledge is socially constructed, and understand the worldviews of others. Interprofessional Education (IPE) – bringing students from different disciplines together during their qualifying training – would seem therefore to provide the ideal opportunity to establish this way of thinking at the outset of practitioners' careers. Clark (2006) suggests that students must be empowered to ask 'who am I ... and what do I know?', 'who are the others ... and what do they know?' and finally 'who are we collectively ... and what do we know?' (Clark, 2006, p. 585).

Many professional courses now include at least some element of interprofessional learning, yet while interprofessional education is frequently cited as a vital feature of the future success of working together, there has been a lack of any conclusive research evidence of its effectiveness (Zwarenstein et al., 2001, 2005). Clark (2006) similarly argues that IPE remains poorly theorised and poorly evaluated. He proposes several models or theoretical approaches to learning that could enable a more critical discussion of IPE. While some of these models overlap, each emphasises the importance of a different aspect of learning that will help inform some of the discussion later in the chapter.

Practitioners as students learn with, from and about each other

Cooperative, collaborative and social learning

> IPE's essence is the knowledge students learn 'with, from, and about' each other in interdependent work groups. Indeed, observers have noted that the skills needed to function in interprofessional teams are most often those that are gained by using problem- or case-based educational methods.
>
> (Clark, 2006, p. 579)

Through these methods (rather than the more individualised approaches common in education) students learn about each other and also teamwork skills such as 'leadership, communication, and conflict management that are critical for collaborative practice' (Clark, 2006, p. 580).

For students this also partly follows the real-world models of informal knowledge acquisition. The idea of how this social learning occurs in 'communities of practice' will be explored later in the chapter.

Experiential learning

Experiential learning is closely related to the idea of social learning in that it too emphasises the importance of collaborative learning. Learning together should be in a real environment or on realistic case studies. The emphasis here is that the learning is the process rather than the outcomes, and students need to be enabled to reflect on the process of this learning to integrate their learning into new situations. Mellor et al. (2013) emphasise the importance of the context for this process, that it is likely only to be successful if students feel 'empowered to interact freely without fear of reproach'.

Cognitive and normative maps

Understanding where other professionals are coming from is an important element of any interagency education. IPE provides the opportunity to explore this in a more fundamental way. The emphasis in this approach is to examine the roots of the core knowledge and values of professional groups. Clark (2006) draws on the idea that these core features can be characterised as 'maps'; thus a 'cognitive' map:

represents the entire paradigmatic and conceptual apparatus used by a profession and includes its basic concepts, modes of inquiry, problem definitions, observational categories, representational techniques, standards of proof, types of explanation, and general ideas of what represents a discipline.

(Clark, 2006, p. 582)

A 'normative' map charts the areas of values, beliefs, moral reasoning and ethics. Enabling students to understand the cognitive and normative maps of other professions is essential because 'they may look at the same thing but not see the same thing' (Clark, 2006, p. 582). In day-to-day practice, practitioners need to be able to reach a common understanding of the problems and issues they are confronted with before being able to move on to finding effective solutions. The previous chapter noted how some integrated teams were able to work collaboratively once a shared theoretical perspective had emerged.

Ultimately, the process can also advance interprofessional knowledge and practice by enabling professionals to 'borrow' the 'tools' of another discipline once they have gained an understanding of them (Lattuca, 2002).

Thinking point 5.4: Can you think of an experience when you and a colleague from your own or another group of practitioners were looking at the same thing but clearly not seeing the same thing?

Cognitive and ethical development

This perspective suggests that understanding the developmental process that students go through during education can give IPE insights into how transformations can occur in their thinking about other professionals and knowledge bases. The theory argues that students move from a belief that knowledge is an accumulation of facts, to accepting that ambiguities exist, to 'relativism'– accepting that knowledge is constructed. Only at this stage can students make informed choices about which knowledge and values they will commit to in relation to other professional knowledge and value bases.

Reflective practice

As noted above, effective experiential learning relies on students being able to 'reflect' on the process of their learning. Schön (1987), a key figure in the development of reflective theory, argued that reflection is a mechanism for enabling practitioners to integrate both the knowledge and value bases of their practice. A reflective practitioner is also able to manage the uncertainties beyond the technical knowledge of the profession. Reflection is discussed in more detail in a later section and in the next chapter.

Many of the same issues relate equally to post-qualifying education and training. The example of training in relation to safeguarding illustrated both the strengths and limitations of bringing professionals together, and even more highly structured qualifying courses cannot guarantee that merely by bringing people together they will understand each other's worldviews. The methods and models employed need careful consideration.

Key points

1   Interagency training has been a long-standing strategy in protecting and safeguarding children to enhance closer working together, yet its exact impact is still not well researched.

2   Evidence-based practice provides an important benchmark for the content of learning, one that has been increasingly stressed in policy and practice.

3   A range of formal learning mechanisms can also be used in the workplace although they overlap with more informal learning; making clear distinctions between them can be artificial.

4   A central aim of interprofessional education is to create opportunities for different professional groups to understand each other's worldviews – knowledge, skills, values and beliefs.

---

2 Learning together with children and families

Just as children and their families have a contribution to make to shape the services they receive, so they can contribute to the development of practice and practitioners. This can happen at many levels through evaluation, feedback, consultation and research, as well as direct involvement in training. Practitioners and the organisations they work for need to recognise that children and their families have specific knowledge that cannot be 'learnt' from anywhere else:

> Children are party to the subculture of childhood which gives them a unique 'insider' perspective that is critical to our understanding of children's worlds.
>
> (Kellett, 2005, p. 4)

This in turn raises further questions about knowledge and knowing – recognising that versions of knowledge are not value free, and questioning the difference between 'lay' and 'expert' knowledge (Brechin and Siddell, 2000). Frost (2001, p. 14) argues that lifelong learning can be seen as a way of 'deconstructing the professional elitist model of training by having direct input into that training from lay people'.

Taylor (2004) suggests that despite an increasing acceptance that service users are part of the network of relations within which practitioners operate, there is little research focusing on their involvement or the impact of it on practitioners, practice or themselves. While arguing for the importance of the involvement of children and families in practitioner learning, Taylor questions whether in expecting the greater involvement of service users the issues of power, trust and communication have been sufficiently addressed.

Only through participatory ways of working and being open to learning can this knowledge be accessed. Strategies for empowerment need to be integral to our expectations of family involvement.

Thinking point 5.5: How are children and families involved in the learning of practitioners? In what other ways might they be involved?

Some qualifying training courses have required the involvement of service users in course development. The Scottish Institute for Excellence in Social Work Education (SiSWE) developed good practice guidelines to promote the involvement of service users and carers in the education of social work students (SiSWE, 2005). These recognised the need for involvement to be properly enabled and acknowledged that making it more than tokenistic required addressing existing structures:

> Building new systems and structures and changing systems and structures within universities is needed to empower and enable service users and carers to participate in a meaningful way.
>
> (SiSWE, 2005, p. 4)

The guidelines also highlighted the range of areas of learning that service users can contribute to: case studies, curriculum design, large and small group teaching, role play and evaluation. Many universities have also developed ways in which service users can contribute directly to the assessment of students' practice (see Practice box 5.4) and indeed the initial selection of students. A survey of eighty-three universities in England (Wallcraft et al., 2012) reported many examples of good practice. The strongest areas were reported as being in recruitment selection and teaching, with less direct involvement in assessment.

Practice box 5.4

'Service User Conversations', a method used at the University of Plymouth to assess readiness to practise, provides feedback on communication skills, links between theory and practice, writing reports, exploration of assumptions and values, time management, self assessment skills. The process includes a conversation with a service user or carer, followed by the student's self-assessment and the service user's or carer's feedback. A report of the conversation is written by the student and verified by the service user or carer.

(SiSWE, 2005, p. 6)

Cooper and Spencer-Dawe (2006) looked at user involvement in interprofessional education with students from a range of settings (drawn from medical students, nurses, social workers, occupational therapists and physiotherapists). Their study concluded that involvement of service users particularly enabled a bridging of the theory/practice 'gap' and reinforced for students the principles of 'service user-centred' care. They argued that 'when learning addresses complex issues, such as interprofessional team working, it has to be amenable to new and creative ways of teaching' (Cooper and Spencer-Dawe, 2006, p. 616). At the same time service users also felt they had made a contribution to breaking down barriers not only between service users and professionals but also between the different professional groups. The SCIE review (Wallcraft et al., 2012) found many examples of high levels of satisfaction amongst students of their experience of service user involvement in their teaching, including that from children and young people who had been in care.

2.1 'Total Respect'

In 1999 the Department of Health (England) commissioned a training course to promote the participation of children looked after by the local authority (Children's Rights Officers and Advocates (CROA), 2000). This recognised, from the research and conclusions of inquiry reports, that the voices of Looked After children and young people had long been insufficiently heard (Utting, 1991; Waterhouse, 2000). The aim of the training was to focus on:

- children's and young people's participation in individual care planning
- making sure children and young people are taken seriously when they make complaints or allegations of abuse or poor practice
- children's and young people's participation in local authority policy and service development.

(CROA, 2000, p. 2)

A training pack was produced after extensive consultation with Looked After children and young people to ensure that the material reflected their priorities. The training itself was designed to be delivered to practitioners with the children's and young people's direct involvement, as reflected in the work within one local authority which has continued to develop the training:

'The training has brought together young people and staff in workshops over 2 days. The emphasis is on listening and understanding each other and practical exercises in body language, listening skills and jargon busting proved a real winner. During training, young people suggested ways care reviews could be less boring, meetings less intimidating and social workers more approachable.'

(Children's Participation Officer quoted in Funkee Munkee, 2007, webpage)

Children and young people evaluating a conference activity with practitioners (Swindon Children's Fund)

Emphasising these messages from children and young people about how they feel about their reviews – crucial meetings for agreeing their future care – can provide valuable learning for all practitioners who are involved in these meetings (see Practice box 5.5). The training also promoted the sharing of good practice from other agencies or local authorities who had developed information packs, or systems of advocacy or other mechanisms for enabling the participation of children of all ages and abilities.

Practice box 5.5

Spotlight on reviews

Many children and young people find review meetings difficult because:

• They feel uncomfortable when there is conflict between adults

- There are too many people at the meeting who know all about them but they know nothing about the adults
- They do not feel able to say what they want in front of carers or parents
- They do not want a particular adult to attend or to have access to minutes (such as a parent or teacher)
- They prefer a neutral venue
- Adults in the meeting often focus on their 'difficult behaviour', and forget to celebrate their achievements.

(CROA, 2000, p. 43)

'[Review meetings are] boring and they can be embarrassing. Jargon – don't understand half of it.'

(Young person quoted in CROA, 2000, p. 42)

As well as adding to the value of the training that staff receive, such initiatives can enhance the skills and self-esteem of those involved:

'The young people are now becoming trainers and will be passing on the skills they've learned to other adults and young people. So the programme is set to grow and grow.'

(Children's Participation Officer quoted in Funkee Munkee, 2007, webpage)

This view was also voiced by the young people themselves, some of whom reported that they had 'Gained confidence in communicating' and 'Enjoyed busting social work jargon' (Funkee Munkee, 2007):

'When I went on total respect, it really influenced me to join the team and to work with young people, even though I am a young person myself, I would still like to work with others and to get involved.'

(Young person quoted in RAW, 2007, p. 1)

The Total Respect training was also an opportunity for practitioners to learn about additional issues for children who are Black and from minority ethnic groups, such as the limited investigation of racial abuse, dealing with cultural needs and lack of placement choice (CROA, 2000).

The organisation closed in 2012 through lack of funding but the training continued to provide a valuable example of how children can contribute directly to the learning of practitioners.

2.2 Children's contribution to learning

It has been increasingly recognised that children are social actors in their own right and can make a contribution to the shape of services that they receive and the environments in which they live (James and Prout, 1997). Government policy acknowledges the importance of children's views, although the acknowledgement can sometimes be experienced as tokenistic or a matter of rhetoric, and most new policy and practice initiatives require elements of consultation or the participation of children and young people. This principle extends to the learning that practitioners can derive from listening to children's views more broadly, as was emphasised in 2005 by the then Children's Rights Director for England:

> Like many who regularly consult children and young people, we find that their views are always serious, concise, thoughtful and highly relevant – and cut through the pre-existing agendas and diplomatic avoidances that beset many consultations with 'professional' adults. We find that even very young children are more than able to analyse and give clear views on many issues within their experience.
>
> (Morgan, 2005, pp. 181–182)

The potential mechanisms for learning can be diverse. There are direct contributions to training as in the case of the Total Respect initiative, but the voices of children are more likely to emerge through consultation, research, and other forms of participation.

Kellett (2005) advocates the value of research not just on children but by and with children themselves. Adults can no longer access the perspective of a child without filtering it through the adult perspective they have acquired since their own childhood. Adult researchers still retain the power and the framing of the questions, and so need to work alongside children to enable them to develop their own questions, ways of collecting data and evaluating outcomes.

> Children observe with different eyes, ask different questions – they ask questions that adults do not even think of – have different concerns and have immediate access to peer culture where adults are outsiders. The research agendas children prioritise, the research questions they frame and the way in which they collect data are substantially different from adults and all of this can offer valuable insights and original contributions to knowledge.
>
> (Kellett, 2005, p. 8)

Enabling children to participate: voting at a school council

The views of young children have been more difficult to access because of uncertainty about the methods of ascertaining them. However, approaches such as 'Mosaic' have attempted to use mixed methods (for example, observation, children's photographs, map making) to compile an overall children's perspective (Clark and Moss, 2001). This approach has demonstrated how the views of young children can be valuable learning for practitioners. Clark and Statham (2005) discuss how the method can be used both in broader discussions such as redesigning a play space and in individual cases enabling children to contribute to decision making in fostering and adoption situations.

Research techniques have also been developed in work with disabled children. Watson et al. (2007) illustrate how children with complex healthcare needs can contribute their views to inform service developments when methods are adapted (for example, photos, drawing, choosing faces with a range of expressions). Similarly, Rabiee et al. (2005) describe other visual methods developed for work with children who do not communicate through speech. Computer-assisted questionnaires have also been used to facilitate consultation and participation with disabled young people (Davies and Morgan, 2005).

Key points

1   Children, parents and carers have unique knowledge about their own lives and can make valuable contributions to practitioners' learning.

2   Children, young people and adults can be enabled to make direct contributions to the education and training of students and practitioners in all areas of children's services.

3   Research by and with even very young children can ascertain their views and support practitioners in making decisions with them about their lives, both day-to-day decisions and in more difficult circumstances.

3   Learning as social activity

While there is clearly an important role for formal training and formal structures, there is an increasing recognition that 'social' learning also occurs in a more informal and unstructured way. This has been theorised in different ways but perhaps most significantly by Etienne Wenger (Lave and Wenger, 1991; Wenger, 1998) in the concept of 'communities of practice'.

Communities of practice are not just descriptions or models of what happens in the workplace. Wenger stresses that 'communities of practice are everywhere', in social settings – families, churches, online – as well as in offices and institutions; they are an experience common to us all. In the work context a community of practice is not synonymous with a team; a community of practice can be much broader or smaller than the formal parameters of a single team. Similarly, just because a team is created does not mean a community of practice is instantly formed (it could even potentially survive after a team is dissolved); such communities are organic in nature. However, the theory of learning contained within this idea has a potentially valuable application to our discussion and in particular to interagency working and integrated teams. It also provides another perspective on how practitioner identities are shaped through participation in such a community.

A community of practice is defined through three key dimensions which we can think about in relation to both single agency and multi-agency groups and teams in children's services:

- **Mutual engagement** – all of its members are engaged in specific joint activities.
- **Joint enterprise** – the collective process of negotiation as people are jointly finding some way of managing the tasks they need to perform. This process also creates a mutual accountability between those involved and a shared idea of why they are all working together.
- **A shared repertoire** – this represents a common set of shared resources – for example, routines, tools, concepts, techniques – and structures that members of the community have developed over time.

Thinking point 5.6: From Wenger's definition, can you identify a community of practice that you belong to outside of work? What is its 'shared repertoire'?

Wenger argues that there are processes within communities of practice that generate new knowledge through the daily interaction of members of that community. This knowledge is created by two different, but complementary, processes which he describes as *participation* and *reification*.

Participation is the 'active involvement in social enterprises' (Wenger, 1998, p. 55). Essentially this involves the daily interactions and shared experiences of members of the community. These individual activities combine to generate new, shared forms of knowledge and practice that are greater than the sum of their parts. This participation shapes practitioners' individual identities, but equally individuals contribute to the identity of the community. This does not mean that it is a process which is necessarily harmonious or free from power dynamics.

Reification refers to the process whereby abstract knowledge is made into more solid form in the shape of law, procedures, schemes of work, assessment tools, etc. This includes not just objects; it also includes a wide range of processes – common ways of naming, describing and encoding. In the context of a multi-disciplinary team, effective working will depend to some extent on this reification, the creation of new shared procedures and policies.

> However, procedures are simply pieces of paper until they are enacted through practice by the front-line professional staff involved in building the actuality of joined-up working.
>
> (Frost and Lloyd, 2006, p. 12)

Wenger suggests that 'communities of practice can be thought of as shared histories of learning' (Wenger, 1998, p. 86). Learning is not always explicitly identified as such by the practitioners involved as it is not static or discrete but occurs in their very participation in developing practice. A community of practice is a place for the *acquisition* of knowledge, for example from colleagues, but can also become 'a locus for the creation of knowledge' (Wenger, 1998, p. 214).

Informal learning at work

Research by Anning et al. (2010) within five integrated teams (including a nursery team, child development team, and youth offending team), attempted to specifically explore the applicability of this concept in practice. They assessed that all these teams were operating as communities of practice to varying degrees. The example of integrated teams being able to develop a shared theoretical perspective could be seen as part of the process of building such a community. This process was not straightforward, as different practitioners joined teams with different theoretical perspectives, knowledge bases and views on childhood; for example medical, social, and needs-based models. However, despite some conflict, common dominant models and ways of working did emerge, which helped draw teams together. The successful development of a community of practice depends in part on the ability of workers to learn from each other and move on from fixed positions.

So professionals will argue and defend their value bases, but will also review their assumptions in the light of these discussions. The role of learning through working together mirrors a key theme throughout this book of practitioners retaining specialist knowledge and core values while accommodating new knowledge and values through the process of working with others. Clark (2006), in his analysis of interprofessional learning, suggests that practitioners can have two communities of practice – the professional one and the interprofessional one; practitioners need to be able to operate in both, acquiring two sets of skills.

As in all communities of practice, in interagency or integrated teams the level of engagement may vary between workers, which can affect the degree to which they are 'signed up' to the shared core values. Minority members, seconded workers, part-time staff, and practitioners who feel that their status is not as high or as valued as others, can all experience a lack of inclusion:

> 'all the core members have a voice and I think we do it together. But some of the people who only come in for two sessions a week may not feel like that because they're much more on the periphery.'

> (Psychologist quoted in Frost et al., 2005, p. 192)

Understanding the roles and valuing the contributions of all members, including those who are peripheral or marginal, is important to maximising the sharing of knowledge.

If communities of practice and the learning within them occur regardless of organisational structures, this raises the question of whether organisations can enable this form of learning. Wenger argues that this is possible if the structures of learning and education are examined in order to facilitate and support communities of practice. Organisations need to be able to strike the balance between being institutional but flexible enough to enable practice development. Policies and procedures are important but should not result in practice 'serving the institutional apparatus, rather than the other way around' (Wenger, 1998, p. 244). Organisations can facilitate communication, encourage learning to be seen as a participative activity and provide support in terms of communal space and finance. This could involve negotiation with communities themselves about how learning can be enhanced (Wenger 2002). However, beyond this, the role of the agency in developing communities of practice may be limited:

> That is not to say that they do not require energy, commitment, work, or financial wherewithal to pursue their enterprise; nor is it to say that they are best ignored or left to themselves. But it is to say that they are driven by doing and learning rather than by institutional politics.
>
> (Wenger, 1998, p. 251)

Wenger reinforces the idea that formal and informal training are not mutually exclusive and can overlap, and training can supplement learning in practice. Smith (2003) argues that these ideas have implications for educators as they refocus attention on learning occurring between people, which can be lost in the emphasis on individual accreditation. This in turn can also lead to reflection on the nature of knowledge and practice. Like organisations as a whole, educators need to explore how communities can be engaged with to enable everyone to participate. This model is also potentially transferable to work within children's services, for example, in schools where 'learning activities are planned by children as well as adults, and where parents and teachers not only foster children's learning but also learn from their own involvement with children' (Rogoff et al., 2001, quoted in Smith, 2003).

Can the principles of 'communities of practice' be transferred to schools?

Other theories place more emphasis on the conflictual nature of knowledge creation:

> Wenger argues that communities of practice are not necessarily harmonious and co-operative but essentially his model is about working steadily towards agreement and stability in work-based learning.
>
> (Anning et al., 2010, p. 83)

Activity theory (Engeström, 2001) argues for the need for conflict within teams in order to generate new learning. This theory also takes place within a community, but one 'of multiple points of view, traditions and interests', which are 'a source of trouble and a source of innovation' (Engeström, 2001, p. 136). It proposes that 'contradictions' are the catalyst for change, development and learning beyond that which can be taught. Engeström used the example of a children's hospital to explore how traditional ways of working come into question (experience 'disturbances and contradictions') when confronted by evidence that they do not work that well. In this instance, current practice in the hospital showed a lack of coordination and communication between the different care providers in the area, excessive numbers of visits, unclear lines of responsibility, and failure to inform other involved care providers (including the patient's family) of the practitioner's diagnoses, actions and plans. Engeström describes how new innovations resulted from the network of practitioners involved, from a range of professional backgrounds, focusing on these core problems. But innovations emerged only after the collision of new and old ideas (Engeström, 2001).

In a stable network, it is suggested that learning is likely to be limited (National Evaluation of the Children's Fund (NECF), 2004), which may run counter to what many interagency contexts are aiming to achieve. Identifying difficult issues as barriers to interagency working, which must always be overcome, might be ignoring the creativity of working and learning in unstable environments (Warmington et al., 2004).

This theory has been used in relation to developing children's services. The government in England introduced the Children's Fund (2001–2008) in response to concerns by the social exclusion unit that improved services for 8–12 year olds were needed to prevent the negative effects of child poverty and reduce the risk of social exclusion. When the programme was being evaluated, the researchers used activity theory as a way of analysing the working of partnership boards and promoting further learning. For example, in a series of workshops, evidence was presented to the partnership boards of individual local Children's Fund programmes of the differences in understanding between its members that the researchers had observed. Similarly, 'contradictions' were pointed out between what people said they wanted to develop and how they were going about achieving it:

> An example of difference might be two descriptions of the purpose of participation which reveal different ambitions for the participation of children and families in the programme. A contradiction might be that Board members argue that they are aiming at interagency service provision, but are not using a commissioning process that encourages it. We show the evidence as quotations or video clips at the workshop and so create an opportunity for participants to discuss quite fundamental matters in a safe environment.

Differences and contradictions are not seen as weaknesses, but as points from which individuals and organisations learn and move on.

(NECF, 2004, p. 17)

Ultimately, no one theory is complete in being able to account for the complexity of informal learning but these approaches can provide insight into the processes within teams that are contributing to their development.

> **Key points**
>
> 1 There is a range of theories about knowledge creation, which stress that it occurs in an unstructured way in the workplace as well as in formal settings.
> 2 The theories of 'communities of practice' and 'activity theory' illustrate in different ways how teams can be challenging but also create new ways of working together. This can be particularly relevant to the development of interagency and increasingly integrated teams.
> 3 Organisations can recognise the value of communities of practice and, to a certain extent, support their development.

4 Reflecting and learning

Reflective practice has emerged as a key approach to learning at the heart of much practitioner training and professional development, with its own substantial and complex literature. The principle has even been adopted by government guidance to all practitioners working with children in that they should '[k]now how to use theory and experience to reflect upon, think about and improve [their] practice' (DfES, 2005, p. 12). Reflective practice stresses that learning can be a perpetual process and that for practitioners in areas such as health, education and social care, knowledge based on 'technical rationality' will take you only so far (Payne, 2002). Practitioners need skills to develop theory and knowledge in new and complex situations. Reflection is also seen as a cornerstone of 'relationship-based' approaches to practice in social work (Ruch, 2005), in the classroom (Pollard, 2008), and in nursing (Bulman and Schutz, 2013), where knowledge of and use of self is emphasised as a vital element. Despite some notes of caution about the difficulties of evaluating the theory (Mann et al., 2009), reflection is now widely advocated as a crucial element of learning.

Reflection is usually portrayed as a cyclical process: current practice experiences can be reviewed – 'reflected' upon – and new ideas and strategies can be formulated and then tested out again in practice (Kolb, 1984; Schön, 1987). From this reflective cycle and its consideration of alternative approaches, new learning will emerge to support the improvement of future practice. Idealistically this has been portrayed as an upward spiral where continual reflection on current practice will consistently enhance professional competence (Pollard, 2008). This circular reflective process can be carried out when looking back on the event (reflection-on-action), but also can occur simultaneously with practice (reflection-in-action) (Schön, 1987). Given that practitioners do not always see theory as related to real-life experience (Eraut, 1994), reflection can also provide the opportunity for them to integrate theory into their practice. The literature is full of circles and spirals illustrating variations on this theme, each model attempting to take account of different dimensions of the complexity of day-to-day practice. That proposed by Kolb (1984) is often seen as a starting point (see figure).

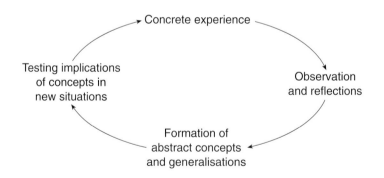

A model of experiential learning (Kolb, 1984, p. 21). 'Learning is the process whereby knowledge is created through the transformation of experience' (Kolb, 1984, p. 38)

Eby (2000) argues that successful reflective practice is much more than being able to reflect back thoughtfully on an incident, but requires the synthesis of the skills of reflection with those of 'self-awareness' and 'critical thinking' (Eby, 2000, p. 52).

Self-awareness requires the recognition that much practice is intuitive. The stress on self-awareness is crucial in encouraging practitioners to understand their own impact on the situation. We all bring our own histories, cultural frames of reference, beliefs, values and experience to any interpersonal interaction. Practitioners need to be 'self-aware' if they are to be able to understand the process and outcomes of their practice.

Concerns that reflection can be a very individualised process – one practitioner reflecting on one interaction – have led to an emphasis on the need for the 'critical' aspect of reflection. Practice continually takes place within a changing social, political and cultural environment, and is affected by a whole range of other issues such as those relating to resources or staffing levels. Critical thinking emphasises the importance of questioning in this broader context in which practice takes place, including power relations between workers and those they are working with. This can be a key part of the process of challenging some of the roots of oppression and issues often taken 'as a given' in practice, establishing reflection as part of an empowering process (Eby, 2000).

Thomas (2004) draws on a model proposed by Taylor (2000) in a health context which brings together some of the strands discussed above. This suggests that there are three elements that reflective practitioners can focus on: technical, practical and 'emancipatory'. These categories reflect a theory developed by **Habermas** of the different ways in which knowledge is constructed:

Jurgen Habermas (1929–) is a major figure in modern sociology and philosophy who has written on critical theory, political theory and ethics.

- *Technical reflection* – for example, assessing and evaluating particular treatments. This emphasises that evidence-based practice and reflection can be linked.
- *Practical reflection* – which focuses less on the 'external' knowledge and more on the personal encounter within the process of the treatment (internal knowledge, feelings, intuition, etc.).
- *Emancipatory reflection* – which involves looking at structures and power issues. 'In this type of reflection the learner is encouraged to look at the constraints on their practice and how to challenge them' (Thomas, 2004, p. 106).

This critical reflection overlaps with one other frequently cited concept in this area – that of reflexivity. This too emphasises the need for practitioners to question the basis of their assumptions, the political context in which they work and even the knowledge base they are drawing on:

Epistemology is the theory of knowledge, a branch of philosophy which is concerned with the nature and scope of knowledge (what we know and how we know it).

So reflexivity has an **epistemological** dimension: it involves a process of 'bending back' which allows the practitioner to analyse what they know and how they know it.

(Turney, 2007, p. 82)

One further dimension of reflexivity is the recognition that just as practitioners influence the practice encounter, so in turn they are influenced by it (Eby, 2000).

In order to maximise learning from practice experiences, reflection can be approached in a structured way. To achieve this, Thomas (2004) advocates the use of 'critical incident analyses'. A critical incident is a moment of practice that has important consequences for the practitioner, or those they are working with. Specific questions rather than open-ended discussion can draw out the knowledge, values and issues. It can be done as an individual exercise, but more can be gained by using it within teams or with 'critical friends' (Thomas, 2004).

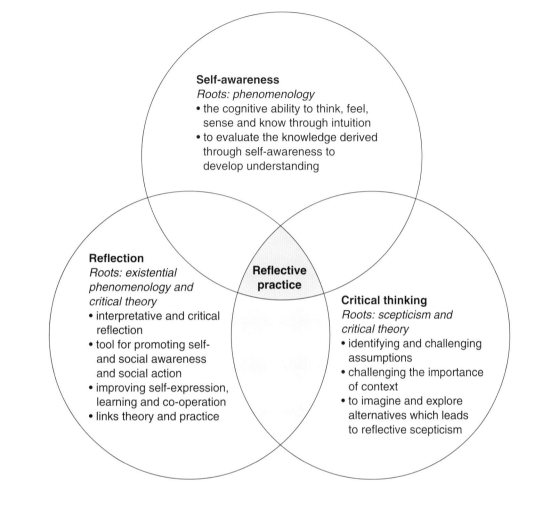

The skills required for critical reflection (Eby, 2000, p. 53)

Practice box 5.6

Critical incident analysis

Practitioners are encouraged to choose one incident – a family interview, a drop-in session, a review of a Looked After child, a telephone call – then use these structured questions to start a reflective process. The questions could be adapted for use in any practice setting.

- Give a brief outline of the situation, what happened, who was involved, where it took place. Include any relevant issues of oppression or discrimination that you were aware of.
- Describe what you did or said, what action you took, and the responses of others.
- How were you feeling at the time and how do you think others were feeling?
- What were the main challenges for you?
- What went well and what did you do to enable this?
- What underpinning knowledge and theories did you use? What methods of intervention did you use? How were these informed by research and evidence-based practice?
- What values underpinned the work and how did you demonstrate or convey these?
- What value conflicts were you aware of and how did you deal with these?
- What skills did you draw on?
- If you were undertaking a similar piece of work again is there anything you would do differently? If so what? If not, why not?
- What do you think you learnt from the work?
- What have you learnt from reviewing the situation and your practice within it? (This question is posed after the incident has been discussed in small groups.)

(Adapted from Thomas, 2004, p. 107)

It is this team experience that can be useful for promoting reflection across disciplinary boundaries. Through this process, individual practitioners are making explicit the values and knowledge that underpin their practice. Many of the key processes for successful interagency working discussed in these chapters rely on exactly this type of process – understanding each other's cognitive and normative maps as suggested by Clark (2006) above. It is through the ability to reflect that a perspective on 'who am I and what do I know?' and also 'who are the others and what do they know?' can be achieved. The theory suggests that the process also creates new learning from the sharing of practice experience and identifying alternative approaches.

Many practitioners will feel that their practice is at least in part intuitive. Reflective practice can enable the implicit to be more explicit and open to critical questioning; however, some commentators argue that there may be limits to this. In dynamic and complex interactions, practitioners can respond without accessing explicit knowledge and it is possible that the value of intuition merits greater recognition. Atkinson and Claxton (2000) suggest that intuitive skills could also be developed alongside those of analysis and reflection.

4.1 Learning organisations

As Thomas (2004) stresses when advocating critical incident analysis (see above), revisiting the initial incident can be emotionally demanding, and exposing practice and knowledge of self in a team situation needs to be done in an environment safe enough to explore issues, doubts and problems. Frequently a problem for teams is protecting this time to learn together. While on the one hand all practitioners are encouraged to develop their knowledge and skills and acquire qualifications, on the other they can experience the pressured working environment reducing opportunities for learning. One child and adolescent mental health team described how important this time and space for development was in their successful transition to a well-functioning multi-disciplinary team:

> Despite pressures from increasing demand, clinical work was undertaken jointly in order to learn about each other's skills and abilities and establish best practice with regard to assessment and interventions. ...

> Progress was co-ordinated through a schedule of team days, where discussion and team building activities took place. The mixture of personalities, paces and an ability to contain differences of opinion, and even at times to value and celebrate differences, has led to considerable development.

> (Wiles, 2005, p. 49)

This question of whether practitioners have time to reflect inevitably relates partly to the organisations in which they work. As well as the onus on individuals to update their knowledge and skills, there has been considerable interest in the idea of the 'learning organisation'. How can organisations promote, enable and sustain such lifelong learning?

Thinking point 5.7: Are you aware of any ways in which your organisation (or one you know of) successfully promotes reflection or informal learning?

We have already noted how reflective practice requires time and space in order to be effective. The concept of communities of practice also raises issues for organisations to consider – how can informal learning in the workplace can be encouraged? Similarly, the advancement of research evidence in practice discussed above requires the organisation to find strategies to enable appropriate access to research by practitioners

Taylor (2004), considering the learning organisation in the increasingly interprofessional environment, argues that rapid change brings into question assumptions about what an organisation is, given the reality of changing structures, management structures and the arrangement of many practitioners in new 'cross-agency' configurations (compounded by pressures on financial resources). She suggests that Wenger too assumes a certain degree of stability for the emergence of a community of practice. While organisations clearly have a key role in supporting the learning of practitioners, lack of research knowledge about how this operates makes it difficult to develop any clear model of the learning organisation supporting increasingly integrated working.

Key points

1 Reflection is widely seen as a key skill in developing and integrating new learning into practice.
2 Critical reflection and reflexivity promote a more serious questioning of the assumptions within work with children and their families, and potentially support a more empowering form of practice.
3 The success of 'learning together' can be enabled by the way in which organisations support both formal and informal learning.

Conclusion

Analysing learning, particularly that supporting more integrated working, is multi-faceted with pre- and post-qualifying structures and formal and informal elements. A closer examination of the ways in which practitioners from different disciplines learn together should guard against any assumptions of guaranteed success. However, there is clearly the potential for learning together to support more effective working together and make a significant contribution to better practice and better services for children.

References

Anning, A., Cottrell, D., Frost, N., Green, J. and Robinson, M., (2010) *Developing Multiprofessional Teamwork for Integrated Children's Services* (2nd edn), Maidenhead, Open University Press.

Atkinson, T. and Claxton, G. (eds) (2000) *The Intuitive Practitioner: On the Value of Not Always Knowing What One is Doing*, Maidenhead, Open University Press.

Brandon, M., Sidebotham, P., Bailey, S., Belderson, P., Hawley, C,, Ellis, C. and Megson, M. (2012) *New Learning from Serious Case Reviews: A Two Year Report for 2009–2011*, Department for Education.

Brechin, A. and Siddell, M. (2000) '*Ways of knowing*', in Gomm, R. and Davies, C. (eds) *Using Evidence in Health and Social Care*, London, Sage, pp. 3–25.

Bulman, C. and Schutz, S. (2013) *Reflective Practice in Nursing* (3rd edn), Oxford, Blackwell.

Charles, M. and Horwath, J. (2009) 'Investing in interagency training to safeguard children: an act of faith or an act of reason?', *Children and Society*, vol. 23, no. 4, pp. 364–376.

Children's Rights Officers and Advocates (CROA) (2000) *Total Respect: Ensuring Children's Rights and Participation in Care*, London, CROA and DH.

Clark, A. and Moss, P. (2001) *Listening to Young Children: The Mosaic Approach*, London, National Children's Bureau.

Clark, A. and Statham, J. (2005) 'Listening to young children: experts in their own lives', *Adoption & Fostering*, vol. 29, no. 1, pp. 45–56.

Clark, P.G. (2006) 'What would a theory of interprofessional education look like? Some suggestions for developing a theoretical framework for teamwork training', *Journal of Interprofessional Care*, vol. 20, no. 6, pp. 577–589.

Clyde, J.J. (1992) *Report of the Inquiry into the Removal of Children from Orkney in February 1991*, Edinburgh, HMSO.

Cooper, H. and Spencer-Dawe, E. (2006) 'Involving service users in interprofessional education: narrowing the gap between theory and practice', *Journal of Interprofessional Care*, vol. 20, no. 6, pp. 603–617.

Davies, P.A. and Bynner, J. (1999) *The Impact of Credit-based Systems of Learning on Learning Cultures*, ESRC report of the Learning Society Programme, London, City University.

Davies, M. and Morgan, A. (2005) 'Using computer-assisted self-interviewing (CASI) questionnaires to facilitate consultation and participation with vulnerable young people', *Child Abuse Review*, vol. 14, no. 6, pp. 389–406.

Department for Education and Skills (DfES) (2005) *Common Core of Skills and Knowledge for the Children's Workforce*, Nottingham, DfES.

DHSSPSNI (2003) *Co-operating to Safeguard Children*, Department of Health, Social Services and Public Safety, Belfast.

Eby, M. (2000) 'Understanding professional development' in Brechin, A., Brown, H. and Eby, M.A. (eds) *Critical Practice in Health and Social Care*, London, The Open University/Sage, pp. 48–70.

Engeström, Y. (2001) 'Expansive learning at work: toward an activity theoretical reconceptualization', *Journal of Education and Work*, vol. 14, no. 1, pp. 133–156.

Eraut, M. (1994) *Developing Professional Knowledge and Competence*, London, Falmer Press.

France, A. and Utting, D. (2005) 'The paradigm of "risk and protection-focused prevention" and its impact on services for children and families', *Children & Society*, vol. 19, no. 2, pp. 77–90.

Frost, N. (2001) 'Professionalism, change and the politics of lifelong learning', *Studies in Continuing Education*, vol. 23, no. 1, pp. 5–17.

Frost, N. and Lloyd, A. (2006) 'Implementing multidisciplinary teamwork in the new child welfare policy environment', *Journal of Integrated Care*, vol. 14, no. 2, pp. 11–17.

Frost, N., Robinson, M. and Anning, A. (2005) 'Social workers in multidisciplinary teams: issues and dilemmas for professional practice', *Child & Family Social Work*, vol. 10, no. 3, pp. 187–196.

Funkee Munkee (2007), *Young People's Participation*, available online at <http://www.funkeemunkee.co.uk/young_people_part.html>, accessed 19 September 2007.

HM Government (2010) *Working Together to Safeguard Children: A Guide to Inter-agency Working to Safeguard and Promote the Welfare of Children*, London, The Stationery Office.

Institute for Research and Innovation in Social Services (IRISS) (2013) *Early Years Evidence: Reviewing the evidence and effectiveness of preventative approaches*, available online at <http://www.iriss.org.uk/project/early-years-evidence>, accessed 17 April 2013.

James, A. and Prout, A. (eds) (1997) *Constructing and Reconstructing Childhood: Contemporary Issues in the Sociological Study of Childhood*, London, Falmer Press.

Jarvis, P. (2007) *Globalisation, Lifelong Learning and the Learning Society: Sociological Perspectives*, London, Routledge.

Kellett, M. (2005) *Children as active researchers: a new research paradigm for the 21st century?*, available online at <http://www.ncrm.ac.uk/research/outputs/publications/methodsreview/MethodsReviewPaperNCRM-003.pdf>, accessed 2 November 2007.

Kolb, D.A. (1984) *Experiential Learning: Experience as the Source of Learning and Development*, Englewood Cliffs, NJ, Prentice Hall.

Laming, Lord (2003) *The Victoria Climbié Inquiry*, London, The Stationery Office.

Lattuca, L.R. (2002) 'Learning interdisciplinarity: sociocultural perspectives on academic work', *Journal of Higher Education*, vol. 73, no. 6, pp. 711–739.

Lave, J. and Wenger, E. (1991) *Situated Learning: Legitimate Peripheral Participation*, Cambridge, Cambridge University Press.

Macdonald, G. (2001) *Effective Interventions for Child Abuse and Neglect: An Evidence- based Approach to Planning and Evaluating Interventions*, Chichester, Wiley.

Mann, K., Gordon J. and MacLeod, A. (2009) 'Reflection and reflective practice in health professions education: a systematic review', *Advances in Health Sciences Education*, vol. 14, no. 4, pp. 595–621.

Mellor, R., Cottrell, N. and Moran, M. (2013) 'Just working in a team was a great experience: students' perspectives on the learning experiences of an interprofessional education program', *Journal of Interprofessional Care*, vol. 27, no. 4 , pp. 292–297.

Morgan, R. (2005) 'Finding what children say they want: messages from children', *Representing Children*, vol. 17, pp. 180–188.

National Evaluation of the Children's Fund (NECF) (2004) *Collaborating for the Social Inclusion of Children and Young People: Emerging Lessons from the First Round of Case Studies*, Research Report No. 596, London, DfES.

O'Brien, S. (2003) *Report of the Caleb Ness Inquiry*, available online at <http://www.nhslothian.scot.nhs.uk/news/annual_reports/publichealth/2005/ar2003/caleb/cnr.pdf>,, accessed 21 September 2007.

Ogilvie-Whyte, S.A. (2006). *Baselines: A Review of Evidence about the Impact of Education and Training in Child Care and Protection on Practice and Client Outcomes*, Dundee, Scottish Institute for Excellence in Social Work Education.

Payne, M. (2002) 'Social work theories and reflective practice' in Adams, R., Dominelli, L. and Payne, M. (eds) *Social Work: Themes, Issues and Critical Debates* (2nd edn), Basingstoke, Palgrave/The Open University.

Pollard, A. (2008) *Reflective Teaching: Effective and Evidence-informed Professional Practice* (3rd edn), London, Continuum.

Rabiee, P., Sloper, P. and Beresford, B. (2005) 'Doing research with children and young people who do not use speech for communication', *Children & Society*, vol. 19, no. 5, pp. 385–396.

RAW (2007) April 2007 Newsletter, available online at <http://www.raw4us.co.uk/newsletter/Spring%20newsletter%201.pdf>, accessed 19 September 2007.

Reder, P. and Duncan, S. (2003) 'Understanding communication in child protection networks', *Child Abuse Review*, vol. 12, no. 2, pp. 82–100.

Research in Practice (RiP) (n.d.) *Research in Practice: About us*, available online at <http://www.rip.org.uk/about-us>, accessed 17 April 2013.

Rogoff, B., Turkanis, C.G. and Bartlett, L. (eds) (2001) *Learning Together: Children and Adults in a School Community*, New York, Oxford University Press.

Ruch, G. (2005) 'Relationship-based practice and reflective practice: holistic approaches to contemporary child care social work', *Child & Family Social Work*, vol. 10, no. 2, pp. 111–123.

Schön, D.A. (1987) *Educating the Reflective Practitioner: Toward a New Design for Teaching and Learning in the Professions*, San Francisco, Jossey-Bass.

Scottish Executive (2002) *It's Everyone's Job to Make Sure I'm Alright: Report of the Child Protection Audit and Review*, Edinburgh, The Stationery Office.

Scottish Government (2010) *National Guidance for Child Protection in Scotland*, Edinburgh, Scottish Government.

Scottish Government (2012) *National Framework for Child Protection Learning and Development in Scotland*, Edinburgh, Scottish Government.

Scottish Institute for Excellence in Social Work Education (SiSWE) (2005) *Service User and Carer Involvement in Social Work Education: Good Practice Guidelines*, available online at <http://www.sieswe.org/files/IA33GoodPracticeGuidelines.pdf>, accessed 19 September 2007.

Smith, M.K. (2003) 'Communities of practice', *Encyclopaedia of Informal Education*, available online at <http://www.infed.org/biblio/communities_of_practice.htm>, accessed 19 September 2007.

Social Care Institute for Excellence (SCIE) (2004) *Improving the Use of Research in Social Care Practice*, Bristol, The Policy Press.

Taylor, B. (2000) *Reflective Practice: A Guide for Nurses and Midwives*, Buckingham, Open University Press.

Taylor, I. (2004) 'Multi-professional teams and the learning organization' in Gould, N. and Baldwin, M. (eds) *Social Work, Critical Reflection and the Learning Organization*, Aldershot, Ashgate, pp. 75–86.

Thomas, J. (2004) 'Using "critical incident analysis" to promote critical reflection and holistic assessment' in Gould, N. and Baldwin, M. (eds) *Social Work, Critical Reflection and the Learning Organization*, Aldershot, Ashgate, pp. 101–116.

Trinder, L. (ed.) (2000) *Evidence-based Practice: A Critical Appraisal*, Oxford, Blackwell Science.

Turney, D. (2007) 'Practice' in Robb, M. (ed.) *Youth in Context: Frameworks, Settings and Encounters*, London, Sage/The Open University.

Utting, W. (1991) *Children in the Public Care: A Review of Residential Child Care*, London, HMSO.

Wallcraft, J., Fleischmann, P. and Schofield, P. (2012) *The Involvement of Users and Carers in Social Work Education: A Practice Benchmarking Study*, SCIE Report 54, London, Social Care Institute for Excellence

Warmington, P., Daniels, H., Edwards, A., Brown, S., Leadbetter, J., Martin, D. and Middleton, D. (2004) *Learning in and for Interagency Working: Conceptual Tensions in 'Joined Up' Practice*, Teaching and Learning Research Programme, Bath, University of Bath. Also available online at <http://www.tlrp.org/dspace/retrieve/247/Daniels+full+paper.doc>, accessed 3 January 2008.

Waterhouse, S. (2000) *Lost in Care: Report of the Tribunal of Inquiry into the Abuse of Children in Care in the Former County Council Areas of Gwynedd and Clwyd since 1974*, London, The Stationery Office.

Watson, D., Abbott, D. and Townsley, R. (2007) 'Listen to me too! Lessons from involving children with complex healthcare needs in research about multi-agency services', *Child Care, Health and Development*, vol. 33, no. 1, pp. 90–95.

Welsh Assembly Government (2008) *All Wales Child Protection Procedures*, Cardiff, Welsh Assembly Government.

Wenger, E (1998) *Communities of Practice*, Cambridge, Cambridge University Press.

Wenger, E., MacDermott, R. and Snyder, W. (2002) *Cultivating Communities of Practice: A Guide to Managing Knowledge*, Boston, Harvard Business Press.

Wiles, C. (2005) 'Developing integrated mental health services for children and young people in Moray' in Glaister, A. and Glaister, B. (eds) *Inter-Agency Collaboration – Providing for Children*, Edinburgh, Dunedin Academic Press.

Zwarenstein, M., Reeves, S., Barr, H., Hammick, M., Koppel, I. and Atkins, J. (2001) 'Interprofessional education: effects on professional practice and health care outcomes', *Cochrane Database of Systematic Reviews*, Issue 1, available online at <http://www.cochrane.org/reviews/en/ab002213.html>, accessed 19 September 2007.

Zwarenstein, M., Reeves, S., Perrier, L. (2005) 'Effectiveness of pre-licensure interprofessional education and post-licensure collaborative interventions', *Journal of Interprofessional Care*, vol. 19 (supplement 1), pp. 148–165.

Chapter 6 Children's services: the changing workplace?

Nick Frost

Introduction

This chapter aims to explore key questions in relation to change and development in the workplaces where a wide range of children's services operate from, often in an inter-agency setting. It will be argued that children's services workplaces are undergoing rapid change that can be understood as being underpinned by wider social factors. There are many influences at play which have a tangible and everyday impact on staff working with children, young people and their families. This chapter will analyse a number of factors, particularly the role of interagency working, and look at which enhance this form of working, and which militate against it.

Children's services are usually understood to include the full range of child-focused professional activities – including children's centres, social care services, youth and play work, youth crime services, and some aspects of universal education and health services – although they are organised within different structures across the UK. There are also related but distinct activities that take place in the 'third' (or voluntary) sector and the private sector. In some jurisdictions in the UK the unifying element for many of the public sector services is that most will be managed ultimately by the Director of Children's Services: this demanding and overarching role symbolises the unity of work with children and young people under the 'children's services' banner. Even where this distinct role does not exist, all relevant organisations – including agencies such as the police and health services – will usually come together to plan strategic approaches to work with children and young people. These arrangements are a fundamental development of the early twenty-first century in children's services – a shift towards integration, cooperation and the joint planning and delivery of services. This move in both 'mindset' and practice seems to be with us for the foreseeable future (Brock and Rankin, 2011).

Children's services across the United Kingdom expanded during the 1990s and 2000s as an inclusive and 'joined-up' definition of such services evolved. This expansion reflected an increasing expenditure on children's services and was associated with a stronger emphasis on interagency working (Frost and Parton, 2009). During this period some workplaces retained a distinctive 'silo', single-profession identity – but many have changed and evolved to reflect the changing landscape.

Core questions

- How does organisational and workplace culture affect work with children and young people?
- What has the impact of the growth of audit, inspection and managerialism been on these workplaces?
- How have the growth of children's rights and participation and the expectations of parents/carers influenced children's services workplaces?
- What has the impact of child abuse and related scandals been on the children's workforce?
- How has the growth of multi-disciplinarity changed the workplace?
- How are contemporary challenges being addressed and what does the future look like?

1 Theorising the interagency workplace

There are many theories that help us understand the workplace: these theories come originally from sociology, organisational theory, psychology and business studies. In this context we draw on the work of Etienne Wenger, who contributed to the development of the concept of 'communities of practice' (Wenger, 1998), which is discussed in Chapter 5 of this book. The concept can be very helpful in understanding the interagency workplace.

Wenger's concept is complex and involved (see http://wenger-trayner. com and Wenger, 1998). He argues that new knowledge is created in 'communities of practice' by the related processes of participation and reification. In applying this thinking, Wenger utilises three key ideas for the process of developing a community of practice in the workplace:

- mutual engagement
- a joint enterprise

- a shared repertoire

Mutual engagement is how in working together we actually do things together in the workplace. This might be meetings, joint visits or running a group together, for example.

A joint enterprise is having a shared idea of why we are working together and what we are working towards: this may be summarised in a shared 'mission statement', for example.

A shared repertoire is how we work together: the language, the tools and techniques and the style of our work.

This theory can be useful in helping us understand the workplace. There is an exercise below that helps to apply communities of practice to our own workplace.

Thinking point 6.1: Think about a children's workplace you know well and assess how effective it is in terms of Wenger's concept of communities of practice. How successful is it at having:

- **a joint enterprise**: having a clear shared goal
- **mutual engagement**: working together towards the joint enterprise
- **a shared repertoire**: having shared ways of working and communicating.

What could be done to make the workplace a more effective 'community of practice'?

2 The impact of audit, inspection and managerialism

Alongside the expansion in children's services there has been a growth in what can be identified as 'pressure from above'. Governments in the UK have wanted to see clear and measurable results from investment in children's services, which has been partly driven by a genuine commitment to promoting the welfare of children. Alongside such a commitment has been a renewed focus on children and young people as carriers of 'all our futures', a burden which has become greater in an age of global competition, where standards of education and skills have to compare to the best in the world if any particular nation state is to thrive. Pressure from above has taken the form (particularly in England) of more extensive, rigorous and demanding inspection and audit regimes, embodied in Ofsted and equivalent agencies such as Estyn in Wales, Education Scotland in Scotland and the Education and Training Inspectorate in Northern Ireland. This target-driven culture has had a profound impact on the workplace. There has been an increasing emphasis on data gathering, record keeping, action plans and often incessant preparation for the next inspection. Alongside this, and related to it, has been a focus on 'leadership': highlighted in the children's services field by developments such as the government-funded National College for Teaching and Leadership (www.nationalcollege.org.uk). These developments have changed the experience of children's services workers and their sense of control over their workplace.

The Ofsted inspection (Ros Asquith)

Every children's services worker will have their own story of the experience of audit and inspection. These will vary according to the exact activity and whether the organisation is within the public, private or third sector. In England the greatest pressure for most, of course, has come from Ofsted inspections. Whether these are unit-specific inspections of, say, a children's home or wholesale inspections of the children's services in a local authority area, they bring with them anxiety, tales of sleepless nights, the relentless cycle of producing data and the tensions and drama of the feedback meeting. In Practice box 6.1 a head teacher gives a graphic account of what it is like to be subject to an inspection by Ofsted.

Practice box 6.1

The inspection – a head teacher's account

I'd been living with the expectation of The Phone Call for some months and had been nervously eyeing the clock every day around noon. However, when the call finally came, I was just trying to calm a child in my office who had been having a huge, violent tantrum in the hallway. Still breathless from carrying him, I picked up the phone and heard the fateful words: 'Inspector for you.'

Under the new Ofsted framework, the call is now from the lead inspector herself. There is no time for gathering oneself together. That's it. She is on the phone. It requires a level of composure that I don't always have, but somehow, I managed to hold a sensible conversation. This consisted simply of the practical arrangements for the inspection, which would start the next day.

My staff soon adopted a 'bring it on' attitude. Outside, so did I. Inside, I was quaking. I know our strengths, but I also know what we still need to improve.

On the way back to my office, I saw my deputy head struggling up the corridor with the boy, and looking anxious. He had been attacking children in our support group, punching them, kicking and biting, tearing paper off the walls and throwing things at everyone. Together we managed to get him into my office and were able to let go of him as he was now contained. He started pulling everything off the walls and pushing furniture over. Then he opened my cupboard, grabbed a pot of yellow glitter, pulled the lid off and started throwing it everywhere, and on us.

How to deal with this when I needed to get so much done for the inspection and I could not even get near my computer? The boy started to swear. He then, quite deliberately, kicked my deputy head in the stomach. He moved so fast that we were not quick enough to stop him.

Later, when his mother came to pick him up, she insisted that he clean up the mess on the floor. As she passed the hoover to him, he flinched in a way that made my colleague and me shiver as we exchanged glances. But his behaviour had been so extreme and violent that I had no choice but to exclude him, and so I arranged for him to attend our local pupil referral unit for a couple of weeks.

It was an hour and a half before we could get on with preparations for the inspection. I don't always manage well under this sort of pressure: the flight response is very strong in me and my adrenaline levels rocket. Just like some of the children we are supporting. We started to collate all the information needed. Staff were ensuring that their planning was good and that their rooms were tidy. We left school at 11 pm.

Usually the anticipation of an event is worse than the event itself. This is not my experience of Ofsted inspections. This is my fifth full inspection as a head and still my anxiety levels are high each time. I didn't sleep that night.

There were two inspectors in the team, and a trainee. First part of the inspection process, after the initial meeting, was joint lesson observations. A good start. This was followed by a team meeting. But it soon became clear that the view they were forming of the school was one that was very different from the reality. I had to struggle to hold it together. I couldn't quite believe what they were saying. Another sleepless night, this time sobbing, fearing everything I had fought so hard for was slipping through my fingers.

On day two, I asked the lead inspector for a meeting to express a concern that I was developing about the conduct of the inspection. She was actually very sympathetic at this point and the attitude and feel of the inspection seemed to change. In the next few meetings, we bombarded them with evidence and eventually it seemed that they were listening and taking on board our self-evaluation. In the next team meeting, the inspectors had read my behaviour logs and risk assessments and they began to develop a better understanding of just how many socio-economic and emotional barriers to learning we have to overcome in this particular primary school for our children to make progress. I was still pacing the corridors.

My staff and the children were magnificent. The children really impressed the inspectors, as did my senior leadership team. But the last meeting, to discuss the final judgments, was difficult. Under the new framework, you are allowed to be a part of the discussion, which is much better than before. I tried to argue, backed up by myriad evidence, against one of the judgments, but I could not budge them. The verdict was to be that – like many schools in this latest round of inspections – we 'require improvement', but we were given 'good' for leadership and management and also for behaviour and safety, which is a real credit to the staff.

The hardest part of any inspection in some ways is the days that follow, with all the staff feeling shellshocked and exhausted. I could hardly string a sentence together. We are left dazed and battered in their wake.

And in the midst of all of this, a tragedy was unfolding. One of our parents was critically ill in hospital and we had just found out that they might not recover. We are supporting the child as best we can, but it's hard, when everyone is so emotional at the moment, not to just sit and sob at the futility of it all.

Things, however, have to go on as normal and we have been soothed by the ethereal sound of children's voices floating through the corridors as they practise for our carol concert. We are OK, my school and me, and we will do anything it takes to get the best for our children.

(Bergistra, 2012)

The head teacher quoted above describes an experience comparable to one that many readers of this book will have been through. Thinking point 6.2 at the end of this section will allow you to reflect upon such experiences.

It is important to note that the impact of inspectoral regimes spreads beyond the period of the inspection: it acts as a form of regulation and control throughout the year. The relentless pressure to produce data and complete audits and to 'have your records up-to-date' exerts an extensive and continuous pressure on practice. Exactly how 'scientific' this inspection process actually is remains problematic. A former auditor, Mike Power, provided perhaps the classic account of 'the audit society' and how we have an inspection and 'audit explosion'.

Power argued that:

> Methods of checking and verification are diverse, sometimes perverse, sometimes burdensome, and always costly.
>
> (Power, 1997, p. 1)

Power explored how audit and inspection regimes exist in tension with ideas of trust. If we could trust professionals to do their best for children, perhaps we could downscale the inspection industry. Perhaps surprisingly for someone from an audit background, Power explained at some length how audit and inspection regimes and methods are not simply technical processes but are socially constructed and contested. He argued, convincingly, that we live in 'an audit society':

> Society that endangers itself because it invests too heavily in shallow rituals of verification at the expense of other forms of organisational intelligence...

(Power, 1997, p. 123)

By this he meant that inspection evidence has more power and influence than other forms of knowledge such as our own experience and the views of service users. While Power was not explicitly writing about children's services, his arguments certainly chime with those of us immersed in the children's services world.

The contemporary British workplace delivering services to children is a location that is constantly audited, measured and inspected. The emphasis on standards and standardisation is greater than that on flexibility and diversity. While many nations have inspection regimes, overseas visitors are often surprised at the extent of standardisation in England. A Danish researcher reflected as follows when comparing English and Danish approaches:

> I likewise concluded that for cases in which there is little time for consideration, e.g. serious abuse or neglect, the English professionals can act more efficiently because they have these standardised procedures and methods. Hence these procedures and methods serve a purpose, but the danger is that they will dominate the rest of the work with vulnerable children which would profit more from a freer and more time-demanding interplay between various professionals' distinctive perspectives.

(Midskard, 2012, pp. 263–264)

This drive towards 'standardisation' raises a profound question about democracy and the control of services. If children's services are constantly responding and changing due to the demands of organisations such as Ofsted, can we be said to have genuine local control of services? In reality there is a complex tension and interplay between elected politicians, professionals, demands from service users, inspectorates, national ministers and civil servants. The exact balance of power between these parties will vary from situation to situation; but there can be little doubt that the power of the inspectorate in children's services is considerable. In the 'third sector' the experience may well be different. This sector is extensive and varies from large-scale national organisations to small community groups. However, many of the larger organisations have adopted similar internal inspection regimes, and while smaller organisations may be largely 'community-led' and relatively informal they are still heavily influenced by changes in workplace configurations in the statutory sector, as discussed in Chapter 1.

Audit and inspection are common across all areas of the public sector

Thinking point 6.2: Think about inspection processes. What are the potential positive and negative impacts of inspection? Could the system be improved? If so, how?

Key points

1 The structure and roles of the workplace are heavily influenced by monitoring and inspection regimes.
2 Inspection regimes can help to enhance the welfare of children but there are concerns that their dominance can have negative impacts on services for children.

3 Children's participation in the workplace

The previous section examined pressures from 'above' which have had an undoubted impact on the children's services workplace; in this section we explore pressure from 'below' – such as children's rights and participation alongside the expectations and demands of parents and carers. The United Nations Convention on the Rights of the Child (UNCRC) has had a major impact on shifting children from being seen as passive recipients towards being active participants in services.

The United Nations Convention on the Rights of the Child has led to children playing new roles in children's services

This shift and its implications, and the distance yet to be travelled, will be explored in this section. Alongside calls for children's rights, comparable demands have come from parents and carers as 'citizens', 'consumers' and 'partners' no longing willing to be passive recipients of 'monolithic' state-delivered services.

Perhaps one of the major changes during the last few decades has been the increase in the quality and quantity of children's participation. The author of this chapter recalls that in the early part of his social work career (in the late 1970s) teenagers in care were often called into 'their' review meetings at the end to be **told** about the future plans for their lives. Today, with the existence of roles such as Independent Reviewing Officers and advocates and the emphasis on children's voices being heard, such practices hopefully belong well and truly in the past.

The drivers for the enhanced role for children's participation are arguably threefold: first, a general societal trend towards liberalisation and the decline of deference; second, the specific impact of the UNCRC

(Jones, 2009); and finally, the campaigning work of children's rights movements, including those that have organised children's voices collectively (Stein, 2011). The third sector has often led the way in the drive for participation. Let us look at each of the three drivers for children's participation in turn.

First, across society we have witnessed more liberal approaches to a range of social issues. Attitudes to homosexuality, divorce, single parenthood and disability shifted markedly during the second half of the twentieth century. A trend towards 'individualisation', a decline of deferential attitudes to authority and increasing toleration of diversity and difference have all in some way shifted power towards previously marginalised and stigmatised groups (Giddens, 1991). The strongest example is probably in relation to homosexuality, which has shifted during a sixty-year period from being illegal to being celebrated in 'gay' weddings. What do these wide-ranging social changes mean for children? Phrases which resonated in post-Second World War childhoods ('because I said so', 'you'll get a good belting') are heard less frequently. Children's voices are heard in School Councils, Children in Care Councils and Youth Parliaments. Children and young people are often asked to speak at local authority meetings and youth workers are funded to work with them as participation officers. Such participation has moved from the often tokenistic to having a real impact, as Mike Stein graphically illustrated in his book *Care Less Lives* (Stein, 2011). Stein started with the origins of the children in care movement. The story he related begins in the late 1960s, when he recalls that:

> There was no recognition at that time of the rights of children in care, or more modestly, any legal requirement for their views to be considered by those responsible for them.
>
> (Stein, 2011, p. 6)

Stein steers us through thirty years of social history and the growth of the children in care movement and concluded that:

> By 2003, 30 years later, a lot had changed. Young people in care were far more likely to be living in foster care or very small children's homes. Their rights movement, including its struggles and campaigns over these years, had brought about significant changes in how young people in care were seen: no longer were

they to be ignored, they were, as of right, to participate in decisions about their lives. In this respect their care had, over time, been shaped by their own actions and resilience.

(Stein, 2011, p. 185)

This is one story of change in children's lives which can be seen across the globe: the fight for girls' education in Pakistan, for trade union rights for child workers in India or for equal Black education in South Africa all provide examples of how children and young people have been involved in struggles to gain more control over their own lives. By quoting Stein and the other examples we are not trying to romanticise this movement; there remains much to be done. It is noteworthy that the children's rights movement has perhaps been stronger in relation to children in care than it has been for children at school, for example. However, in this author's day-to-day involvement in children's services, I witness young people presenting their views to senior managers, and young people being genuinely consulted.

Practice box 6.2

Viewpoint

Viewpoint is an online consultation tool and City of Bradford Metropolitan District Council has purchased a licence to use Viewpoint to engage with looked after children and young people at the time of their looked after review meeting.

Viewpoint is a computer assisted, self-directed interview tool. It assists us to ascertain the views of children and young people through specific, age related and issue based questionnaires. Viewpoint consists of a series of online questionnaires that children and young people complete on their own. These questionnaires are displayed in an engaging dialogue with animated cartoon assistants.

Once a child or young person completes a questionnaire online the Independent Reviewing Officer is alerted and has access to the completed questionnaire. This information is then used to represent the views of the child or young person in the review meeting. Viewpoint should be viewed as a tool which can be used with children and young people to ensure that their views are known and are included in decision making about their lives.

> If Viewpoint is to be successful, children and young people need to be encouraged and supported to use the tool.
>
> (City of Bradford Metropolitan District Council, n.d.)

Practice box 6.2 describes Viewpoint – an online tool for collecting the views of children about their own experiences of review meetings. Viewpoint is one example of how children and young people can actively participate in influencing services. It reflects how we are increasingly interested in hearing the voices and opinions of children and young people – although of course there is a long way to go.

Thinking point 6.3: What could be done to improve the active participation of children and young people, a) in service provision for children and young people and b) in society more generally?

Key points

1 Children and their families are becoming increasingly involved in shaping the services they receive.
2 These changes can also be seen in the context of broader social changes in society.

4 The impact of child abuse and related scandals on the children's workplace

To the outsider or lay person many children's workplaces suggest child abuse: unfortunately 'children's homes' often have this resonance, as do sometimes day nurseries and other care settings. We have over the last three decades seen an extensive list of abuse scandals emerge, to name but a few:

- sexual abuse across a range of children's homes and other settings in North Wales (Waterhouse, 2000)
- physical abuse in the Magdalene Laundries in the Republic of Ireland (Ryan Commission, 2009)

- sexual abuse of children and vulnerable people in institutions across the United Kingdom by Jimmy Savile (Gray and Watt, 2013)

A 'Magdalene Laundry'; some institutions trusted to care for young people have betrayed that trust

Thinking point 6.4: Why do you think some children's workplaces have become sites of child abuse, when they were designed to work in the best interests of children and young people?
Think about what you know about the Jimmy Savile case: what were the social, cultural and situational issues that allowed him to abuse vulnerable people?

The list could unfortunately go on for many pages. Why is there this tragic link between the children's workplace and abuse? Abuse can be seen, quite simply, as the misuse of power that one person or group of persons has over others (Finkelhor, 1986). Where the powerful group are adults and the other group are children there is a clear power difference. Where the children are vulnerable (in care, disabled, 'troublesome') then the power differentials become even greater: and the children more likely to become abused. If this analysis is correct then children's workplaces are potentially most abusive when the power differentials are at their greatest, and children's workplaces are safest if power differentials are minimised. This is why children's rights and participation are fundamental to protecting children.

The French philosopher/historian Michel Foucault wrote about how power is built in to everyday life – in the buildings, routines and structures we work in (Foucault, 1991). By this he meant that power is designed into the structure of buildings. So, for example, the idea of the 'staff room' may seem innocent enough – but it carries with it messages about power, difference, segregation and secrecy. The staff room is the centre of the professional culture and attitudes developed by teaching staff. Buildings, as Foucault argued, are never innocent. It is easy to forget how issues about child abuse are designed into our workplaces: the CCTV, the Criminal Records Bureau checks, the identity check at reception, the coded locks on doors, the rules about cameras and phones, aside from the more obvious 'child protection procedures' all demonstrate how child abuse – its prevention and detection – are core to our workplace experience and its design.

Most of us probably feel a sense of betrayal when someone in our profession is found guilty of abusing a child they have worked with. As a social worker the current author has felt that sense of betrayal a number of times throughout my career – a feeling that I am sure is shared by the majority of teachers, nurses, sports coaches or priests when a new allegation of child abuse from their professions emerges.

How does this paradox occur? How can a child-centred workplace, perhaps somewhere designed to nurture and care for children, become a centre of abuse and cruelty?

Wardhaugh and Wilding (1993) developed a framework for suggesting how care becomes corrupted. They suggest that there are eight factors that contribute to the 'corruption of care':

1   The corruption of care depends on the neutralisation of normal moral concerns …
2   The corruption of care is closely connected with the balance of power and powerlessness in organisations …
3   Particular pressures and particular kinds of work are associated with the corruption of care …
4   Management failure underlies the corruption of care …
5   The corruption of care is more likely in enclosed, inward-looking organisations …
6   The absence of clear lines and mechanisms of accountability plays an important part in the corruption of care …
7   Particular models of work and organisation are conducive to the corruption of care …
8   The [particularly vulnerable] nature of certain client groups encourages the corruption of care.

(Wardhaugh and Wilding, 1993, pp. 6–27)

Perhaps we can invert the work of Wardhaugh and Wilding and suggest how to make a place safe for children?

- Make sure care and professional commitment are central to caring for children.
- Ensure that power imbalances are reduced.
- Support staff and make sure vulnerable workplaces are safe.
- Strive towards high quality management and leadership.
- Make sure institutions are open and outward looking.
- Ensure the workplace is transparent and accountable.
- Address work cultures in vulnerable settings.
- Ensure vulnerable client groups are particularly protected.

No doubt great progress has been made since many large-scale workplaces, such as children's homes, were found to be abusive. However, we should never be complacent: it is fairly safe to predict that some current day children's workplaces will, in the future, be found to be the site of abusive practices. We can recall the disbelief and shock of those who knew and worked with Jimmy Savile as his crimes against children and vulnerable adults were exposed: it can be happening close to us without us even realising (Gray and Watt, 2013). The role of 'whistle-blowers' – people who decide to disclose what is going on in a particular organisation – can be crucial. Alison Taylor spent many years telling people what was going on in North Wales children's homes (Waterhouse, 2000). She was ignored, disbelieved and sometimes disparaged – but bravely continued to put her case and in the end she was proved to be correct.

While most child protection systems and procedures are essential, it can be argued that procedures alone can fail to address the core issue at the heart of child abuse – the misuse of adult power over children and young people. By addressing power imbalances, and by empowering children and young people, ensuring adults treat children with respect, we can make sure that our workplaces are safer places for children. Of course, power differentials can never be completely eliminated, so some procedures and safeguards will always be required. But policies and procedures can be ignored or bypassed so safe practice is better based in truly empowering practices. This is another reason why the continued development of children's participation as discussed above is so vital. The nature of these empowering practices will vary from setting to setting and according to the age of the children and young people worked with, but empowering practices might include:

- youth parliaments/councils
- Children in Care Councils
- involving young people in inspections/case audits
- gathering the views/perspectives of children on service provision, even with the youngest children
- 'takeover' days, such as that described in Practice box 6.3.

Some workplaces are not afraid to address power structures, if only for a day

---

Practice box 6.3

Children's Commissioner's Takeover Day

(extracts from publicity material for the event)

Takeover Day gives children and young people the chance to work with adults for the day and be involved in decision-making.

The Children's Commissioner for England said: 'Organisations get the opportunity to show their commitment to their communities and tell us they gain a fresh perspective on what they do, often with new solutions. Every sector can take part – it's a flexible event which can be tailored to suit your needs.'

Top 5 reasons for organisations to take part

1   Improved links with customers or service users and the local community

2   Fresh ideas, insight and creativity and ways to improve what you do

3   A better understanding of how children and young people experience issues involved in your work

---

---

4   The chance to demonstrate your commitment to listening to young people, and encourage their commitment to the success of your organisation

5   It's easy to do and the benefits far outweigh the work needed to make a really successful day!

How to achieve a really successful Children's Commissioner's Takeover Day in 3 simple steps

Step 1- Engaging

Discuss with your colleagues which group will lead activities, approach your local school, college or youth group to invite them to participate.

Step 2- Develop your activities for the day

Whatever your size with careful planning and there are always opportunities for children's ideas and creativity and to bring a fresh perspective to your work.

Step 3- Manage the practicalities for your day

Advance preparation with your colleagues and children and young people will help ensure that everyone gets the most out of the day.

(Children's Commissioner, 2013)

Practice box 6.4 gives an example of how children and young people can be engaged in processes which help to redress the power imbalance between children and adults. The LILAC project (Leading Improvements for Looked After Children) involved supporting young people in care to become active in promoting high-quality care provision.

Practice box 6.4

The LILAC project (Leading Improvements for Looked After Children)

The work

Undertaken in only 10 months the work has included:

- *Recruitment of the team.*
- *Training weekends and days, including training as inspectors.*
- *Developing and refining standards and criteria.*
- *Compiling the LILAC manual.*
- *Piloting the work in two local authorities.*
- *Evaluation and dissemination.*

The standards

Shared values

The local authority adopts shared values that enable children and young people to be actively involved in services that directly affect them, including honesty about what can and cannot be changed and any limitations due to the organisation's responsibilities.

Style of leadership

Senior managers and elected members adopt a style of leadership that champions and promotes the involvement of young people at all levels of the local authority. They demonstrate the need to work in partnership with young people.

Structures

Structures are in place that ensure that young people are involved in:

- the planning and evaluation of services
- developing and reviewing individual packages of care
- mechanisms to handle complaints and provide advocacy.

These structures are flexible, do not rely on the involvement of a small group of articulate young people and take account of everyone's different abilities.

Staff

Staff support and contribute to practice and policy on the active involvement of children and young people in services that affect them.

Recruitment and selection

Young people should be involved in the recruitment and selection of all staff and carers who will work with them or be responsible for them.

Care planning and review

Children and young people should feel involved in the decision making that affects their lives and all decisions about them should be fully explained. All decision making, planning and review processes should be easily understood.

Complaints and advocacy

Children and young people should know what to do if they are not happy with the way they are being treated and feel that their complaint will be listened to and treated seriously. The local authority complaints procedure should comply with all statutory regulations and have had young people involved in its drafting. Young people should have access to an advocate if they wish.

The messages: what have we learnt?

- *The value of the subtle and intricate observations and judgements that care-experienced young people can make because they are **experts by experience**.*
- *Looked-after children and young people are more willing to open up and share truths with care experienced inspectors.*
- *You need a culture, willingness and confidence on the part of a local authority, especially senior managers, to be open and willing to adopt a care experience-led approach to reviewing*

> *their policies and practices in relation to the services they provide for children and young people.*
>
> - *The same culture needs to be adopted in the training, supervision and attitude of staff who work directly with care-experienced young people.*
> - *The opportunity has given the pilot inspectors new, transferable skills and a new found confidence that should be made available to other young people.*
> - *LILAC can stand alone, but it also has a unique contribution to make to the development and work of other key inspector bodies such as OFSTED.*
>
> (The Fostering Network, LILAC project, 2007)

Key points

1 Workplace culture can be very powerful and can maintain negative and abusive environments.
2 Children's workplaces are safer if power differentials between adults and children are minimised. This is why rights and participation are fundamental to protecting children.
3 Addressing power structures within organisations can contribute to making workplaces safer for children.

5 What has the impact of multi-disciplinarity been on the workplace?

A major theme of this book has been the development of interagency working and the related tendency towards co-location. In this section we investigate how the shift towards interagency working has changed the interprofessional children's services workplace. In another chapter in this book we focus on the 'what works' issue – 'what works' in improving the lives of children and their families. Here the focus is more on professional experience of the workplace: we analyse, in particular, the co-located workplace and the professional experience thereof.

There is now a large amount of research on interagency working, which is discussed throughout this book. It is argued here that eight main themes emerge from this literature:

1 **Complexity and ambiguity**: the literature suggests that interagency working is complex, challenging and ambiguous. There is no 'recipe book' or 'magic wand' that interagency work can deliver. It has to be worked at and developed and obstacles have to be addressed and overcome (Anning et al., 2010).

2 **Professional identity**: professional identity in interagency teams is subject to change and development (see Wenger, 1998).

3 **Power, status and difference**: working together, even in co-located settings, does not do away with difference based on status and power. Nor does it do away with those differences that arise from social inequalities, such as gender, ethnicity and (dis)ability (Wenger, 1998).

4 **Leadership**: how teams are led in interagency settings requires a different set of skills to those required in more traditional 'silo' organisations. Leaders need to gain authority with professionals from backgrounds which will be different to their own (Purcell et al., 2012).

5 **Information sharing and communication**: this is often the biggest challenge facing interagency teams. Different professionals often have differing approaches to confidentiality and information sharing. It is important that clear protocols are established and that effective information sharing takes place (Atkinson et al., 2007).

6 **Outcomes**: the ultimate challenge. The issue of the outcomes for service users arising from interagency working is complex and uncertain (Atkinson et al., 2007). It is an issue explored fully in Chapter 4 of this book.

7 **Structural and organisational issues**: multi-agency working involves complex organisational structures, often with complicated interactions, between funding streams, line management and supervisory arrangements (Anning et al., 2010).

8 **The Team Around the Child**: this represents a flexible and multi-agency way of working with children and young people. The aim is to start from the needs of the child and for professional roles to be responsive to their needs (Siraj-Blatchford et al., 2007).

Thinking point 6.5: Reflecting on these key eight issues, think of a children's services workplace that you are familiar with. Where would you rate it in terms of interagency working? Can you identify ways in which interagency working in this service could be improved?

5.1 What does the effective interagency workplace look like?

There is powerful evidence that professionals find working in the multi-professional workplace a stimulating and fulfilling experience. Anning et al. (2010) concluded their work on learning in the interagency workplace as follows:

- Much knowledge in the workplace remains tacit, but professionals working in multi-agency teams are required to make it explicit for their colleagues.
- There are two types of knowledge – codified and personal – and professionals need to be trained to deploy both in the workplace.
- Professionals generate theories about their work through daily situated experiences of and reflection on delivering services.
- Multi-professional teamwork offers opportunities for professional knowledge and expertise of individuals to be distributed across the team.
- The team carries the sociocultural histories both of individual workers and of the institution, and all this changes as the nature of work and team membership fluctuates.
- Knowledge and expertise are shared in informal exchanges in the workplace and social events.
- Knowledge and expertise are shared in the formal planned contexts of meetings and training events, and in joint activities between professionals in the workplace. …
- Service providers and users can learn from each other in cycles of expansive learning to deepen their understanding of and refine workplace activities.

- It is important to respect and deploy distinctive specialisms, as well as general understanding, if professionals are to gain job satisfaction and retain opportunities for career advancement beyond the life of the multi-professional team in which they currently work.

(Anning et al., 2010, pp. 85–86)

As we saw in Chapter 4 (section 2.3), it has been suggested by Brock et al. that the following factors are crucial to the successful integrated workplace: communication, assertive leadership, a supportive culture, individual qualities and organisational issues.

Key point

There is now good evidence that practitioners are able to work effectively and ethically in a multi-professional workplace, although there are quite complex and deeply rooted issues to be addressed by individuals, their leaders and by service users.

6 What does the future look like?

This section will bring together the disparate trends discussed so far and take a more holistic approach to the workplace. How is the workplace changing? What are the trends and general direction? How is this likely to look in the future?

There have been a number of factors identified in this book which are having an impact on many workplaces, including:

- the impact of recession and austerity
- the increasing dominance of information technology
- the changing nature of society: globalisation and new migrant communities, for example
- the rapid pace of change
- changing consumer/service user expectations.

More specifically, a number of factors have been identified which are leading the children's workforce towards more interagency working. These factors include:

* government policy, regulation and legislation
* the persistence of complex and seemingly intractable social problems
* the need to work as efficiently and effectively as possible.

The specific impact of these changes will differ from workplace to workplace, from profession to profession. However, it is possible to prepare, with the use of the evidence we have, for change within workplaces. What might the children's services workplace of the future look like?

Perhaps the only change we can predict with some certainty is change itself. Whereas the workplace of the past offered some stability and consistency, the modern workplace is one of rapid change. Some thinkers have characterised the modern period using concepts such as 'post-modern', 'fluid' and 'liquid' (Bauman, 2000). This means that change is a persistent factor in modern society: driven by technology, globalisation and social change.

Such change makes life difficult for professionals: it is hard to learn lessons from the past when everything is constantly changing; we have to make sure that we are always up-to-date (through lifelong learning) and that we can engage with change.

Below, a thinker on organisation in general reflected on why our modern workplace is changing (Ouye, 2011). He gave five reasons:

1　'**The continuing distribution of organizations**'. Ultimately, workers, work and workplaces serve the needs of the organisations, and they will reflect the continuing spatial and organisational distribution of these organisations with more distributed work styles and workplaces.

2　 '**The availability of enabling technologies and social collaboration tools**'. Technologies for collaborating with co-workers wherever they are will continue to become cheaper, easier to use and ubiquitous. They are already being combined and synthesised into platforms which feature a wide range of tools to collaborate asynchronously and synchronously, cheaply and ubiquitously.

3 **'The coming shortage of knowledge workers'**. There will be a shortage of younger knowledge workers in the coming years as the Baby Boomer generation retires and younger workers take their place. Organisations will have to compete for workers who are more comfortable with and seek flexible work, including alternative workplaces.

4 **'The demand for more work flexibility'**. Workers will demand more work flexibility—the ability to decide how they should define and tackle specific problems and tasks, and when and where work is done.

5 **'Pressure for more sustainable organizations and workstyles'**. Organisations will have to examine all major sources of greenhouse gas emissions, including tapping the potential of how, where and when we work: group locations, building efficiencies, commute patterns, and air travel practices.

(Adapted from Ouye, 2011)

Compare our modern experience of change at work with the classic account below from Charles Dickens of the office in *Great Expectations*; one can feel the slow pace of work and the predictability of the unchanging workplace.

Mr Jaggers's room was lighted by a skylight only, and was a most dismal place; the skylight, eccentrically patched like a broken head, and the distorted adjoining houses looking as if they had twisted themselves to peep down at me through it. There were not so many papers about, as I should have expected to see; and there were some odd objects about, that I should not have expected to see — such as an old rusty pistol, a sword in a scabbard, several strange-looking boxes and packages, and two dreadful casts on a shelf, of faces peculiarly swollen, and twitchy about the nose. Mr Jaggers's own high-backed chair was of deadly black horse-hair, with rows of brass nails round it, like a coffin; and I fancied I could see how he leaned back in it, and bit his forefinger at the clients. …

Of course I had no experience of a London summer day, and my spirits may have been oppressed by the hot exhausted air, and by the dust and grit that lay thick on everything. But I sat wondering and waiting in Mr Jaggers's close room, until I really could not bear the two casts on the shelf above Mr Jaggers's chair, and got up and went out.

(Dickens, 1992, p. 125)

In reading these two accounts we can compare and contrast the 'contemporary' workplace with the 'traditional' workplace. In the modern workplace we have come to expect change: we have to live with change. But also workplaces can be resistant to change: we are all attracted by what feels safe, comfortable and familiar. When a specific change is suggested we all need to position ourselves in relation to this change. The Practice box 6.5 allows the reader to reflect on this.

Practice box 6.5

In a survey about a specific change in children's services, those who responded fell into the following categories:

The enthusiasts

This group were very keen on the change. They acted as champions: they, spoke about the change to others and were actively engaged in implementation.

The optimists

This group thought the change would be positive, although they needed to see the evidence of change and feel that the change would be successful.

The unsures

This group had not yet made their minds up. They needed to know more, to see evidence and see positive results.

The pessimists

This group were against the change: they had 'seen it all before' and thought 'everything was alright as it was'.

(Adapted from Cater and Frost, 2007, p. 22, evaluation of West Leeds Project)

Key points

1 Research with teams in integrated workplaces has identified some of the factors crucial to their successful development.
2 Workplaces delivering services for children will continue to change in response to global as well as local pressures.

Conclusion

This chapter has explored the children's workplace, how it is changing and the particular influence of interagency working on this. It has been argued that the workplace is changing rapidly and the forces contributing to this have been explored. It also seems to be the case that the move towards interagency working is fundamental to these changes, and that this is a trend that is with us for the foreseeable future. Understanding what is happening in our workplaces is central to our shared work in trying to promote the best interests of children and young people in the future.

References

Anning, A., Cottrell, D., Green, J., Frost, N., Robinson, M. (2010) *Developing multi-professional working for integrated children's services*, London, Open University.

Atkinson, M., Jones, M., Lamont, E. (2007) '*Multi-agency working and its implications for practice: A review of the Literature*', CfBT.

Bauman, Z (2000) *Liquid Modernity*, Cambridge, Polity Press.

Bergistra (2012) 'Ofsted is the last thing you need when a pupil is having a tantrum', *The Guardian*, 17 December, available online at <http://www.theguardian.com/education/2012/dec/17/headteacher-on-a-knife-edge>, accessed 15 August 2013.

Brock, A., Frost, N., Karban, K., Smith, S. (2009) *Towards Inter professional Partnerships: a resource pack*, Leeds, Leeds Metropolitan University.

Brock, A. and Rankin, C. (2011) *Professionalism in the Interdisciplinary Early Years Team*, London, Continuum, 2011.

Cater, A. and Frost, N. (2007) *An evaluation of the West Leeds Project*, Leeds, Leeds Metropolitan University.

Children's Commissioner (2013) *Children's Commissioner's Takeover Day 2013*, Office of the Children's Commissioner, available online at < http://www.childrenscommissioner.gov.uk/takeover_day>, accessed 24 August 2013.

City of Bradford Metropolitan District Council (n.d.) *Viewpoint briefing note*, available online at <http://bso.bradford.gov.uk/userfiles/file/ Children%20in%20Care/Viewpoint%20Briefing%20Note.doc>, accessed 22 August 2013.

Dickens, C. (1992) *Great Expectations*, London, Wordsworth.

Finkelhor, D. (1986) *A Source Book on Child Sexual Abuse*, California, Sage.

Fostering Network (2007) Lilac: Leading Improvements for Looked-After Children, available online at <http://www.fostering.net/all-about-fostering/resources/reports/lilac-leading-improvements-looked-after-children#.UZy3z_twY0Q>, accessed 23 August 2013.

Foucault, M. (1991) *Discipline and Punish*, Harmondsworth, Penguin.

Frost, N. and Parton, N. (2009) *Understanding Children's Social Care: Politics, Policy and Practice*, London, Sage.

Giddens, A. (1991) *Modernity and Self-identity: Self and Society in the Late Modern Age*, Cambridge, Cambridge University Press.

Gray, D. and Watt, P. (2013) *Giving Victims a Voice: Joint Report into Sexual Allegations Made Against Jimmy Savile*, London, NSPCC.

Jones, P. (2009) *Rethinking Childhood*, London, Continuum.

J.A. Ouye (2011) *Five Trends that are Dramatically Changing Work and the Workplace*, Knoll, available online at <http://www.knoll.com/media/18/ 144/WP_FiveTrends.pdf >, accessed 23 August 2013.

Midskard, J. (2012) *Action and Thinking: An Investigation of How Social Workers Influence School Professionals Regarding Vulnerable Children's Issues*, Roskilde, Roskilde University.

Power, M. (1997) *The Audit Society*, Oxford, Oxford University Press.

Purcell, M., Christian, M., and Frost, N. (2012) 'Addressing the challenges of leading children's services in England', *Journal of Children's Services, vol.* 7, no. 2, pp. 86–101.

Ryan Commission (2009) *Commission to Inquire into Child Abuse,* Dublin, Republic of Ireland Government.

Siraj-Blatchford, I., Clarke, K., Needham, M. (2007) *The Team Around the Child,* Stoke, Trentham.

Stein, M. (2011) *Care Less Lives: The Story of the Rights Movement of Young People in Care,* London, Catch 22.

Wardhaugh, J. and Wilding, P. (1993) 'Towards an explanation of the corruption of care', *Critical Social Policy,* vol. 37, pp. 4–31.

Waterhouse, R. (2000) *Lost in Care: Report of the Tribunal of Inquiry into the Abuse of Children in Care in the former County Council Areas of Gwynedd and Clwyd since 1974,* London, HMSO.

Wenger, E. (1998) *Communities of Practice,* Cambridge, Cambridge University Press.

Wenger, E. (n.d.) home page, at <http://wenger-trayner.com>, accessed 22 August 2013.

Acknowledgements

Grateful acknowledgement is made to the following sources:

Text

Page 69: Hudson, B. (2005) 'Partnership Working and the Children's Services Agenda: Is it Feasible?', *Journal of Integrated Care*, vol. 13, no. 2, April 2005, Pavilion; Page 65, Practice box 2.1: Welsh Government (2011) 'New integrated family centre for Powys', National Assembly for Wales. © 2011 Crown Copyright, reproduced under the terms of OGL, http://www.nationalarchives.gov.uk/doc/open-government-licence/version/2/; Pages 151–5, 160–161, 171 and 173: Easton, C., Featherstone G,. Poet, H., Aston, H., Gee, G. and Durbin, B. (2012) *Supporting families with complex needs: Findings from LARC 4* Slough: NFER. © National Foundation for Educational Research 2012; Page 235, Practice box 6.1: Bergistra (2012) 'Ofsted is the last thing you need when a pupil is having a tantrum', *The Guardian*, www.guardian.co.uk. Copyright © Guardian News and Media Ltd 2012; Page 242, Practice box 6.2: City of Bradford Metropolitan District Council (2013) Viewpoint Briefing Note, Viewpoint: Helping Children to be heard/City of Bradford Metropolitan District Council, www.bradford.gov.uk; Page 249, Practice box 6.4: The Fostering Network (2007) *LILAC: leading improvements for looked-after children*, the fostering network, a national voice, nlcas, csci and scie

Illustrations

Page 18: © Jeff Gilbert/Alamy; Page 26, Top left: Francis, R. (2010) Independent Inquiry into care provided by Mid Staffordshire NHS Foundation Trust January 2005 – March 2009: Volume 1, The Stationery Office. Copyright © Crown Copyright 2010. Reproduced under the terms of OGL, http://www.nationalarchives.gov.uk/doc/open-government-licence/version/1/open-government-licence.htm; Page 26, Top right: Local Safeguarding Children Board (2009) *Serious Case Review: Baby Peter – Executive Summary*, Local Safeguarding Children Board (LSCB) Haringey; Page 26, Bottom: North Wales Police (2013) *Operation Pallial: Public Report on Progress*, North Wales Police Press Office; Page 32: Copyright © Swindon Children's Fund; Page 34: Copyright © 2005 TopFoto; Page 51: www.JohnBirdsall.co.uk; Page 59:

Blaenau Gwent County Borough Council (2013) 'Blaenau Gwent Team Around the Child', Blaenau Gwent County Borough Council, reproduced under the terms of OGL http://www.nationalarchives.gov.uk/doc/open-government-licence/version/2/; Page 68: Measuring Child Poverty: A Consultation on Better Measures of Child Poverty: HM Government (2012) *Measuring Child Poverty: A Consultation on Better Measures of Child Poverty*, Department for Education and Department for Work and Pensions, reproduced under the terms of the Open Government License, http://www.nationalarchives.gov.uk/doc/open-government-licence/; Page 72: Perry, B.D. (2002) 'Childhood experience and the expression of genetic potential: what childhood neglect tells us about nature and nurture', *Brain and Mind*, 3: pp. 79–10, Kluwer Academic Publishers. Copyright © 2002 Kluwer Academic Publishers; Page 76: Copyright © Crispin Hughes/Photofusion; Page 82: Copyright © Karen Robinson; Page 95: Copyright © John Phillips/Photofusion; Page 102: Copyright © Clarissa Leahy/Photofusion; Page 106: Copyright © Karen Robinson/Panos Pictures; Page 108: Copyright © Anwar Hussein/Getty Images; Page 125: www.JohnBirdsall.co.uk; Page 126: Tiers of Need, from *DfES Children's Services: The Market for Parental and Family Support Services*, 2006, PriceWaterhouseCoopers; Page 127: Mapping provider types against different tiers of need, from *DfES Children's Services: The Market for Parental & Family Support Services*, 2006, PriceWaterhouseCoopers; Page 129: Copyright © samc/Alamy; Page 145: © John Chillingworth/Getty Images; Page 155: © Photofusion Picture Library/Alamy; Page 156: © Nytumbleweeds/Dreamstime.com; Page 159: www.JohnBirdsall.co.uk; Page 163: Copyright © David Mansell (www.reportdigital.co.uk); Page 172: © HighScope Educational Research Foundation; Page 185: Copyright © Ulrike Preuss; Page 191: www.JohnBirdsall.co.uk; Page 195: © MBI/Alamy; Page 197: Copyright © Lisa Woollett; Page 204: Copyright © Swindon Children's Fund; Page 207: Copyright © Swindon Children's Fund; Page 210: Copyright © Chapman Wiedelphoto; Page 213: Copyright © Chapman Wiedelphoto; Page 234: © Ros Asquith/Guardian News & Media Ltd; Page 239: © Pat Tuson/Alamy; Page 240: © Children's Commissioner for Wales; Page 247: © Children's Commissioner for England; Page 249, Practice box 6.4: The Fostering Network (2007) *LILAC: leading improvements for looked-after children*, the fostering network, a national voice, nlcas, csci and scie.

Every effort has been made to contact copyright holders. If any have been inadvertently overlooked the publishers will be pleased to make the necessary arrangements at the first opportunity.

Index